SELF-SELECTED
ESSAYS

J. B. PRIESTLEY

SELF-SELECTED
ESSAYS

Essay Index Reprint Series

BOOKS FOR LIBRARIES PRESS

FREEPORT, NEW YORK

First Published 1932
Reprinted 1968

LIBRARY OF CONGRESS CATALOG CARD NUMBER:
68-22938

PRINTED IN THE UNITED STATES OF AMERICA

CONTENTS

CONTENTS

Introduction

MORE than half the essays in this collection have never appeared in any volume before, and represent what seems to me the pick of my more recent contributions to the *Saturday Review* and the *Week-End Review*. The other·essays have been chosen by me from four volumes, *Papers from Lilliput, I For One, Open House,* and *Apes and Angels,* and appear here by the courtesy of their respective publishers. There are about eleven years between the earliest of the essays published here and the latest. That is not long, but it is a year or two longer than my life as a professional writer. During most of this time, the short essay was my favourite literary form. It is not my favourite form any longer, though I can well believe that some day I shall return to it, with renewed interest and hope.

J. B. PRIESTLEY.

Home From the Sea

To return from a long voyage is almost to be born again. There is one brief moment, after landing, when you discover your old life as Columbus discovered America, when you play stout Cortez not on a peak in Darien but on a bleak English quayside. It seems to you, if only for a second or so, that not one of the places you have seen—lands coloured like the rainbow, ports with names that are themselves three-volume romances—is so fantastic as the grey little island to which you have returned. Then familiarity comes crashing down and everything round you is clear and solid and something known to you all your days, whereas all your voyaging has crumbled into the fragments of a dream. Because I had made a good many voyages, lasting from a few hours to a week, I thought I knew something of the sea; but actually I knew nothing. Those short voyages do not allow you sufficient time in which to forget your old existence as a land animal or to see the life afloat as anything but a brief episode, a queer interlude of rocking decks and berths and alleyways and white paint. Now that I have spent week after week in this strange world, when ten thousand miles have foamed past, when two score suns have risen from the encircling waters and plunged down into them again, I understand many things that were before a mystery.

Thus it was not long before I began to see the world as long-voyage sailors must always have seen it. In spite of the blue expanses on the map, I had always thought of the sea as a kind of happy accident, a bright novelty that made its appearance here and there so that landsmen might enjoy their holidays. Now I saw that the maps had told even less than the truth, that the world was indeed a waste of tumbling waters in which it was the land that was the happy accident. By observing narrowly the sun and stars, poring over charts and cunningly turning a wheel, you might, with luck, arrive where some solid stuff peeped out of the water and grew trees and grass and even streets and houses. We flatter ourselves, we men and apes and beetles, that the world belongs to us; but in truth it belongs to the fishes who can go round and round the globe with never a break in the rhythmical play of their fins and tails. We are mere interlopers. Look in at the nearest fishmonger's and you will observe in the round eyes of the dead creatures there a look of pained surprise, of wounded dignity. Now, I can understand that look, for the fish, well aware of the fact that the world was made for him and his kind, suddenly finds himself the prey of an insolent upstart with feet and lungs, who has only a fraction of the earth's surface on which to live. An alderman kidnapped by a turtle could not be more surprised or feel more wounded in his dignity.

It is true that the ship itself was in a sense nothing but a floating bit of land, on which we could lead a life

not surprisingly different from our customary one.
But there were differences. The background, the
vague ring of sea and sky, was all strange, so that
even the ordinary things we did took on a new significance. Some people never notice this difference, and
that is why they find sea voyages so tedious. Let us
admit at once that long voyages, even to places with
names like rich sonnets, are not the exciting affairs
that the romantic fancy paints them as being. Compelled to pass the time somehow between one meal
and the next (and how important meals are on board!
—the four stout pillars of the day), you find yourself
doing things that would be beneath your notice
ashore: reading books that you have despised for
years, playing crudely devised games with almost un-
sporting eagerness, encouraging your companions to
tell their longest and dullest stories, indulging in naps
without stint or shame. The days can be so empty of
incident that the sight of a rusty old buoy that has
drifted out into mid-ocean, a few floating spars, the
mere idle rumour of a distant ship, will send every
one crowding to the rails. No one can complain here
of the hurrying hours, the day gone by like a flash,
for time stretches out as empty and vacant as the
shining space surrounding us. There is time for everything, even to work through all the games of Patience
or to read the story of Clarissa Harlowe.

If you have no sense of the changed background, of
having been born again into a strange little world,
then this life may seem tedious enough; but most of

us found it had a curious, fascinating quality of its own. Our old life faded like a dream. Our old interests, the familiar routine, were lost with the horizons of home. We were in a new world, and became, as it were, new people, strange even to ourselves. Our days may have seemed empty enough, passed in trivialities, entirely lacking that excitement with which our fancy had dowered them; and yet they came to have a significance and charm of their own, a kind of rhythmical flow, beating to the throb of the ship's engines, that we were sorry to find broken, in spite of all the bustle and interest of an arrival in port, when we came to the land again. Even those who complained most of the tedium of sea voyages found themselves, rather to their astonishment, half regretting that they were leaving us at this port or the other, that the queer interlude was at an end. There was, at least to me, a curious sweet melancholy that pervaded this easy empty life of ours and gave it a fascination, an indescribable charm. The background against which we performed our little antics seemed nearer to eternity than the familiar one of our ordinary life. The crowded, cosy, painted world we knew had faded into the silent universe of bright stars and black space. Night after night, when they danced on the boat deck, I would watch them with a kind of sweet trouble about my heart, a strange lovely melancholy like that of a boy in love through one long dreaming summer. The quaint tunes on the gramophone—those wistful dance tunes of our time that would be so bright and carefree if

they only could—blown into a whisper by the tropical
breeze; the little circle of coloured electric globes, the
bare arms of the girls, the black coats and white coats
of their partners, against the huge staring night, the
stars and the restless shadow of the sea: all this held
me night after night, for in this tiny patch of sound
and light—something so little and lovely, foolish and
yet half tragic—there seemed to be all our human life.
Nor was it any different when we held carnival and
capered there as pierrots and shepherdesses and cow-
boys and gipsy maidens, for, once we had surged from
below up into the night, these our revels shrank to a
pin-point of light, a whisper in the darkness.

Now that I have set foot on shore again, it is, as if
I had never been away, had only dozed for a minute
or two in my chair and been visited by a confused
dream of a long journey. The seas and flaming sunsets and islands and tropical jungles have been packed
away like the tattered scenery of some bankrupt
theatrical company. That life on the ship which had
blotted out all other existence is now nothing but a
few coloured scraps in the memory, shredding away
with every tick of my watch. Those people who made
up my whole world only a little while ago, what are
they now but ghosts? Where is the general with the
extraordinary eyebrows (they were far larger than
any subaltern's moustache); and pretty Miss N.,
whose fancy dress was so daring, who won so many
prizes and stayed out so late, it was said, on the boat
deck; and the baronet who had been a cow-puncher

and grumbled because there were no hard biscuits and
salt junk on the menu; and the parson's wife, whose
voice was too shrill and who danced far too many
times with the sleek cavalry captain? Where are the
three planters who never left one corner of the smoking-room; and the spectacled American who was so
angry when his favourite game of shuffle-board was
not included in the ship's sports; and the three dark-
eyed girls from Demerara who had just seen snow for
the first time in England and could talk of nothing
else; and the "bookie" from Yorkshire who was
always getting up complicated decimal sweeps on the
day's run; and fat Mr. S, from Baltimore, who ate so
much and so quickly that he seemed to be warehous-
ing rather than eating his food; and the mysterious
grim man who was going up the Orinoco; and the very
old gentleman who sat opposite me at table and would
always pinch all the rolls (as if they were little boys'
cheeks) at breakfast-time? Where are they, these
ghosts, dimming now while the cock crows in my
memory? And where is the ship that once carried
them and me and was once all our world? Already it
it is as remote and insubstantial as the Flying Dutch-
man.

A London Hotel

WE are staying in an hotel in one of those squares at the back of Oxford Street. You will say that we ought to have more sense, but we have our excuses. We had to come up suddenly; the rooms we usually have were engaged; we were told that this was a good hotel. It is one of those hotels that like to describe themselves as quiet places for gentlefolk. They are, I believe, a distinct type. They have no bands nor dancing nor cocktail bars; they do not advertise themselves in the illustrated weeklies; they are not very expensive but neither are they very cheap; and they maintain, very firmly and consistently, a fairly high standard of inconvenience and discomfort. They occupy a middle position between those dreary bed-and-breakfast warrens that are always near the big railway stations, so that provincial noncomformist parsons may dive into them five minutes after giving up their tickets, and those palatial hostels where innumerable pageboys may be seen flitting above ten-pile carpets, carrying Martinis and the *Chicago Tribune*, places indeed that the likes of me only visit in the company of American publishers. There must be scores of hotels of this middle kind in London. I have stayed at a round dozen of them myself, probably more, for I have never stayed twice at the same one: I am not such a fool as that; but nevertheless I am fool enough

to imagine at times that I shall stumble upon one that
is really different from the others. If possible, however, I try to make other arrangements: my optimism
has reasonable bounds.

Here we are, then. Once more we are quiet dignified
gentlefolk staying at a quiet dignified hotel. My room
is more fantastic than usual. It has all the appearance
of having been at some time a corridor, though possibly it is really a section of what was once an immense
drawing-room. Whatever it was, it is now an extraordinarily, inhumanly long and narrow apartment, a
place ripe for a German film producer. At one end is
a long narrow window and at the other is a long
narrow wardrobe, which has a mirror that always
offers me a monstrous distortion of myself, who
appear in it as if I were fully as broad as I am tall.
This is, of course, an obvious optical illusion, but it
adds nothing to my pleasure. It is quite impossible to
have a night's sleep in this room, which must have
been designed by some one who either never slept or
never did anything else. Over the door is a large fanlight that is brilliantly illuminated all night because
the lights in the corridor outside are never turned out.
(They will be to-night, however, even if the bodies of
the night-porter and the Boots are found afterwards
near the switch.) There is no escaping this illuminated
fanlight once you are in bed, and no doubt advertising
people will soon take advantage of the fact. But that
is not all. This room is on the first floor, just above the
main door of the hotel, and my pillow is not more than

a yard from the window, through which all the noises
of the street, taxis starting up and hooting away, come
at all hours. For two nights now this room has. offered
me glimpses of eternity. It is determined to make a
thoughtful man of me. Mere reading will not do. The
electric light is so placed that you can only read at the
cost of having smarting eyes. Moreover, when you have
read yourself into feeling sleepy again, you must then
get up to turn out the light, with the result that you
are wakeful once more. If any man wishes to know
what he thinks about life at quarter to three in the
morning, let him occupy this room for a few nights.

The only meal we are taking in this hotel is, of
course, breakfast. There is something very queer
about these London hotel breakfasts. Everything
seems to be there, porridge, fish, sausage, kidney, eggs
and bacon, toast and marmalade, tea and coffee. These
viands are not merely names on the menu but solid
bodies set on the table for you to eat. You may spend
twenty minutes disposing of them. Yet there is a
curious unreality about these meals. They are like
those dinners that actors pretend to eat in the second
act of comedies. At the end of them, you feel you have
had enough, indeed more than enough, but you cannot
help suspecting that you have only been playing a
trick on your interior and that the trick has not quite
succeeded. These sausages and eggs and bacon are
somehow not real sausages and eggs and bacon; they
are not the things in themselves, but mere appearances, part of some phantasmagoria of the kitchen. It

B

is all like eating food in a dream. And the waiters themselves are in the secret. There is mockery in the gusto with which they set before you these spectral eggs and rashers. I have never been one of those members of the audience who go on to the stage to keep an eye on the conjurer, but I fancy such people must have the same sensation I have when I am break-fasting in this fashion. Those liquids that the conjurer pours out of his magic kettle—I will wager that they taste exactly like hotel tea and coffee. Possibly these are conjurers' eggs, coming not from a hen but a hat. And the waiters *know*, of that I am certain. That is why the younger ones can hardly keep a straight face.

The head waiters are grave enough, but they are also sinister. I have noticed that time after time. The head waiter here, for example, could walk straight into a mystery play and be worth fifteen pounds a performance as a collector of suspicions. He has a villainous bald front, a crooked nose, and deep-set but quite colourless eyes, and you could swear that he had disposed of the body only five minutes before he walked into the dining-room.

There is a room here asking for a murder. It is one of the three lounges. The first lounge is to the right of the entrance hall, and is always full of middle-aged Scotswomen playing bridge. (Why are these hotels always full of middle-aged Scotswomen?) The second lounge is to the left of the entrance hall, and is a leathery, railway-guide and illustrated-paper sort of place. One end of it is always occupied by young wives sitting up very stiffly and waiting for their husbands, who are at the telephones asking if Mr. Murchison will be in or telling somebody that they can offer 2,500 at 3¾. The other end appears to have been annexed by a man with a vaguely military appearance, who yawns a great deal but contrives to look as if he has only to have two more to be tipsy. It is the third lounge, at the far end of the entrance hall, that is ripe for a murder. It is much bigger than the others but hardly used at all.

Yesterday, I happened to be in the hotel about half-past four, and so ordered tea. After waiting about ten minutes, I asked the waiter where it was. "I've put it in the Brown Lounge for you, sir," he said, and then it was that I discovered this mysterious room at the end of the hall. It was closely shuttered and very dimly lit, full of enormous chairs and settees, and there were dim acres of engravings and photogravures on the walls. I groped my way to a very large chair and a very little table with a tray on it. The only other people there were two old women who talked in whispers; and if one of them had turned out to be Dickens' Miss Havisham I should not have been surprised. All the noises of the hotel and the streets outside were banished with the closing of the door, and there was no sound at all but the vague whispering of these two old women. Usually I linger over tea, but yesterday there was no lingering. It seemed like eating bread-and-butter in a mausoleum. If ever I want to murder a man, I shall take him in there.

I can see the whole thing. I shall pretend that I want to have a quiet chat with my victim and shall suggest coming to this hotel for tea. As soon as we arrive, I shall seek out the head waiter, that sinister figure. "I want tea for two," I shall tell him, softly but with the right emphasis. "Ah, tea for two," he will say, looking at me with those colourless eyes. "The Brown Lounge?" There will be a kind of cold flicker in those eyes. "Yes," I shall reply, very softly. "The Brown Lounge. Tea for two. And a sharp knife." Then I shall rejoin my man, and, talking very loudly and cheerfully, with many a clap on the back, I shall march him down the hall and into that shuttered room. "Rather a dreary sort of hole this, isn't it?" he will say, staring about him. "Not a bit of it," I shall reply. "Just a quiet hotel for gentlefolk, that's all." The head waiter himself, I trust, will bring the tea and the knife, and as he goes will nod casually towards a gigantic sideboard not far away, and I shall understand. The rest will be easy. It is possible, indeed highly probable, that the two old women will be sitting there, but I do not imagine for a moment that they will interfere or pay any attention to my business with the knife and the sideboard. They will, I fancy, just go on whispering together, like true gentlefolk staying at a quiet hotel.

Caledonian Market

On most days this open market off the Caledonian Road is very open and very Caledonian, so grey and bleak that you might be bargaining on the summit of one of the Cairngorms. That it is possible to do a brisk trade in ice-cream and glasses of sea-green lemonade on that windy height only proves that man is a romantic and imaginative creature. Indeed, the whole Caledonian Market proves that. Consider the American visitors, who may be seen any Friday, looking a little pinched, at the stalls where jewelled brooches and silver dishes and amber and ivories are offered for sale. The people who own these stalls are either dark-skinned young men or fat, needle-eyed women, and a glance at them tells you that they would rather die than sell a thing for less than a hundred and fifty per cent. profit. But these visitors from America, the place where all good legends go to when they die, see these brooches and ivories against the grey Caledonian background, and so imagine there are tremendous bargains to hand. And so there are. You may pay ten shillings more for a silver bowl or an amber necklace in the Caledonian Market than you would pay in a decent shop in the centre of the city, but then you are being given more than ten shillings' worth of romantic legend with the articles. The story of how you picked them up will be worth a whole heap of dollars to you, once back in the home town.

This is a trivial example, however, and does not touch the Market proper, which these artful merchants of jewellery have no real right to attend. Wander down those long aisles there into which the oldest lumber-rooms—nay, the very dustbins—seem to have been emptied, and then you can begin to understand how this one surviving pedlar's market or rag-fair fosters the kindliest romantic illusions. It does this by patching together, every Tuesday and Friday, the last shreds of self-respect in broken men. You are, we will say, nearly sixty years of age and in a wretched state of health. It is ten years since you were sacked from your last little regular job. You have a bent back, flat feet, no teeth, a wheezing voice, and you cannot even shave yourself. If your son (who drives a bus) and your brother (who still keeps the fried-fish shop in Hoxton) did not slip you something, and your daughter occasionally share her dole with you, no doubt you could not exist outside the workhouse.

Nevertheless, you are no mere beggar, even if things are not always going too well. As a matter of fact, you have a little business of your own. You are in the second-hand, the buying and selling line. You are a trader in the Caledonian Market. Out of your dilapidated suitcase you produce certain articles—perhaps a dirty cushion, two egg-cups, an under-skirt, the *Letters of Charles Kingsley,* and a broken alarm clock—and these you offer to the public. There you stand from ten to four, exchanging remarks about the weather and the state of trade with your fellow merchants, and even though nobody ever buys anything from you, the fact remains that you are in business, just as Dick Whittington was and Mr. Selfridge is. Every Friday, dignity returns to you.

That is why most of these unshaven and toothless traders of the Caledonian Market are so aloof. If you want to make an offer for the Banjo Tutor, the two sodden tennis balls, the cracked vase, the bowler hat, the photograph of General Buller, you may do so, and they will talk to you, bargain with you, man to man, but they do not make any of those shameless appeals to the passer-by so characteristic of the traders in other open markets. The man with the Wild West hat —who pretends to quarrel with his wife all the time he is virtually giving sweets away—may resort to all manner of tricks, and so may all the clever young Jews who sell imitation silk stockings and girls' dresses for eighteenpence, but then these fellows are keen money-makers, with pocket-books stuffed with pound notes, and do not mind mountebanking it a bit. They are not there to recover some of their self-respect, so they need not stand upon their dignity. These others, the humblest of traders, whose shop is a piece of brown paper and whose stock is nothing but the siftings of the rubbish heap, are almost condescending in their talk to possible customers. "Oh, yersh," you overhear them saying, "I've 'ad them boxin' pickshers. Might 'ave annuver shoon, p'raps nexsh week, p'raps not fer a munf or tew. Cawn't tell, reelly."

It is now some years since I saw what has always seemed to be the queerest stock-in-trade of any merchant, even for Caledonian Market. He was a tall, shambling, melancholy fellow, a vague ruin of a man, and he stood beside an immense map, about six feet square. He had nothing else for sale but this map. It was not recent enough to be of any service, this map, and not old enough to be of any interest. It was a completely useless map, and even though this world is crowded with people mad enough to buy anything, you could not imagine that anybody would ever buy that map. There was nothing in the attitude of the owner to suggest that he himself dissented from this opinion. He was obviously a man who did not believe in miracles, but nevertheless was waiting for one to happen. And I think it will be agreed that there is only one country that could possibly be the subject of that forlorn monster of a map. Yes, it was Ireland.

The last time I was up there I noticed a number of cards in a basket. At first these cards looked as if they were crowded with bone buttons, but as there seemed to be something peculiar about these buttons, I bent down to examine. They were false teeth. In the Caledonian Market you can now buy false teeth by the card, and it is high time most of the stall-holders, whose remaining blackened stumps wreck all their sibilants, tried a few cards. But the favourite merchandise is still the rubber heel. You pass thousands and thousands of rubber heels, though nobody

ever appears to buy any. But then, who would buy
one of those old-fashioned frilly parasols, especially
when they are very dirty and full of holes.

Yet a man there, the other day, was putting up one
parasol after another, and was so convinced that he
had struck a good line that he was shouting at the top
of his voice: "Oo, muvver, look what I got!" Only a
few yards away, a man who looked like a kind of obscene bird—for he had an enormous beak of a nose and
a round glaring glass eye—was saying "Perfect! Perfect!" For a minute or two I could not understand
what he was talking about—for the glass eye was
misleading—but then I saw that he was referring to
the ugliest wash-hand-stand I have ever seen. It had
a pink marble top—with a place for a mirror, but no
mirror—and was made of a greeny-yellow deal. A
cynical little boy, with an uncommonly large head,
was busy opening the drawers of this nightmare piece
of furniture, for the benefit of a dubious patron, and
it was these drawers that were perfect. Behind was a
card that said "Free Delivery Within Reason," which
might serve as a good motto for a philosopher.

A young conjurer was in attendance on this last
visit of mine. He was dressed in a greasy frock-coat,
blue uniform trousers and hobnailed boots, and he had
two objects in life, one to make the little boys "stand
back, there," and the other to induce twelve sportsmen
to throw a penny each into the ring before he began his
next and greatest trick. Nevertheless, he seemed to be
a very good conjurer, making things appear and dis-

appear as though these few square feet of market were the stage at Maskelyne's. The only thing he could not control, apparently, was dirt, for he was almost lost in it. A little magic with soap and water and he would have seemed a new conjurer altogether.

It was when I had left his audience, after taking the part of all twelve sportsmen, and had decided to leave the Market that I saw the only thing there I wanted to buy. The reason why I did not buy it was simply that it was too big. I saw among the usual jumble of stuff on one of the humbler stalls, a very large framed certificate, with crossed English and American flags at the top; and this is what it announced to the world: "Anglo-American School of Embalming. Diploma. The O.K. Buckhout Chemical Company, Ltd., of Kalamazoo, Michigan, U.S.A., and London, England, hereby certifies that Arthur Sherry of London has attended a series of Lectures and Demonstrations and has under the instructions of Professor Renovard become thoroughly familiar with the science of Embalming." What a diploma, and what a world! Arthur Sherry—Embalming—the O.K. Buckhout Company of Kalamazoo, Michigan!

Well, if the worst comes to the worst—as it may have done with Arthur Sherry and even O.K. Buckhout—we can always put some odds and ends in the last of our suitcases, and set up as traders in the Caledonian Market.

The Ring

NOT Wagner's but the boxing-hall in the Blackfriars Road. It was once the Old Surrey Chapel, and it still suggests a chapel. I remember that when I first saw it, all that remains of my Nonconformist boyhood was wickedly thrilled at the thought of seeing some boxing matches in such a setting. Dick Burge, who was responsible for the transformation, must have been the sort of man I dreamed about when I was a boy, compelled to sit, hot and glowering, under a Children's Address. Its deaconly appearance gave me no thrill last night, however, though it was my first visit for several years. It was not a night for easy thrills. The Blackfriars Road, black and dripping, was being swept by sleet, and I trust that Mrs. Burge, now the director of The Ring, will forgive me if I say that, even after the miserable Blackfriars Road, her hall did not seem very snug and lively. The big lights above the ring itself had not been turned up, for it still wanted some minutes to eight; the place was still dim, chill, cheerless; the cries of the youths who offered us apples and bars of chocolate went echoing hollowly, forlornly; and there was nothing to see, to do. I was alone—with a whole row of ringside seats to myself—and I began to wish I had stayed at home. The programme looked dull. Even the "Important 15 (3-min.) Rounds Contest" did not suggest anything very exciting.

Then the officials made their appearance. The referee climbed into his high chair, and the timekeeper sat down beside his stop-watch and bell. The fat men in white sweaters brought out their pails of water, bottles, and towels, and stumped round to their corners. The announcer climbed into the ring, which was immediately flooded with hard bright light. I like the announcer at the Ring. He looks as if he were taken over from the original chapel. He has an air of mellowed Nonconformity. His trim white hair and white moustache, his black tie, black morning coat, and dark, striped trousers, these things give him dignity; and even when he bellows "Ler-hay-dees an' Ger-hentle-men, Ser-hix Rer-hound Contest," you still feel that he is probably the last of the Old Surrey deacons.

Two thin but muscular youths, whose street-corner faces seemed almost an insult to their excellent bodies, climbed into the ring, grinned, touched gloves, and then instantly began pummelling one another. They were poor boxers but good stout-hearted fighters, and they pleased the rapidly growing audience. One of them got a cut early in the contest, with the result that both their faces were quickly crimsoned and there were marks of blood on their bodies. Somebody who knew nothing about the sport might have imagined that they were trying to kill one another and that the roaring crowd in the cheap seats was filled with blood-lust, but of course actually they were both good-humouredly slogging away, doing little or no harm to one another, and the crowd was merely applauding their lively spirit. It ended in a draw, a great round of applause, and an astonishing shower of coppers in the ring, so many indeed that it took the announcer and an assistant several minutes to pick them up. These two novices had pleased the crowd, and so it had rained pennies on them. The man sitting in front of me—a fellow with huge shoulders, a battered face, and a professional air—had registered the general verdict when he cried: "A bloody good fight!"

The next two were not so satisfactory. They were dapper dark lads, better boxers than the others but far less pugnacious. One of them was a trifle affected in his footwork and had a funny little trick of his own, a sort of back-kick not unlike that of a stage dancer. This amused the crowd at the back of me. They decided that these antics were effeminate, and immediately, unanimously, christened the author of them "Cissie." They indulged in waggish irony. "Oh, Cissie!" they screamed, as if in girlish terror. "Don't 'urt Cissie," they implored. In the last of their six rounds, however, these two improved and hammered one another to such a tune that the crowd was won over, dropped all talk of "Cissie," and gave them a round of applause as a benediction.

The contest that followed, though it rose to the dignity of twelve rounds, pleased nobody. The two boys appeared to be engaged in a kind of double-shadow boxing. They seemed determined to get through their twelve rounds without giving one another any real trouble at all. "Oh, 'ave a fight, 'ave a fight!" cried a disgusted sportsman at the back. The referee stopped them at one point and apparently uttered words of reproof. But they did not have a fight. The crowd at the back, tired of giving them ironical congratulations, now began to stamp in unison and to whistle "All by Yourself in the Moonlight." The announcer appealed for order, but not very passionately. The timekeeper chatted with his neighbour, smoked cigarettes, and mechanically shouted "Seconds Out" and sounded his bell. The referee yawned harder than ever. The two boys danced round and round the ring, went back to their corners, were slapped and towelled and massaged, returned to the centre each time looking very ferocious, but did not fight. We were all glad to see the last of them.

Now came the event of the evening. The fat men with cigars and the little hard-bitten men with cigarettes stopped roaming up and down the corridor that led to the dressing-rooms. They all came out, looking knowing and important. The lights above the ring looked harder and brighter than ever. You could not see the other side of the building; everything there was a mysterious blue haze, in which a match occasionally twinkled. "Cher-hoc-lait" cried the white-coated youth, more hopefully. "Fine Aipple," retorted the opposition caterer, sticking his tray of green fruit under our noses. The announcer entered the ring, and there waited, grave, important. There was a cheer.

Tom had come out, an old favourite and a Bermondsey lad. A grin lights up his broad flat face; he
puts his two gloves together, holds them up to salute
friends and patrons. He is attended by several enormous fellows with cauliflower ears, old hands. Another round of applause. The Frenchman is out, with
Messieurs Dubois and Dupont in close attendance.
"Ler-hay-dees an' Ger-hentle-men." Tom has cast
aside his beautiful silk dressing-gown, to reveal himself as a brown, stocky little fellow in blue shorts. The
Frenchman is performing those mysterious exercises
with the elastic ropes that girdle the ring. He is taller
and longer in the reach than Tom, but does not look
so strong or so fit—a queerly-made, ugly fellow, this
"Froggy," as they quickly decide to call him. He
does not look as if he will last more than a round or
two.

At first Tom seems to have it all his own way. You
hear the thump-pad-thud of his glove on Froggy's
lean body. But Froggy does not seem to mind. Now
and then that long left of his flashes out and sends
Tom staggering. "Don't take it too easy, Tom," the
crowd tells him. The other Bermondsey lads at the
back are full of advice. "Poke it out, Tom," they cry;
and then "Turn 'im round, Tom." And Tom is only
too anxious to do all these things, but somehow the
ungainly Frenchman never allows himself to be hurt.
Now and then, it is true, he blinks and gives a queer
little grin, all of which suggests that Tom's blows to
the body have made some impression, but he comes

back from his corner as fresh as ever. Indeed, somewhere about the tenth round, it stops being Tom's
fight, and there is now no talk of his taking it too easy.
Froggy is not only very quick with that long left of
his, but he is also a crafty fellow. Every time Tom
rushes in, he is stopped, and you hear the dull thump
of the wet glove. And there are moments when Froggy
drives Tom round the ring or bounces him against the
ropes. If Tom were softer, he might easily find himself on his back, with the timekeeper's voice measuring out his doom; but Tom is very tough, an old
taker of punishment. The last round sees him almost
as lively as ever, but now it is Froggy's glove you hear
thump-pad-thudding. The final clang—and the referee jerks a thumb towards Froggy's corner. The
announcer cannot be heard above the cheers. We do
not know Froggy and—to speak candidly—do not like
the look of him; but he has proved himself the better
man; and so we give him the best cheer of the evening. (Perhaps Froggy's friends in Paris would do the
same for Tom—perhaps; it is just possible.) Tom
puts his gloves together, shakes them at us, still grinning, and we give him a cheer too. Everybody is
good-humoured.

There was more to come, but a great many people
were drifting out, now that the great event was over,
and I followed them. The Blackfriars Road looked
exactly as it had done when I hurried out of it earlier
in the evening, a black misery, but the thought of the
good-humour I had left behind me kept me warm.

When the old Ring is transformed into a gigantic boxing arena, where really big purses are won and lost in a few minutes under glaring film-studio lights, I hope it will keep its good-humour. I hope it will, but I have my doubts.

Petticoat Lane

THAT curious smoky loneliness which is London on a winter Sunday morning was shattered, as if a gigantic bomb had burst, the moment I turned the corner from Aldgate High Street into Middlesex Street. This will not seem odd to anybody who remembers that Middlesex Street was once called Petticoat Lane, and is still Petticoat Lane every Sunday morning. At first I saw nothing except the tops of stalls because I was wedged in the crowd. We pushed, and they pushed— not angrily but in quiet good-humour—and gradually we began to move until we achieved something like a yard a minute. Then suddenly the crowd thinned and I found myself ejected—and a little man was dangling gaudy suspenders not six inches from my nose. "Take a look at 'em," he was roaring.

After escaping from these suspenders, I joined the group in front of a seedy-looking man who was talking in an astonishingly loud and angry voice. He had not shaved that morning or perhaps the morning before either, and wore neither collar nor tie, but nevertheless his stall glittered with gold watches, dozens and dozens of them, and not very far from the dirty fist he kept banging down was a heap of money, a whole heap of it, pounds and pounds. There was nothing very Jewish about his appearance, but never before have I heard such a strong Hebraic accent.

When you heard his talk of "dese vatches" you would
have sworn he was doing it on purpose. "In de Vest
End you go and pay six tibes de prize for dese
vatches. And vy? Because, I tell you," he cried, in a
towering rage, "dey're all robbers." And in a more
tender mood, that man, I am convinced, would not
have hesitated to call you "ma tear."

I had imagined such accents were no longer heard
in this world. Indeed, I have never met them except
in the harum-scarum novels of the thirties and forties
of the last century, early Dickens and Thackeray and
Valentine Vox and *Ten Thousand a Year*. But indeed
I might have suddenly been plunged into a chapter
of one of those novels. When I was a boy and stared
at those old illustrations by Cruikshank and "Phiz,"
so fantastically crowded and crazily energetic, I
thought that London was probably like that, but afterwards I came to the conclusion that there was nothing
realistic about those old illustrators, who merely re-
ported the doings in some dingy elfland of their own
invention. Now I see I was wrong. I am prepared to
believe they really drew the London of their day.
That London still persists, every Sunday morning in
Petticoat Lane. I had pushed my way into a "Phiz"
drawing. Here was one of his streets—not simply
crowded but *bursting* with humanity, and not ordinary
humanity, of course, but queer gargoyle-like beings,
monstrously fat, lean as hop-poles, twisted, shaggy,
battered, sinister. This fellow serving jellied eels, that
squinting jovial man, accompanying a cheap gramo-

phone record with a solo on a little tin toy trombone, this vast waddle of womanhood offering us a saucer of green peas, the curly Jew there smoothing out a pair of second-hand trousers—where have we seen them before? Why, in those queer scratchy illustrations we used to stare at, half fascinated, half repelled, so many years ago—in *Nicholas Nickleby* and *Oliver Twist.*

All the furious energy was still there. It was commerce turned into pandemonium. A Dionysiac frenzy possessed nearly everybody who had anything to sell. There were rows and rows of men selling overcoats, and no sooner had I set my eyes on the first of them than I thanked Heaven I was wearing an overcoat. If I had not been, they would have pounced upon me at once and hustled me into one of their "smart raglan overcoats I tell you people at Eighteen Shillings, I tell you Eighteen, all right then, Seventeen Shillings, for the last time this overcoat at *Sixteen Shillings!*" A youth in front of me was jammed into one and compelled to buy it, and later I saw him wandering about in it, still with a dazed expression on his face. One little man, all nose and bowler hat, was savagely cutting trousers to pieces with a carving knife. I do not know why he did it, but nobody seemed surprised. Men selling large pink vases would hit them with a hammer. A fellow with razor strops to sell looked like a homicidal maniac. The sweat was streaming down his face, and one hand was bandaged and bloody. "I'll now first take the edge off this razor," he bellowed, and then, in a fury, he picked up the razor and attacked a block of wood with it. Later, when I passed, he was yelling, "As the basis of this strop, people, you've got Carbonorum, the hardest substance known. Cuts glass, glass!" And the next moment there were showers of cut glass falling round him, through which you saw his eyes gleaming wildly.

It was a cold morning but the innumerable young men who were selling cheap sweets were in their shirt sleeves and even then looked uncomfortably hot. "Not One," they cried in a kind of ecstasy, slapping packets of chocolate and butterscotch into paper bags, "Not One—Not Two—Not Three—But *Four!* Who'll have the next?" Whenever one of these people had a drink, as they frequently did from bottles that no doubt came from Mr. Hyman Isbitsky's saloon across the way, you expected to hear a sizzling. Two young Hebrews who were offering us cutlery rescued, they said, from a great fire, had worked up the evidence with such energy that it was hardly possible to see either them or the cutlery for masses of slightly charred tissue paper, which they tossed about all over the place. What appeared at first sight to be a fight finally assumed the shape and sound of a very large man selling pull-overs at "arf a dollar." All the silk stockings were the centre of what looked like a riot. You saw them swaying in the air, above the massed heads, and then heard a voice that from the frenzied sound of it might have been prophesying the destruction of the city. "They're not rubbish," I heard one

of those gigantic voices cry. "Look at 'em. Feel 'em.
I've sold rubbish, people. The other day I sold some
at threepence a pair, and they *were* rubbish. I admit
it. These are the real thing. Shilling a pair." Even
your very character and destiny were hurled at you
as if Doomsday were already darkening the horizon,
for the three or four fate-readers I saw (all in M.A.
gowns) were summing up their victims and scribbling
their prophecies on slips of paper at an astounding
speed.

The first armies of the French Revolution could
never have known a more militantly democratic spirit
than the one that seemed to inspire all these frenzied
salesmen. "I don't care who you are," they would
roar, time after time, scores and scores of them. No
matter whether they were selling pink vases or milk
chocolate or watches or overcoats or mechanical toys or
stockings or cheese sandwiches, they did not care who
we were. All these things were being sold elsewhere,
especially in the West End, at prices so monstrous
that the salesmen's perspiration broke out afresh at
the thought of them and their voices cracked when
they came to record the infamy of it. In a passion
of fair-dealing, they shook in our faces their licences
and various mysterious documents that proved somehow they were speaking the truth. They brought out
handfuls of money to show that it was not merely that
they were after. And they did not care who we were.

In all that bustle, sound and fury, it was strange
and arresting to discover a quiet little space, a dumb

salesman. I saw a number of people, apparently quite absorbed, around one stall where there was no noise, and I was so curious that I pushed my way through to see what was happening. It was a little stall covered with second-hand gloves of every description, from the lordly fur gauntlet to the dirtiest twisted cotton pair, and all the people were quietly busy looking them over and trying them on, while the proprietor, very tall, thin, and depressed, sat staring, lost in a reverie. And then here and there, I came upon small brown men, from some unknown Orient, standing motionless, with cheap gaudy scarves hanging over their arms. They said nothing and I never saw them sell anything. They merely looked at us and Petticoat Lane, their eyes a dark mystery. And then there was the dimmest and most hopeless figure of all. I remember only a drooping cap, drooping moustache, drooping chin—and his stock-in-trade, which consisted of three shiny red notebooks each labelled "The Giant Memo Book." I appeared to be the only person there who noticed his existence; nobody wanted to buy a Giant Memo, and his silence, his whole attitude, suggested that he knew that as well as I did. I thought of him trailing home with his three Giant Memos, the very dimmest shade of a stationer. "I don't care who you are," they still roared. But I should like to have learned who he was, where he had been, what he had done, this dingy Cousin Silence of Petticoat Lane.

The Magic City

IT was one of those fat, shiny, expensive American magazines that you sometimes find in hotel lounges, marking the trail of the American tourist here. Its special subjects appeared to be travel and geography. It offered me a little travel too, for the moment I opened its vast and sumptuous advertisement section I was wandering in a foreign land, "A Loving Thought for Mother," one page began, and then gradually introduced the topic of Whitman's Sampler chocolates. "The Amber East is calling," cried another page. "Answer the lure of the great bronze image with eyes of gold." It was suggested too that I should bring the family to Minnesota, where apparently game fish await the swish of my line. I caught sight of six very tense-looking gentlemen, ready, it seemed, to spring at one another's throats at any moment, and underneath this tableau I read, "Planning high-speed business." I was warned against dull, discoloured teeth, asked to safeguard baby's health, and told definitely not to experiment with Oil Heat but to take the advice of more than 80,000 owners of William's Oil-O-Matic Heating. "Roads are White Pages of History in Virginia," another page informed me. And of course there were pictures of very aristocratic people, apparently

eight feet high and made of wood, looking at enormous
cars: "To step from your library or drawing-room
into Cadillac or La Salle involves no change of environment," from which I gather that these cars now
contain rows of bookshelves and grand pianos. "Tell
your Travel Story with Filmo Movies," cried another
genial bully. But why go on? Everybody knows these
advertisement pages, which take toll of all America's
literary and artistic cunning.

Well, I turned over dozens of these shiny leaves,
feeling as usual like a very poor and distant relative
of the people to whom such pages are addressed.
Everybody who subscribed to that magazine seemed
to be in for a far more gorgeous time than you and I
can ever hope to have. I was only peeping in through
the palace windows of this new world. I saw some
very fine photographs of "eagles in action," and came
to the conclusion that a mere snapshot of a sparrow
or two would be better suited to my station—or yours
—in this life. And then—why, everything was
changed almost apocalyptically, in something under a
dozen twinklings of an eye. You see, in the middle of
this rich magazine, I came upon some coloured photographs of a place. I will try to describe some of them.

There was one of a broad blue river. You looked
across it and saw, high above a line of trees, grey
towers topped with little dark turrets, standing out,
solid and clear, against a pale silken sky. Then, on
the next page, you looked into a sunny courtyard,
with the glimmer of leaves above the ancient paving,

and in this courtyard was a little company of fantastic soldiers, dressed in round black hats, white ruffs, gold and scarlet tunics, with red knee-breeches and stockings and buckled shoes, and all holding tasselled pikes. They might have marched straight out of a fairy tale. Anything might happen in a place where such soldiers mounted guard. Another photograph pretended to show me "one of the fairest corners" of this place, but obviously it was either all made up or miles and miles from anywhere, a secret. What you saw was a long sunken garden, buried among trees. In the middle was a rectangular pool, surrounded by paved walks, beyond which were beds bright with flowers. In the foreground were enormous lupins, and you never saw such blue and purple spikes. And everything there, the trees, the soft mirror of water, the walks and the flower-beds, seemed to be shimmering in a dreamy haze, and not a soul was to be seen. A man might look at that sunken garden, just peep through the tallest lupins for a minute or two, and then find he could be happy with the thought of it for a month.

These were all obviously very special places that you and I would never be able to see. But one photograph was of a street, because it said so. In the background you could see some tall buildings, but they did not look very amusing. It was what was happening in the street itself that was so curious. There was a white line running across it, and, standing a foot or two behind this line, was a tall fellow in blue holding out his arms, which were fantastically gauntleted in white. Behind him, again, was a number of great vehicles, waiting there, near the line, as if they were about to run a race and the man in blue would give the signal to start; and what made the scene so pleasing was the fact that all these vehicles were coloured a bright vermilion. You should see what a show they made on that page! I could see people, so many pink dots, sitting on top of these vehicles, waiting for the race to begin or perhaps dreaming of those romantic assignations to which such scarlet chariots must be carrying them, and I must say that when I first turned the page and saw them, I envied these people. They seemed to be even luckier than the people in the advertisements, who had been called by the Amber East and had answered the lure of the great bronze image with eyes of gold, or had taken the family to Minnesota and had fished like anything, or were able to step from their libraries and drawing-rooms, without change of environment, into Cadillacs and La Salles.

Beneath the picture of this bright and Babylonish street was something quite different, though apparently it could be seen in the same city. It was a tiny house and shop that somehow had been able to survive an immense conflagration that had happened nearly three hundred years ago. Not only that, but it had been written about by a man of genius, whose tales have been read by everybody, all over the world. And there it was, the little shop, with its low roof, its worn stones, and ancient windows, and mysterious

dark doorway. A very nice girl in a blue coat and
skirt and silk stockings could be seen, in the picture,
looking in the cosy little window. Imagine being able
to see that shop any time you wanted, and perhaps
knowing the nice girl in the blue coat too! Or, if you
do not care for that kind of thing, there are "the
masses of beautiful dahlias in bloom." You see them
in a picture of some garden somewhere in this city.
Across the right foreground there runs a row of sharp
iron spikes, which are there no doubt to prevent the
country's enemies charging down the flower beds.
Then, bang in the middle, in all the hues that photo-
graphy ever knew, are the dahlias themselves, bloom-
there in their hundreds, and every one of them nearly
as big as your hand. Behind there are some trees, and
behind them, exquisite, remote, mysterious, the upper
stories of some large building in white stone, probably
a palace.

And I must say these coloured photographs killed
everything else in that magazine for me. After seeing
them, I did not want to "Plan now for a healthful,
happy vacation in Maine," nor to change my mind,
cast off my Occidental worries for a while, and "watch
the monkeys skipping over the walls of Jaipur" (which
would, I feel sure, remind me of my Occidental
worries), nor to go beyond the high Sierras where,
apparently, there is a land singularly blest by Nature,
nor to "savour the charm of three centuries ago, while
cruising in modern luxury through the picturesque
heart of French Canada." These are all very fine

things to do, and in the ordinary way I might have dismissed them with the tribute of a sigh, but they did not haunt my mind as that magic city did, with its rivers and palaces and gardens and fantastic soldiers and great vermilion carriages. And I only wish they had not put at the top of these enchanted pictures the heading: "High-lights of London Town," because this piece of editorial carelessness prevented me from learning what the place really was. It can't be London, I know, because I live there and it is all quite different, a stupid medley of dirty river and buses and policemen and dusty parks.

The Underworld

A MAN must be prepared to make many sacrifices for his art, and I was ready to take my place in an orange-coloured motor-coach and be condescendingly shown a number of places I had seen before. But there are limits. When I saw that board, I said at once: "If you go, then I stay behind." For on that board was printed in the boldest letters: "Tour of London's Underworld." I could not possibly go riding through the East End, from nine until eleven, above a notice that said "Tour of London's Underworld." It is bad enough merely to use your neighbours for sight-seeing purposes, to go gaping at them. But to announce to every little Jewish tailor's hand or Chinese laundry-man that in your opinion he was living in an under-world, this would be intolerable. Fortunately, however, the notice-board was put away, having done its duty by tempting us into the coach. But it did not disappear from our imaginations, where it was still prominently displayed. We were on our way to the Underworld. A glance at the tourist agency's leaflet could reassure us. There were three conducted tours of London: in the morning you could do the City, in the afternoon the West End, and in the evening— there it was, far plainer than that mysterious thing, the pikestaff—Underworld. We must not be in too great a hurry to jeer at the tourist agencies. In a world

that is rapidly becoming disillusioned about everything, they alone show us the bourgeoning romantic
imagination. These are the Cooks who say the broth
cannot be spoilt.

Our party was not a large one, and it was chiefly
composed of middle-aged American ladies, who
perhaps had come all the way from San Francisco and
Chicago to see a real Underworld. Our guide had been
specially created by a generous and wise Nature for
such ladies. He was a young man with a store of
sound information, a horribly false accent, and an
enormous conceit of himself. He had been explaining
London so long to open-mouthed tourists that not
unnaturally he had arrived at the conclusion that he
himself was chiefly responsible for all the fine things in
it. Prospero himself at the revels could not have been
more condescending. He did not take us straight to
the Underworld. We began with Bloomsbury and
Clerkenwell, and there, in what was still broad daylight, we stopped in front of churches and ancient
hospitals while he told us all about "Dickens, the
great wraitah," or "Henrai the Aith," the "plarntin' of
ewld trees," the "faounding of ewld sepewlcars." At
times he was so overcome by the wonder of it all, more
especially his own knowledge and wisdom, that he had
to close his eyes—they were small, pinkish, hot, the
result of too much close study or too many bottles of
beer—while addressing us. When not engaged in
pouring out information, he was good enough to talk
with the nearest middle-aged ladies, to whom he ex-

plained why he never wore a hat or overcoat. When
he stopped the coach, stood up and lectured us, small
Cockney boys gathered round and looked at him and
at us with sardonic eyes, like so many little Sam
Wellers.

Dusk fell upon us, mercifully, and now we made for
Shoreditch, and ran on through Whitechapel and
Shadwell. The Underworld. There could be no doubt
about it. I had been this way before, but then I had
merely taken buses and tubes in the ordinary way,
had gone poking into pubs or stared into little shops
with outlandish names written above them, and so of
course it had never occurred to me that I was exploring an Underworld. Why should it? I was only
wandering about in another part of London, just
round the corner. I had always thought of the "underworld" as having a spiritual rather than a topographi-
cal reference. It might begin and end anywhere in
London, this real underworld. Postal districts can
have nothing to do with it. Every now and then,
detectives stroll into suites of rooms in the big hotels,
expensive service flats, decaying houses in Bayswater,
Chelsea studios, Bloomsbury boarding-houses, and
then we who read our papers suddenly catch a glimpse
of this real underworld, inhabited by people who go
prowling through this jungle of London like tigers.
It is not an orange motor-coach but one of the vans
of the Flying Squad that could take you for a tour
of this underworld, and I am not sure that even the
detectives could do it properly. They could only show

you a little piece of it, in full flight.

Having offered myself as a tourist of the Underworld, however, I promptly began to see it. Very artfully, our guide told us that we need have no fears, we were quite safe. Then of course it seemed at once as if we were skirting innumerable dangers. Our progress through these melancholy little streets became a series of hair-breadth escapes. Here, for example, are some of our adventures. More than once, our coach was besieged by creatures of the Underworld. If we stopped, they gathered round and clamoured for money. They jumped up at us and contrived to cling hold of the side of our vehicle. Sometimes they threw things at us, with many a yell of execration. With these eyes, I saw them fighting on the pavement, inspired no doubt by the implacable feud spirit of the Underworld. The only thing that tended to reassure me was the size of these Underworld creatures, for they were all very small indeed, so small that I doubt if the oldest of them was more than fourteen.

At last we arrived at Charlie Brown's famous pub, where we made a long stay, ostensibly that we might enjoy at leisure the sight of Mr. Brown's extraordinary collection of Oriental and other antiques and curiosities, but really in order that the guide and the driver might have a few drinks. I do not propose to describe Charlie Brown's, for during these last few years all the papers have discovered it in turn and it is now one of London's show places. But I cannot help wondering what would happen to the man who carefully ex-

D

plained to Mr. Brown, who believes in law and order, Ming vases, and no nonsense from anybody, that he himself, his Railway Tavern, his ivories and bureaux, were part of the Underworld.

And now we were in Limehouse, which I take to be the very heart of this Underworld. We were not shown any Chinese gambling and opium dens because, the guide explained, it was his experience that visitors refused to gamble and smoke opium themselves and he had to do it all. Apparently, these Oriental vices had rather palled upon him. So our coach, like an uneasy monster, merely went creeping about the narrow little dark streets of Limehouse, and the picturesque wickedness of the place was left to our imagination. Once more, the guide referred to "Dickens, the great wraitah," but that was the only author he did mention. Here I think he did less than justice to one of our contemporaries. If a certain imaginative young Cockney, with an eye for sinister effects and a not unpicturesque style, had not written a book or two about this quarter, some years ago, I doubt if these Underworld tours would ever have been planned. It is Mr. Thomas Burke's *Limehouse Nights* that have done the trick. And as life has a queer habit of imitating literature, it is possible that Limehouse and the immediate neighbourhood is gradually becoming more queer and sinister and picturesque. Mr. Burke, who has, I believe, a large public in America, should demand a royalty on the proceeds of these tours. As it is, he is not even mentioned.

We went roaring down into Rotherhithe Tunnel, and then when we emerged on the Surrey side, our guide became very perfunctory indeed. It was not until we reached the Embankment that he awakened up again, and began pumping information about the Savoy and Cecil Hotels into us. By the time we arrived at Northumberland Avenue, our destination, he was talking as hard as he could go. "And thet concludes my tawr," he said, at last, "and if any of you wish to take the morning or afternoon tawrs, please remember I can talk for one hour on Westminster Abbey, half an hour on St. Paul's or the Tower." But even the middle-aged American ladies did not rise to this bait. The thought of his hour's talk in Westminster Abbey sent us hurrying away, happy to be unguided. I returned to Hampstead by tube, and for my fourpence was presented with a genuine underworld, with inscrutable Orientals thrown in—as far as Belsize Park, for which station our Far Eastern visitors have a strange passion. And there's mystery for you.

In The British Museum

"The British Museum, unrivalled in the world for the richness and variety of its contents, occupies a huge building of various dates, which is entered from Great Russell Street, in Bloomsbury, a few yards N. of New Oxford Street. A pigeon-haunted forecourt separates the street from the colonnaded main façade (S.), in the pediment of which are allegorical sculptures, by Westmacott, representing the Progress of Humanity and various personified Arts."

The above paragraph is written by Mr. Findlay Muirhead. I have stolen it from one of his *Blue Guides*, and rigged it up hastily as a sort of colonnaded main façade. In Mr. Muirhead the British Museum met its match. It gives me all the more pleasure to announce this because the place has always conquered me in a few minutes. I hurry along Great Russell Street, walk briskly through the forecourt—pigeon-haunted, as Mr. Muirhead observes—and dive under the allegorical sculptures, feeling as certain as Westmacott himself of the Progress of Humanity; and as I go, I tell myself that this time there shall be no shirking, no incurious idling about and then a sudden bolt for tea and tobacco; I will be a good Museum man, a visitor inspired by a little of that Muirhead spirit. (After all, I possess his *Guide to London*. A man left it in my rooms at Cambridge and I have kept it ever since.) In the old novels, the hero frequently took the heroine round the museums and galleries, and astonished her by the extent of his knowledge and the power he had of making everything live. "Look at this," he would say, pointing to half a Grecian foot, a Roman hand, the bottom of an Egyptian vase, or the remains of a Babylonian water-jug; and then he would sketch lightly the whole background of the civilization, the remote and enchanting past, from which this object came. That is the kind of man I should like to be when I visit one of these places. And I never pass beneath that colonnaded main façade without telling myself very firmly that this time there must be no nonsense.

If there was a little room somewhere in the British Museum that contained only about twenty exhibits and good lighting, easy chairs, and a notice imploring you to smoke, I believe I should become a museum man. I should have time then to look at something properly, to meditate over it. As it is, however, I wander from room to room, floor to floor, in a kind of uneasy dream. I begin to feel like a ghost as I flit past those rows of gilded coffins, down those long aisles flanked by colossal-winged lions and man-headed bulls. I do not say that this is altogether unpleasant. Perhaps extreme old age is something like this, when you drift like a dead leaf through the winter of your years, and your very grandchildren and the younger members of the club seem as remote and fantastic as winged lions and man-headed bulls. Perhaps when we die, we slip quietly into this museum atmosphere, into regions equally quiet and shadowy, warm but sunless, where things out of Nineveh loom gigantically and gems from ancient Crete glitter faintly in the dusk, and it is all one, a dream of life in which Apollo and Aphrodite are stony, dumb—until at last a bell rings and we rush out to tea and Great Russell Street, or find ourselves kicking and mewing on another planet.

Sometimes in the British Museum I entertain myself with a fancy that I have been projected into some Socialistic and Utopian State of the future. The very air, which appears to have been warmed and disinfected in the basement, sustains this fancy. There is Utopia in your nostrils. Then the officials, the uniformed attendants, all help. The visitors as a whole do nothing to destroy the illusion. Different as they are in appearance and manner, they all have that look, intelligent but docile, of good citizens, men and women who would fit snugly into a Socialistic State. Frequently their hair is wild, but all else about them is tame enough. You have a feeling that most of them are quietly pleased to have left behind them the roaring chaos of Tottenham Court Road and New Oxford Street. Their faces light up with a faint gleam of pleasure and interest the moment they first catch sight of these ordered rooms, in which everything is so neatly ticketed and so nicely dead. They happily tiptoe forward, safe in a little world where nothing has escaped the officials and the catalogue. With a sober

pleasure they follow the elderly lecturer, who talks
of Pericles and Pheidias and points to a tiny Parthenon in a glass case, a Parthenon that will never be
disturbed by a wind whistling over from the Ægean,
by the shouts of enraged citizens, by the glitter of
foreign shields and ships. Even the children here are
all dressed alike, subdued and earnest, and have to
march forward two by two, under the eye of a school-
mistress. And shouting, singing, fighting, drinking, and
making love seem to be strange antics of long, long
ago, early habits of mankind that may be discovered
from a study of the specimens and are duly noted in
the catalogue. Reproductions of such specimens may
be obtained, you feel, by students engaged in genuine
research by application to the proper authorities. And
so the fanciful evidence accumulates, though as none
of us happens to know what the well-drilled Socialistic
and Utopian State will be like, obviously such evidence
is not worth much. A fancy, that is all.

I was there the other day, and drifted about as idly
and foolishly as ever, acquiring no information of any
kind. No, that is not strictly true. I made one discovery, relating to the age of the official type, the born
Civil Service man. How long has this type existed?
I do not know, but now I can go back with confidence
to 3300 B.C. He was alive then, because there is a
solid and unmistakable image of him in the British
Museum, labelled "Sumerian official 1st Dynasty of
Ur." There he is to the life, looking as if at any
moment he will slowly open those large grey heavy-

lidded eyes, stare at us solemnly for a minute, and
then declare that "really he hasn't the least idea." His
forehead is small and slopes back sharply; there is no
mistaking the supercilious cut of the large eye-socket;
his eyebrows must have been thin and always slightly
raised, and the eyes themselves must have been of that
bulging stupid kind; his nose juts forward well, a
perky triangle; and his mouth and chin are small and
mean. His arms are folded at ease, and he presents a
figure of repose. He is waiting there until somebody
has filled in the proper form. That somebody has been
dead these five thousand years, but he does not know
it, and even if he knew he would not care. He is very
happy here in the Museum. And nobody will persuade
me that I do not know that man, though few people
can know less about the 1st Dynasty of Ur than I do.
But I am convinced that that Dynasty had its Oxford
somewhere and that this man went there and sneaked
off with a First and a piffling essay prize, and then
hurried into the Civil Service and after that never
hurried again. If I had stayed another minute in front
of him, he would have referred me to another department. Undoubtedly he likes the Museum, but he
would be happier still in Whitehall. One day he will
hear about Whitehall, and will then calmly get down
from his pedestal and go there. I shall not be very
surprised if, one day, I catch sight of him lunching at
one of the more exclusive clubs.

After leaving the Sumerian official, I only halted
for another minute, and that was on the landing of

the mosaic staircase, which offered me a most curious spectacle. A number of little schoolgirls, in blue coats and red-ribboned hats, filed past me on this landing, and I saw them against the background of that colossal head of Rameses the Second, which stands against the wall facing this landing. The head was illuminated from below, and its vast spread of features looked as if they had been newly transported from one of the wilder Arabian Nights. Cutting across the lower half of this nightmare face was a bobbing procession of little red-ribboned straw hats. I knew at once that I should see nothing more fantastic than that if I stayed for hours (unless, of course, I remained all night, and then I do not know what one might see), so off I went. As I stood for a moment at the entrance, meeting the cold air as if for the first time, I happened to glance to the left, and there I encountered the level dark gaze of Hoa-Haka-Nana-Ia, from Easter Island, that remotest and most mysterious of all islands. I asked him who he was and what he was doing, standing quietly there in the very heart of Bloomsbury, but he made no reply. He merely looked at me—sardonically. I have a feeling that at certain odd times, perhaps about two in the morning, he stirs a little and quietly chuckles.

Among The Glass Jars

I was handed over to a youngish man who was wearing a check apron. He was one of those fair, undersized Cockneys who have no features but yet a great deal of character. Mr. H. G. Wells knows all about them and on the whole has dealt justly with them, in spite of his trick of pretending to survey them from a vast biological and sociological height. This one with the check apron was quite capable of saying "Chubes," like Kipps, but on the other hand he could not have shared Kipps's dismay. He was learned in those chubes, for he saw thousands of them every day. I had been handed over to him so that he might show me some of them, for we were in the Museum of the Royal College of Surgeons.

This is, I need hardly say, no ordinary museum. If it had been, I should have avoided a guide, because it is much better to drift about such places by oneself, making one's own discoveries. I do not like to be piloted up and down innumerable corridors and to be prevented from thinking by the chatter-chatter of some well-informed human parrot. If it had been a mere matter of piloting and information, I think I could have got on quite well without my friend in the check apron. His services, however, were more important than that. When we parted, I rewarded him not for knowledge, but for his cheery ignorance.

Where there is a Cockney there is life. In the midst
of death, his sparrow glances, his little ragged moustache, his perky accent, were a constant reminder of
the fact that somewhere outside there still existed a
world of bo'l'd staht an' fegs an' Ally Pally an' Lily
Morris singing "Down't 'ave any mo-wer, Mrs.
Mo-wer"—or, if this is too vulgar for you, a world of
sport and song, conviviality, humour, and affection.
Set me down, if you like, as a weakling because I
stood in want of such a reminder; but I am a layman
and I have just been. There used to be men about the
streets crying, "Any rags, any bones, any bottles to-
day." We leave the rags outside the Museum of the
Royal College of Surgeons, but the bones and the
bottles are there. Perhaps those men were not what
they seemed.

I did not feel very uncomfortable in the presence
of the bones. There is a certain grotesque humour
about skulls and skeletons. Hamlet did not plumb
the depths, for Yorick and the painted lady might
have had a worse end; they might have found
their way into glycerine and a glass jar. There are
rows and rows of skulls in this museum, and if you
wish you may survey bonekind from Piltdown to
Pimlico. (Jonathan Wild is there, by the way, and
looks completely at home.) You may begin with the
Neolithic and come by stages to the modern European in his place of honour, though even then it is
only such grinning honour as Sir Walter had. There
are skeletons ranging from a pigmy lady to the in-

credible eight feet of the Irish giant. I noticed some bony fellows leaning forward in a rather absurd way, and then discovered that they had been anthropoid apes. I was asked to remark how flat the tops of their skulls were, and did so, though without much satisfaction. You scream, scratch, and throw coconuts, apparently, and then, having another inch or so on the top of the skull, you produce the dialogues of Plato, *Macbeth*, the Ninth Symphony, and the catalogue of the Museum of the Royal College of Surgeons. In short, when the skull is the right size, it immediately begins to put itself in museums. I am sorry, but there is something here that eludes me.

There is one long room that is nothing less than a symphony of bone. Man cuts a poor figure in there, though I noticed that the tiger cut a worse. The centre-piece is composed of the vast gleaming arches of the sperm whale, like the ribs of a ship. Melville would have clapped his hands at the sight of his old friend so imperially housed. The prehistoric creatures and the pachyderms are next in order of importance. Nature apparently built these fellows to last, but they have not lasted, except as shining ruins. That little extra bit of skull has seen to that, and as Nature is also responsible for anything that happens to skulls, she appears to be playing a very queer and inconsistent game.

But what about the game that Man has been playing? I caught a shuddering glimpse of it down in the basement, where the Army Medical War Collection

is now permanently deposited. A series of faces
modelled and coloured to the life in wax illustrate the
marvels of plastic surgery. They were, indeed, too
much to the life, for I seemed to have known the very
men. You see a face that stops short at the upper
lip, the rest being nothing but crimson pulp. You
see it again, and something good is happening to it.
You see it once more, and it is a complete face, a little
twisted and scarred, perhaps, but still a face. There
are models of cheeks being restored, of noses being
manufactured out of strips of skin from foreheads. A
glimpse is sufficient to make you grateful for ever for
this patient mingling of art and science. Incredible,
though, that the same species could have produced
both the wounds and the healing, that the same age
will both pulp and mend its creatures. Incidentally,
it might not be a bad idea to duplicate some of those
models and hang them up in various public places
throughout Europe and America. All foreign negotia-
tions might be conducted within sight of those things
that are half faces and half screaming horrors.

After all, there is another war going on all the time,
and you may find a few of its souvenirs in the thousands and thousands of glass jars, filling room after
room. Some of the things in these jars look quite
pretty, and not unlike specimens of submarine life.
Sometimes they are tinted blue or pink or both; their
shapes are strange but not ungraceful; many of them,
delicate, translucent, seem to sway or wave in the
spirit or glycerine that is their element. They did not

fill me with horror, make me feel sick, as I thought they would, these livers and kidneys and bladders and stomachs. I could not associate them with myself or my own kind. If I had learned that they had been brought from another planet, I should not have been very surprised. I understood enough, however, to respect the men who had put them there. It is a good war, this, and it is being fought on ever wider and wider fronts. Unlike Mr. Bernard Shaw—who has all the prophet's contempt for people outside his own line of business—I have always admired the doctors. It is said that the best of them must be something of a charlatan. I should prefer to say that even the worst of them protects us from something worse than a thousand charlatans.

"All these," said my aproned guide, when he came to the last gallery, "are what you might call freaks." Might, indeed! I do not intend to describe these little pranks or mistakes of Nature. Those who have the stomach for it may go and see for themselves. They should do what I could not do, namely, take Science with them. In Science there are no horrors; all is understood and therefore forgiven; and the two-headed thing in its jar can be calmly examined. I looked down and saw two charwomen in blue, dusting some glass jars below, and I wondered what they thought about it all. I looked again and saw a figure in white. Apparently it was Sir Arthur Keith, busy sorting mandibles. I could hear them clattering like dominoes. I did not wonder what he thought about it all, for the simple reason that I know, if there is any truth in the reports of public men's speeches. John Hunter left behind him 13,682 specimens, and since then thousands and thousands of others have been added. No part of us has escaped its little jar. Yet look where you will, you will not find the tiniest jar labelled "Mind of Man" or "Soul of Man." And if you wish to know what it is that is responsible for all this collecting, arranging, cataloguing, what drives men on to study these things so patiently, I can only direct you to that room below on the right, where you will see rows of bottled crinkly greyish-brown stuff—brains, they call them. This stuff is responsible for all this ordered activity and selfless devotion. The unbottled examines the bottled and that is how it is done. And after that, I told myself as I wandered into Lincoln's Inn Fields again, it seems silly that the jars cannot dust and arrange themselves.

At Popular Prices

IF you don't look steadily at anything, if you don't listen carefully, if you don't really think about it all, this place seems miraculous. Happy the age, the city, the people, that possess not one but many such places! A girl with eighteen pence in her purse can dine here in a style that Queen Elizabeth herself never knew and would envy. Men have conquered half the world, looted whole kingdoms, and never arrived at such luxury. The grandparents of these people would have walked miles just to *see* such a towering and glittering palace, just to stare at it from outside, open-mouthed. The idea of marching in and ordering what they fancied would have stunned them. To be made free of a place like that! To have what you liked and only pay a sixpence or a shilling! It looks like a guinea at least, and fit for nobody less than the Queen and Dizzy and the Shah! To go in, caring for nobody, and have a bob's worth! How they would have gaped! And here their grandchildren and great-grandchildren are, hundreds and hundreds of them, none of them anybody in particular, but all nicely dressed, laughing and talking, ordering this and eating that, fairly owning the place. But in truth, they do own the place. They know that this palace was built for them.

Dreamily surveying it, I say again it seems miraculous. It shatters my syntax and for once I become a really modern writer. The marble hall below, piled high with bonbons and cakes, as if we had just sacked the cities of the Indies. The lifts and the stairs, all as busy as Paddington. The carpets, the mirrors, the ten thousand lights, floor after floor. This room, with hardly an empty chair, and an acre of table cloths. The waitresses in their neat black-and-white. The assistant-managers and managers, so dignified, so polite, so grave, so quietly opulent, casting smooth glances upon the Egyptians, the Philistines, the portions of roast pork. Consider the menu with its closely printed columns. Here, it is true, are no nightingales' tongues, no peacocks' brains, yet Nero himself never knew such variety. There is a portion of almost everything edible under the sun to be had for eightpence, a shilling, one-and-six, or two shillings. One of a thousand shining teapots may be yours for an hour for a few coppers. You may eat French and Viennese pastries, as rich and reckless and multi-coloured as eighteenth-century archdukes, with a glittering fork.

There are ices, chocolate, pink, and yellow, that were delivered this morning, by the ton. You may tap the sweet warm flood of coffee for threepence. Nor is that all. Above the clatter and chatter is a sound more sensuous than the golden scented air, the Viennese pastries, the prettiest white-and-vermilion of the girls—it is the orchestra. Yes, there is music here too. It comes from an orchestra as big as any that Papa Haydn ever took for a jog through his symphonies. You can hear it all the time, and from

E

here you can see it, can just catch a glimpse of the
sleek young conductor and his dark first violins. By
the Waters of Babylon they now sit and strum. When
they have finished, we shall applaud, and the conductor will turn and flash an eye at the girls. What a
place!

There is just time, before we cool, to wonder at the
whole achievement. It is one of the characteristic
products of the new democratic-industrial civilisation.
This is the age when the planets can be weighed under
the very roof where the atom is divided up. I suppose
the basis of this amazing piece of organisation is really
some such wizardry with figures. Somewhere in the
background, behind the lights and marble and
napery, behind the thousand waitresses and cash-box
girls and managers and violinists, behind the shimmering bonbons and cakes and cauldrons of hot-pot
and vanloads of coloured ices, are a few men who go
to work juggling with quarter millions and fractions
of a farthing, who know how many units of electricity
it takes to cook a steak-and-kidney pudding and how
many minutes and seconds a waitress (five feet four
in height and in average health) will need to carry a
tray from the kitchen lift to the table in the far corner.
There is, you may say, a scientist in the basement.

None of this would have been possible at any
earlier time. In the nineteenth century these people
would have gone to dingy coffee taverns, little chop-
houses, and the like. This luxury, this variety, was
not for the likes of them. Their forefathers (and

mine) would not have known what to do in such a place; they would have gaped at the glittering marble hall, scratched their heads, and gone away to munch their bread and bacon in some reeking ale-house. But this is the twentieth century, which says, "I don't want the gentleman's guinea, I want your pennies. There are such a lot of you, you see. Give me your pennies and I will work miracles for you. Look, here is a newspaper, and you can understand every single word of it! Here are moving pictures, made specially for you. And here is a white palace where you can have your tea." And here they are, sitting over their "plice an' chips, roll an' burrer, cikes an' po' o' tea," envying nobody, lords and ladies of the miraculous pennies, Demos dining in state.

I wish I could say I liked it all. I am not—as so many writers seem to be—the last of an old and very distinguished family, did not take to writing because the last mortgage was foreclosed, and have no memories of an Elizabethan manor to trouble me. My grandfather, a grim Yorkshire working man, honorary treasurer of the local Co-operative Society in its fighting days, and a hanging judge of meat (he always went on Saturday to buy the joint), would not have dared to enter this place. These people, some trifling and accidental differences apart, are my people, or at least rickety Cockney versions of them. My heart warms at the thought of this new civilisation, which allows everybody, except the very poorest, to sit here in comfort and even luxury, all washed and

nicely dressed, and order their food and drink and
know that it is all well within their means, with the
days when they sullenly envied the rich rapidly
dwindling into a mere social history. Nevertheless,
there comes a moment—it is here now—when one
cannot dreamily rhapsodize any longer, when the
glance becomes steady, the ear acute, and the mind
cannot be put off with fine phrases.

The trouble is, it is all so false. On those amazing
columns of figures, which are real enough, has been
erected a gigantic sham. The marble hall is not really
marble, it is a fake. The bonbons and the cakes are
concocted for the eye. All those hundred-and-one
items on the menu—they look well, but do they taste
well, do they nourish? They do not. I do not mean
to say the food is bad, but nevertheless it is certainly
not good honest solid fare. In a place like this, the
management is far too sensible to use anything
tainted, but it is obvious that all the raw materials of
the dishes have been snapped up as bargains somewhere. (What my grandfather would have said of the
meat is not printable.) The sumptuous looking
pastries should be seen and not tasted. The service
only looks well at a distance. In detail, it is not re-
assuring.

Nothing perhaps is dirty, but then nothing is really
clean either. Tea and coffee are always splashed into
the saucers. The food is slopped on to the plates.
Only the table-cloths at the other end of the room
appear virgin. The waitresses do not survive a more

careful scrutiny. They are over-powdered and under-nourished; they do not look very strong or very healthy; they have far too much to do; there is a suggestion that when at last they do marry, they will have trouble with their babies. The assistant managers and the like are not men with whom one would care to establish friendly relations; they look rather greasy, rather dirty, at once servile and despotic. The customers are not so clean and healthy and happy as one first imagined them to be. Too many of the older ones look ill or worried; too many of the younger look caddish or minxish; and all the younger women, the girls who clap the band, have smothered themselves with cheap cosmetics. Even the band itself will not do. The music it plays is not real music, just fake stuff; and it does not perform as honest musicians should. That excessive tremulo, for example, isn't that the pastry translated into sound? Alas!—is this the new civilization? Do we enter this place in the debit or the credit column? Are we winning or losing. Let's get outside and talk it over.

At Thurston's

BEYOND the voices of Leicester Square there is peace.
It is in Thurston's Billiards Hall, which I visited for
the first time, the other afternoon, to see the final in
the Professional Championship. Let me put it on
record that for one hour and a half, that afternoon, I
was happy. If Mr. Thurston ever wants a testimonial
for his Billiards Hall, he can have one from me. The
moment I entered the place I felt I was about to enjoy
myself. It is small, snug, companionable. Four or
five rows of plush chairs look down on the great table,
above which is a noble shaded light, the shade itself
being russet coloured. Autumn to the cloth's bright
Spring. Most of the chairs were filled with comfortable men, smoking pipes. I noticed a couple of women
among the spectators, but they looked entirely out
of place, just as they would have done among the fat
leather chairs of a West End club. I had just time to
settle down in my seat, fill and light a pipe myself,
before the match began.

It was between Davis and Newman, both of whom
have held the championship. They suddenly appeared,
in their shirt sleeves and holding cues, and we gave
them a friendly round of applause, which they
acknowledged with something between a bow and a
nod. The marker arrived too. He deserves a word to
himself. He was an essential part of the afternoon,

not merely because he kept the score and called it out, but because he created an atmosphere. He was a young man, whose profile was rather like that of the Mad Hatter; his face was all nose, teeth, and glittering eye; and he had an ecclesiastical dignity and gravity of manner. He handed over the rest or the half-butt like one serving at an altar. To see him place the red on the spot was to realize at once the greatness of the occasion. Best of all was to watch him removing, with his white-gloved hands, specks of dust or films of moisture from a ball. The voice in which he called out the scores was the most impersonal I have ever heard. It was a voice that belonged to solemn ritual, and it did as much as the four walls and the thickly curtained windows to withdraw us from ordinary life and Leicester Square. And withdrawn we certainly were. After a few minutes the world of daylight and buses and three o'clock winners receded, faded, vanished. I felt as if we were all sitting at ease somewhere at the bottom of the Pacific.

Davis had a broad face and wore a brown suit. Newman had a long narrow face and wore a black waistcoat and striped trousers. Davis was the more stolid and cheerful. Newman suggested temperament. Apart from these details, I could discover no difference between them. They were both demi-gods. In the great world outside, I can imagine that one might pass them by as fellows of no particular importance, just pleasant, clean, neat men with north-country accents. But in this tiny world of bright-green cloth and white and crimson spheres, they were demi-gods. After the first few minutes I began to regard them with an awe that has no place in my attitude towards any living writer. If one of them had spoken to me (and Newman did speak to the man on my left, who was evidently something of a connoisseur and made all manner of knowing noises), I should have blushed and stammered and nearly choked with pride and pleasure. No modern writer could make me feel like that, simply because no modern writer is great enough. It would have to be Shakespeare; and when you are in this remote little world of billiards, players like Messrs. Davis and Newman *are* Shakespeares: they are as good as that. They have the same trick too: they make it look easy. Watching them, you have to use your imagination like blazes to realize you could not do it all yourself.

I do not know whether I have any right to describe myself as a player, but I have played billiards many a time. If I am staying under the same roof with a billiard table, I nearly always play on it, but on the other hand, I never go out looking for billiard tables on which to play. Public billiard rooms are dreary places, even if you find the game itself fascinating, as I do. Moreover, they are too public for my taste. Once you have a cue in your hand in those places, it appears that everybody who happens to be there has the privilege of advising you. Strangers say, quite angrily: "Oh, you ought to have gone in off the red there!" Then when you try something else:

"No, no, no! The white's the game. That's it. Only put plenty of side on. Oh no, too hard!" And they make little clucking noises and laugh softly behind your back, until at last you bungle every shot. This does not seem to happen in any other game but billiards. If you play bridge in a public room, strangers do not stand behind you and point authoritatively to your Queen of Spades or King of Diamonds. Nobody makes remonstrative noises at you when you are playing chess. But billiards is anybody's and everybody's game. The adventures of those three shining spheres, as they chase one another over the green cloth, are public property, and the moment you have grasped a cue, you yourself are a public character whose actions can be criticised with freedom. And as I happen to be a very poor performer, I prefer to play in private, almost behind locked doors.

The shortest way of describing the skill of Messrs. Davis and Newman is to say that it appeared miraculous when they ever missed anything. Now when my friends and I have played the game, it has always seemed miraculous if anything happened but a miss. The balls always seemed so small, the pockets so narrow, the table so hopelessly long and wide. These professional champions, however, treated every shot as if it were a little sum in simple arithmetic. While they went on calmly potting the red, bringing it back nearer to the white every time, and then collecting cannons by the dozen, we all leaned back and sucked our pipes almost somnolently, secure and happy in a drowsy peace of mechanics and art. It was when they chanced to fail that we were startled into close attention. You could hear a gasp all round you. If the marker had suddenly broken into song, we could hardly have been more astonished. The only persons who never showed any signs of surprise were the two players—and of course the marker. If Davis, after going half way round the table with an amazing number of delicious little cannons, all as good as epigrams, finally missed a shot, Newman quite nonchalantly came forward to make the balls do what he thought they ought to do, for half an hour or so. And the things they did were incredible. He could make them curve round, stop dead, or run backward. But if Newman went on doing this for three-quarters of an hour, quietly piling up an immense score, Davis sitting at ease, nursing his cue, showed no anxiety, no eagerness to return to the table. His turn would come. I tell you, these were demi-gods.

The hall was filled with connoisseurs, men who knew a pretty bit of "side" or "top" when they saw it, smacked their lips over a nice follow through, and heard sweet music in the soft click-click of the little cannons, and when a stroke of more than usual wizardry was played, they broke into applause. Did this disturb either of the players? It did not. They never even looked up, never smiled, never blinked an eyelid. Perhaps they had forgotten we were there, having lost all remembrance of us in following the

epic adventures of the two whites and the red. Of all
games, billiards must be the worst to play when you
are feeling nervous. The least tremor and you are
done. These two players had every reason to feel
nervous, for they were beginning a championship
match, but they showed no trace of feeling, not a
quiver. And when we clapped them at the end of long
breaks, they merely gave us a slight nod. "Ah, so
you're there, are you?" these nods seemed to say. I
felt awed before such greatness. These men could
do one thing better than anybody else could do it.
They were masters. Their world was a small one,
bounded by the shaded electric lights and the stretch
of green light, but in that world they were supreme
conquerors.

To play billiards every afternoon and evening, year
in and year out, might seem monotonous, yet I think
they must lead satisfying lives. What they can do,
they can do, beyond any possible shadow of doubt.
They hit the red and it vanishes into a pocket. They
have not to convince themselves that they have hit it
and that it has probably gone into a pocket, as we
have to do in our affairs. What can I do? What can
you do? We think this, we imagine that, and we are
never sure. These great cuemen are as sure as human
beings can be. I envy them, but my envy is not so
sharp that it robs me of all pleasure in their skill.
When I am actually in their presence, looking down
on the table of their triumphs, my envy is lost in
admiration and delight. When the world is wrong,

hardly to be endured, I shall return to Thurston's Hall and there smoke a pipe among the connoisseurs of top and side. It is as near to the Isle of Innisfree as we can get within a hundred leagues of Leicester Square.

Davis Cup

Iᴛ is always hot when I visit Queen's Club. Baron's Court does not figure in my mind as a part of London, but as some sizzling little tropical town, with red roofs quivering in the heat. It was hot last Friday afternoon, when I went to Queen's to see the second day's play of the Davis Cup match between Great Britain and Germany. When there was no play going forward, women put up sunshades; the players used their towels very freely; many of us felt that our shoes were too tight; it was that kind of afternoon; we might have been sitting on Barbados. When you consider that it was still April and that a day or two before we had all been shivering in our thickest overcoats, you will admit that it was very odd. It seems as if I have only to move in the direction of Queen's to send the temperature soaring. It would have seemed cooler perhaps if the play had been on a grass court. There are few things in this world that look hotter than a new hard court in full sunshine. It looks angrily hot. Staring down at it, you can imagine the most terrible of the deserts. How absurd it is for the hell-for-leather game that is played on these fierce brick-red surfaces, and played by athletic men who are soon drenched with sweat and gasping for breath, should still be called Lawn Tennis! It is a name with the mildest associations. It suggests a companion pastime

69

to croquet, a refined late-Victorian thing, bright with petticoats and delicately clouded with curates.

Some people still think of lawn tennis as a namby-pamby affair. When I told a friend of mine, some time ago, that I was playing a good deal of lawn tennis, he assured me solemnly that it was useless to him because it was "a soft ball game." This amused me, for my own lawn tennis, poor though it is, is far fiercer, more dangerous to life and property, than his cricket. I fancy that if he encountered a few of Tilden's services, Borotra's volleys, or Gregory's smashes, he would, after pausing for breath, arrive rapidly at the conclusion that the game was not quite so contemptible to his fierce masculinity. Contemporary lawn tennis is not a dangerous game (though the great Borotra himself was once laid out, unconscious, by a terrific drive that hit him on the forehead), but it is fast and very hard. It demands more and more from its champions. If you imagine that all modern French literature is written in a sad defeatist spirit, read Lacoste on tennis. The French have put all their grand military energy into the game. Racquet in hand, they have made some of their magnificent raids.

The national character peeps out of the game as it is played by these various representative champions. As I have already suggested, the lawn tennis of the great French players is characteristically French. Watch the Orientals patiently driving from the base-line hour after hour, and you can see the East at play and can understand its multitudinous pagodas and temples and its bewildering carving. Consider the Americans, their coolness, their tremendous efficiency. The match between Great Britain and Germany last week was more characteristic of these two peoples than their efforts during the War. The Germans, though magnificent sportsmen, were grave and anxious fellows, who rarely permitted themselves even a smile. They returned the ball over the net like tennis machines. They were, you felt, officials of the racquet, and had successfully passed many examinations on the game and could easily have given very long and very intelligent lectures on it. The swarthy and amiable Prenn did not look very German, but there was the patient genius of Germany in his extraordinarily accurate play. Nothing could have been more Teutonic than the broad stiff back of Dessart, who toiled away in the doubles like an irreproachable civil servant. The English, as usual, were more casual and cheerful, sometimes breaking into sheer high spirits. They were very much the amateurs. Sometimes they did idiotic things, hitting wildly, even breaking down. There was nothing official about them. They could not have passed an examination on the game or lecture on it. They were not always fully aware of what they were doing. But, on the other hand, there was in their game real personality and an occasional flash of genius.

On Friday, I watched Gregory and Collins, that great doubles team, completely overwhelm the German pair. These two fine players of ours are perfectly matched. Collins is not a brilliant player (though he is a tremendously hard hitter), but he is cool, patient, watchful, impossible to ruffle or depress. When he waits, his tall angular figure all tense, to kill a lob, you know for a certainty that in another ten seconds that lob will be lying dead on the court. Gregory is far more erratic, but at the same time he is also a far more brilliant and splendid performer. He is one of the great personalities of the game. It does your heart good to watch this burly and bouncing young man on the court. He is by profession a doctor, and I seriously advise him to send his more depressed patients to see him in a doubles match. He is Elizabethan England breaking out into lawn tennis. Chapman would have roared his approval of him. No machine-like accuracy, no clever little tactics, no examinations and lectures for him. When he puts on his flannels, he leaves science behind him, and arrives joyously at art. Time after time, he can, with many a comical look of despair, drive the ball into the net, hurling points away. Time after time, he can serve faults. But then he will suddenly do something huge and homeric, whip up a colossal drive, volley from some crazy angle, and smash so that the ball bounces clean over the stand. To play against him must be like trying to argue with Dr. Johnson. The two Germans, the other afternoon, were over-awed by him, but I suspect that it was not merely those tremendous smashes of his that did the trick, but that it was also his bounding zest and his high spirits. His huge grin bewildered them. They were dominated not only by his skill, but also by his fun.

It was impossible not to like the members of the German team. They may have been grave and anxious, but they were real sportsmen, quick in their courtesy. This amateur lawn tennis seems to be one of the last refuges of sportsmanship in this world. In spite of all the fuss, the "ballyhoo," the articles and photographs and autographs and all the nonsense, these young lawn tennis players, though they may be occasionally rather too conceited (in which, of course, they are not at all like authors, a singularly modest and self-depreciating class of persons), seem to me to behave towards one another in an altogether admirable knightly fashion. They all want to win, but not at any cost. They have no desire to cheat their way to a championship. They do not regard their opponents as men who have to be done down one way or another, by fair means or foul. The smile and hand-shake at the end of a game still have a friendly significance, and are not the formal antics of professional boxers. Moreover, although little incidents will sometimes happen, they are not for ever appealing to the umpire, nor does the watching crowd go baying at him.

That is one reason why lawn tennis is so pleasant to watch, and it seems to me nowadays one of the best of all games for a spectator. (Though I prefer the men's game to the women's, which is apt to be very monotonous and, curiously enough, far less graceful and imaginative.) The one drawback to a person who tries to play, like myself, is that the sight of these delightful services and forehand drives with top spin and undercut backhand drives and the rest, makes your own game all the more futile and pitiful. I remember the first time I saw Tilden play, I came home with lovely strokes sailing through my head and tingling in my fingers, rushed to change and get out on to the court, and then promptly made the most miserable exhibition of myself. I must revenge myself for that by reading his novel, which, if one may judge by the reviews, seems to be rather like my lawn tennis.

Man Underground

WHAT is it makes people grumble about the crowded Tubes and swear they will never travel underground again if they can help it? Most of them seem to imagine it is ordinary discomfort, but I fancy it is really a sense of indignity. After all, to be compelled to stand ten minutes or so is no great hardship to most of us, especially when we know that we are being hurled towards our destinations at a tremendous speed. The indignity of these rush hours, however, is undoubtedly unpleasant. Human beings, yourself included, are suddenly turned into parcels. Labels are pushed into their hands; trains are promptly loaded with them to the full capacity; doors are opened and shut to admit them; they are hustled out, shot up in lifts, and only then, when the sweet cold rush of real air comes to meet them, are they allowed to turn back into ordinary men and women. I seem to remember that some years ago shouting machines were employed at several of the busiest Tube stations. "Now pass along, please," these monsters roared, and there was a suggestion that if you did not pass along they would eat you. The mechanical voices are there no longer, but during the rush hours the attendants themselves are not unlike those machines and clearly regard us as so much material for transport, moving parcels of an awkward size and shape. It is only when things

are quiet that the attendants share our common
humanity and are seen as fellows who are interested
in the result of the 3.30 and have an eye for a pretty
girl.

Nevertheless, it is when the Tubes are quietest that
they are queerest. The sense of indignity, the parcel
feeling, during the rush hours is only slight, fleeting;
and the jam of humanity prevents you from noticing
what is really happening. When there is hardly anybody about, however, you cannot help thinking how
queer it all is. A lady of my acquaintance will not
alight at any Tube station by herself; if there is nobody else getting off the train, she goes on to another
station; and she does this not because she imagines
she would run the risk—we will say—of being
attacked by a ruffian lurking in the shadows of the
corridor on the way to the lift, but simply because the
thought of being alone in these underground passages
terrifies her. I have no such feeling myself; and,
indeed, I find a certain pleasure in these mysterious
tiled corridors when they are deserted. If I was not
in a hurry to get anywhere, I should like them to go
on and on, to see them stretching before me, dwindling
to pin points of light.

The other day I went by the Hampstead Tube to
Tottenham Court Road and changed there for Oxford
Circus, and it happened that there were very few
people about, so that I was able for once to think
about my surroundings. At Tottenham Court Road
I was carried up an escalator, went along a passage

and down some steps, found another train that shot
me into Oxford Circus Station, and there, after more
corridors, I mounted an escalator so long and high
that it might have been Jacob's Ladder itself. It was
while I was being carried obliquely upward by this
astonishing thing that I suddenly thought, I am a
creature who is carried about in this fashion. There I
was; I had said good-bye to daylight on the summit of
Hampstead, had stepped into a little box that had
rushed me down a shaft to some passages and a plat-
form somewhere in the middle of the hill, had boarded
a vehicle, a thing as terrifying as a thunderbolt, that
had hurtled me under half London, and after that I
had been going up and down moving staircases. I
remembered that years ago I had read a fantastic
story by Bulwer Lytton called *The Coming Race*, but
that nothing in that story was as fantastic as this
journey from Hampstead to Oxford Circus. I wondered what Lamb or Hazlitt would have said if they
had had a vision of these lifts, tiled corridors, thunderbolt trains, and staircases for ever moving up and
down. They were wise men, but I swear they would
have shuddered and cried: "If this is what will
happen, thank God we have not many years to live
and will be dead long before life becomes so inhuman." They would see us as people living in a
nightmare of machinery, creatures as cold, strange,
and remote as beings from the Moon. They would be
astounded beyond measure to learn that their own
works were still being read and admired—never so

often read and never so widely admired—by these same queer beings. In short, they would feel what most of us have felt when we have read stories about the future, *When the Sleeper Awakes,* and the like. And I saw that what was wrong with such stories was that the sleepers never wakened properly, that they showed us a nightmarish life because they were still half in a dream.

The mistake, of course, is to deduce the inner from the outer facts of life, to imagine that the mere mechanics give the key to everything, to forget that the solid human core of thought and feeling remains. What was I doing—this man of buried tubes and moving stairways? Was I on my way to prostrate myself before some giant flywheel or piston and perhaps sacrifice a child or two to it, to take part in some awful rites suitable to such a being? That is what some horrified observer from the past might well have supposed. But you and I know very well that I was about to do nothing of the kind. As a matter of fact, your Lamb and Hazlitt would have been the first to appreciate the object I had in undertaking this nightmare journey, for I was simply on my way to do what they themselves had done hundreds of times, to see some friends and then enjoy myself in a cheerful playhouse. And the others, moving up and down those escalators, they too were on their way to look at hats and gowns, to be examined by the doctor, to try to sell 350 gross of what-nots at 35s. the gross, to listen to music, to meet their lovers. They were being haled up and down those escalators by motives that were hardly different from those in operation when Cæsar landed in this island.

We must not allow ourselves to be deceived by vivid and fantastic presentations of life in the future. Their showmen are always people who either have a passion for machines and contrivances or a horror and detestation of them, and whether they have one or the other, the result is ever the same, they exaggerate the importance of such convenient devices, turn servants into masters, forget to humanize these things, and so completely falsify life. In fifty or a hundred years' time it is quite possible that people will spend most of their hours either up in the air or deep under the earth, and the thought of such an existence strikes us at first as being horrible, inhuman, unless of course we happen to have that type of mind that puts "gadgets" before anything else. But having made my way from Hampstead to Oxford Circus underground and shed no humanity *en route,* I refuse to be alarmed about the future. The real things will be going on just the same —as we realize at once when we make an imaginative effort and humanize everything—and on the whole life will probably be a shade pleasanter, for these contrivances have a trick of enlarging a man's freedom, enabling him to see more friends and hear more symphonies than he could before.

Yes, and I will go further and—at the risk of being considered hopelessly out of the movement—I will say that there is such a thing as progress and that it is still happening. I am not forgetting the war and I am also not forgetting (as so many people do) the literature that has come out of the war; history shows us innumerable great wars but never before has it shown us such literature of war, fierce and uncompromising in its detestation of the event and its pity for the victims. We ought to be ashamed of ourselves when, because Macaulay's millenium has not arrived, we throw up our hands and admit universal defeat. I am tired of hearing people say that all is lost. And these are not shivering outcasts, mumbling crusts, but well-nurtured, cultivated persons who have delicate dinners served up to them every night and can savour new pessimistic works under shaded lights in quiet cushioned rooms. I am tired of hearing our clever young men and girls say they would rather be living in the eighteenth century. Like children, they imagine they would all have been fine ladies and gentlemen, Horace Walpole and the like. It is more likely they would have been Spitalfields weavers, grenadiers with the lash waiting for them, footmen and maids sleeping in dark holes, ragged and starved ushers, some of Squire Western's oafs and slatterns. A day of what was ordinary life to the average man or woman in the eighteenth century would probably reduce them to screaming imbecility. No, we move on, in spite of all our stupid people—and our clever people.

The Prophets

THERE were four of them, three men and one woman, and I saw them in the public forum in Hyde Park. In the 'Nineties, which were crowded with professional Cockney humorists who gave us "glimpses of life" and jested desperately in and out of season, it was, I fancy, the fashion to regard these public meetings in Hyde Park as a magnificent free banquet of absurdity; the whole staff of *Punch* might have been seen any fine Sunday afternoon, pulling out their note-books in the shadow of the Marble Arch; and women would titter and grow moist-eyed and men would roll about in their chairs and almost suffocate with laughter at the very mention of Hyde Park. In these days, now that we have exploded nearly everything, our gun-cotton, our ideals, and even our standard jokes, it is probably a sign of extreme youth or senti-mental old age to think of these public meetings in the park as a glorious feast of fun. For my part, I have little interest in them, for they are usually con-ducted now by experienced tub-thumpers, old hands, and there is nobody more tedious after a first acquaint-ance than your old hand with his bag of cheap oratorical tricks, his face and voice of brass, his patched sordid dialectic. On the occasion when I saw this little group of four that I shall call the prophets, I walked round the assembled crowds without stopping to listen to any of the speakers. There seemed to be the usual meetings in progress: some orators roaring out their approval of God, others noisily assigning limits to His prestige and power, and others again loudly denying His existence; the philosophers, the saints and the angels were all being butchered by someone to make an artisan's holiday; and any idler present had the choice of some five or six entirely different universes. I was just turning away when I caught sight of the three men and the woman, the prophets, standing in a little empty space between two great knots of people. One was speaking and the other three were supporting him, and apparently they had no audience at all. Something about them, perhaps their pathetic isolation, rather attracted me, and I moved forward; but as I knew that if I planted myself boldly in front of them, all their eloquence would be directly addressed to me, I merely walked forward to the outskirts of the adjoining crowd and drew as near to my four as I could without appearing to listen to them.

This was sheer cowardice on my part and I suffered for it (as one always does), for I could not hear a word they said. On one side there was a noisy political meeting and a great deal of heckling and shouting and booing, and on the other, where I was standing, everybody was singing a very objectionable hymn under the leadership of a perspiring Salvation Army official. I had to content myself with watching my little group, apparently ignored by everybody else and at once

absurd and pathetic in its isolation. All three men had
beards. This was no mere coincidence, for there was
something about these beards that suggested they
were there on principle; they were all long beards that
had obviously been allowed to go their own way,
beards that had demanded and obtained self-deter-
mination. Two of the men were elderly and their
beards were fairly full and satisfying, but the other,
an under-nourished fellow with bulging eyes, was much
younger, and his beard, though longish, was thin,
patchy and straggling—a horrid sight. No doubt it
was a rule in the tiny sect to which they obviously
belonged that all male members should grow their
beards. Many tiny religious sects have, I fancy, some
such rule. There is nothing odd in this, because if a
sect is only small enough all its members become
prophets, and prophecy demands that the chins in its
service should not wag uncovered. Indeed, there is a
type of beard, long and full, that belongs to the
prophet alone. This old and honourable connection
between prophecy and beards is easily explained.
Growing a long beard is the simplest way of going into
the wilderness. The man who shaves is the man who
has come to terms with this world. He who has fore-
seen the impending Doomsday cannot be expected to
lather his face briskly every morning or come out of
his apocalyptic vision in order to strop a razor; nor
can a prophet, no matter how minor, consort with
barbers, who care only for sport and sixpences and not
at all for the wrath to come. Thus, the tiny sects,

made up almost entirely of prophets, are right to insist upon beards, and these three men, in letting themselves be overrun by their strange growths, were only doing their duty.

When I first drew near, one of the two elderly men was taking a turn on the little wooden soap-box and addressing a heedless world, but after some time he was relieved by the others. They were all much less vehement (so far as my eyes could judge of the matter) and more restrained in manner than the general run of park orators; they gave me the impression of men who knew that it was their duty not to denounce, not to argue furiously, not to challenge and criticise, but to testify, without unnecessary violence, to the truth that was within them, a truth, I imagine, of which they had almost a monopoly. Every now and again, the little chorus of three, supporting the speaker, would nod their heads and make some exclamation to show their approval. The younger man, he of the vile beard and the under-nourished look, was the most interesting. When he mounted the soap-box, there happened to be a moment's quietness on either side, where the hymn-singing and heckling were still in progress, and I did actually catch the first two words of his discourse. In a thin reedy voice, the very tones of one who is nourished chiefly on starry and insubstantial fare, who feeds on tea and bread-and-butter and visions, he cried, "We believe . . ." And then the noise began again, and I did not catch another word, nor do I know to this day what they do believe. In all probability the doctrines of their microscopic sect are based on some strange little heresy that has persisted in odd corners, among bakers and saddlers in obscure towns, for centuries; and it is more than likely that there is much talk of the end of the world and the coming reign of the saints in the meetings of the sect. For all their quietness and mild glances, however, there was an apocalyptic gleam in their eyes, particularly in those of the younger man, and their beards had not sprouted on behalf of any shallow, time-serving sort of creed. Perhaps they knew the very date when the world was to be withered away and the stars were to drop from the sky like rotten fruit, and had travelled many a league with their soap-box to give us warning; perhaps they were there ready to barter an eternity of bliss for half-an-hour of our attention, and, because we did not choose to listen, already saw the angel of death making ready his sword above our heads. But no, if they believed that things were at such a desperate pass, surely they would not have been so calm, surely they would have raised their voices and not allowed every roaring fool in the park to catch the attention of the doomed city.

The woman did not speak, though, like the rest, she occasionally nodded her head in approbation. She was a sturdy middle-aged woman, who looked better fed and more sensible than her men-folk. Undoubtedly she had come with one of the men, and was probably his mother, wife or sister; she had accepted the creed when she accepted the personal relation, and being a motherly sort, she probably not only mothered the man, but mothered his poor little creed too. Against the background of these bearded fantastics, with all their starry folly, she looked robust and earthy, as solid as a hill. If her man had taken to drink instead of prophecy, she would have seen him through with that too, and would have gone with him into the public-houses to see that he did not take too much and get himself into trouble. As it was, she had come to Hyde Park to stand by the soap-box and nod her head with the rest, but doubtless all in a dream, her mind being busy with hurrying little images, with shifting faces, vague cries from the past, and the remembered grasp of little children; while outside the sun went down the sky, the crowds sang or cheered or heckled or drifted away, the voice just above her head droned on in the old way she knew so well, and she stood there ("Like a fool," perhaps she thought) with aching feet, still nodding her head though no one listened or stopped to look.

As I watched this ineffectual quartet, in their motives like gods and in their wit like sheep, I pestered myself with vain questions. Where had they come from and where would they go to? To what strange place would they carry themselves, their beards and their soap-box? What did they do for a living? Did they go to workshops and factories and quietly endure the rough chaff of the others, comforted by the knowledge that they were men set apart, men guided miraculously by an inner light to the truth? Were they the only members of their set or were they merely the few who had volunteered for this particular duty? Where did they meet and what did they do? Of what would they talk when they were on the way home from the park? Were they always conscious of their mission, their great destiny, or did they relapse, on ordinary days, into commonplace artisans or shop-keepers, strangely bearded? Were they moved to come to this place by an ecstasy of conviction that left them no choice but to express themselves in public, whether they made converts or not? And supposing, I said to myself, that these people, whom you think absurd, whose beliefs you actually know nothing about, are in the right after all, that by some miracle they have stumbled upon the key to the universe and were busy on the soap-box tearing the problem of good and evil to shreds, that the date when these three men first met will be celebrated down the ages, that the younger one with the bulging eyes will ulti-mately turn human history in a new direction . . . what then? And I went on "supposing" and "what then"-ing to myself for some time, but nevertheless while I was doing this I was hurrying away from the three prophets and the woman, for I knew that time was getting on, and I was anxious not to be late for tea.

Dissolution in Haymarket

SURELY there is hardly a street in London less morbid, more determined in its own sedate fashion to make something out of life, than Haymarket. Indeed, now I come to think of it, Haymarket is one of my favourite thoroughfares. It has a pleasant gentlemanly air, with just a suggestion of the eighteenth century, and has, too, all manner of interesting things in it. To begin with, there are its two large theatres, one of which is associated in my mind with a number of charming plays, and the other—I regret to say—only with camels. There are the Stores and a fine old tobacco shop, and, best of all, the shipping agents with their model steamers and little panoramas. Those steamers alone—and there are quite a number of them—lift the whole street high above the common level. The sight of them prevents London from closing in on you, for it suddenly opens some little windows in what seems the grey wall of the street, and through these windows come flashing the bright dunes and red roofs of Denmark or the shining peaks of the Sierra Nevada. If this is not enough, flanking them you have the actual windows of the little panoramas, which artfully combine in themselves the lure of travel and the excitement of a toy theatre. No, it would be hard to find a London street less morbid, less gloomy, more likely to augment rather than diminish one's zest for life.

Yet as I was journeying on a bus down Haymarket
the other day, about the lunch hour, there suddenly
came crashing down upon me a mood such as I have
never known before. It was as if a huge black stone
had been flung into the pool of my consciousness. It
all happened (as we were told it would) in the twink-
ling of an eye. Everything was changed. The whole
cheerful pageant of the street immediately crumpled
and collapsed, with all its wavering pattern of light
and shade, its heartening sights and sounds, its warm
humanity, its suggestion of permanence, and I was
left shivering in the middle of a tragedy. Not something magnificent, you understand, with funereal guns
roaring out over the battlements of Elsinore or queens
with bright hair dying for love, nothing after the high
Roman fashion; but a dreary tragedy of cheated fools
and illusions blown to the winds, of withering and
decay, dust and worms. I saw this world for a moment
or so through the hollow eyes of the prophets and the
great pessimists, and what I saw left me shivering
with cold and sick at heart. Nor did there remain with
me that cosy painted chamber of the mind into which
I might retire, there to forget in comfort, for it, too,
was desolated, heaped about with cold ashes and with
its tattered curtains flapping in the wind. All the stir
and noise and glitter seemed nothing but fast-shred-
ding pigment on a dead face.

I might have been old Donne himself, brooding over
corruption and putrefaction and the gnawing worm;
and it was his words that returned to me: ". . . all

G

our life is but a going out to the place of execution, to death." What was the bus I was in but a greasy tumbril, and what were all of us, jogging there empty-eyed, littered with our foolish paraphernalia of newspapers, umbrellas, parcels, but a company of the doomed? There we were, so many grinning skeletons masquerading in this brief and bitter carnival as fat citizens, charwomen, bus conductors, chorus girls; idly juggling with thoughts of our destinations, the offices, restaurants, clubs, theatres that claimed us; when, in truth, we had all but one sure destination—perhaps round the next corner—the narrow grave. "The sun is setting to thee, and that for ever." And on the face of every one there, hurrying with me to the place of execution, I read the marks of weakness and decay, and seemed to see that untiring hand at work furrowing the brow and dimming the eyes. Everywhere was dissolution. The whole street was mouldering and rotting, hastening with all that was in it to its inevitable end. The crowds I saw through the windows seemed made up of creatures that were either gross or wasted, shuffling, bent, twisted in limb, already bleached and mangled by disease; and here and there among the crowd, in bright contrast and yet infinitely more pitiful, were the few who had youth and strength and beauty, who moved as if they thought they could live for ever—who had not yet heard, from afar, the hammering, the slow tread, the pattering of earth upon the coffin.

There was something more than the old thought,

death is certain, festering in the heart of that mood. That, indeed, is a thought we are always quite willing to salute, with a mere wave of the hand, but are really very unready to entertain, except when we make its first acquaintance in childhood, when it has a trick of bringing a whole host of grimacing shadows about our bedsides. But there was something more behind that sudden tragic vision I had. There was a sense of universal dissolution, of this life as a pitiful piece of cheating, of bright promise all ruthlessly scattered. Nothing remained but the certainty of decay and death. The more you loved life, delighting in whatever it had of beauty and goodness to offer you, the more openly you bared your breast for the stroke of its dagger. I saw all of us there—my fellow passengers in the bus, the driver and the conductor, the policeman and the hawkers, the playgoers waiting at the pit door, the crowds shopping or loafing—as the victims of this great treachery, lured into worshipping a loveliness that must fade and pass, trapped into setting our hearts upon things we can never keep with us, upon beings who smile for an hour and then miserably perish. It is well, I thought, for the grandest of our old preachers to say: "We long for perishing meat, and fill our stomachs with corruption; we look after white and red, and the weaker beauties of the night; we are passionate after rings and seals, and enraged at the breaking of a crystal," and then to make it plain that these things will not avail us. But other and nobler things, it seemed to me, would avail us even less, for the more we opened our hearts, making ourselves eager and loving, the more certain amid this universal dissolution was our ultimate misery. We are the poor playthings of Time, dandled for an hour and then flung to rot in a corner; and yet we are all born, as was said of Coleridge, hungering for Eternity.

So brimmed with such thoughts, feelings, old quotations, strange images, clustering together like the pieces in a kaleidoscope to form one tragic vision of things, I was carried down the desolated length of Haymarket, where man spendeth his vain life as a shadow. As those last words will suggest, my mood had by that time crystallized into the utter hopelessness of that other and greater Preacher. Vanity of vanities! Had I been a natural man instead of the smooth mountebank demanded by decency and encouraged by my natural timidity, I should have descended from the bus, put ashes on my head, and cried "Woe!" to the assembled hawkers and playgoers and policemen, stunning them with gigantic metaphors. That is what, in my heart, I wanted to do, so surely was I possessed by this sudden hopeless vision and by a mixed feeling of contempt and pity for my fellow mortals. Yet I sat there, quietly enough, and still well aware of the fact that I was on my way to lunch with two friends at a club not very far away. I was, as it were, purely automatically aware of this fact, for in those last moments, so rapt had I been in my vision, I had no sense even of personal identity. But I moved forward, as a man might over a darkening field of battle, towards the club and my friends, and arrived there and greeted them in a kind of dream; and then, suddenly, out of my dream, I looked at them sharply and curiously, these friends of mine, whose grim sentence and that of all they held dear still seemed to be ringing in my ears. How strangely childish, touchingly naïve, their smiling confidence, their little preoccupations, their chatter. I saw them seating themselves opposite me at the lunch table, and it was as if they were people acting on a distant stage; yet I did not feel completely detached from them, but, on the contrary, felt a kind of tenderness for them and all their little toys and antics. Then I heard one of these doomed creatures propose that we should drink Burgundy. I stood out for something lighter, for though I like a glass of Burgundy as well as the next man, I maintain it is far too heavy for lunch.

Too Many People

I HAVE decided that I cannot enjoy London any longer, not even on a short visit. I think it was our experience at the Circus that decided me. As soon as we arrived in town the other day we bethought ourselves of the circus at Olympia and made up our minds to go that very afternoon. It never occurred to us to book seats. Having lunched, we descended upon West Kensington like gods, our minds pleasantly humming with anticipation and full of circuses. For my own part, I was bent on seeing the hundred or so clowns it promised us. Professional clowns and clowning, the silly antics of serious people, are rare enough these days, and would be a refreshing change from the other and unprofessional kind of clowning one knows so well, the serious antics of silly people. We were in good time, and I saw us strolling in and dropping into comfortable seats, surrounded by the enthusiastic youngsters who would make up the larger part of the afternoon audience. But when we arrived at the place, there seemed to be a revolution in progress. Olympia was being stormed as if it were another Bastille. Streams of people were coming away and great throngs were still pressing forward. Uniformed attendants, with very hoarse voices and waxed moustaches, and looking like the ringmaster's poor relations, were bawling out the news that all tickets for the Circus that

afternoon had been sold. Notwithstanding their passionate reiteration, people, thousands and thousands of
them, were still besieging the ticket-offices, perhaps in
the hope of booking seats for the following week.
Clearly we had arrived several days too late, and,
feeling foolish, as one always does in these circum-
stances, we withdrew into the bustling wilderness of
West Kensington, clownless and disconsolate.

This experience, from which I did not recover
throughout our short stay, confirmed a suspicion I
have entertained for some time, and I suddenly saw
why it is that I enjoy these visits to London less and
less. There are too many people in the place. One
does not, of course, expect the city to be empty (how
horrible it would be if it were!); the hum and bustle,
the stream of strange folks, are inseparable from one's
thought of the town, and are indeed part of its attrac-
tion; and I am not crying out here for vacant lengths
of street, empty theatres, and deserted restaurants. I
do not want a whole city to myself, even if, in my heart
of hearts, I believe that I ought to be supplied with
one if necessary. But there is a point past which a
cheerful and comfortable bustle and busyness turn into
detestable overcrowding, not heightening our pleasure
but robbing us of it. We are elbowed out of enjoy-
ment, so hustled and harassed in our search for
entertainment that we had better be working. This is
what seems to me to be happening in London. Not so
many years ago there were just enough people about,
in the streets and buses and shops and theatres and

restaurants to animate the scene, giving it movement and colour and dramatic interest, so that one felt one was seeking pleasure in the world's capital and enjoyed the gregarious thrill; but at the same time there was ample room to move and enjoy at ease, and there was no necessity to push and jostle and book seats and rush for tables. Now it seems—it may be my fancy, for I have no figures to support me; but there it is—that happy state of things has vanished, and as year follows year there seem to be more and more people walking the streets, waiting at shop counters, jumping on buses and tube trains, filling the theatres and hotels and restaurants and tea-shops.

Where they all come from, these people, I cannot imagine; but there they are, and more and more of them. I find the very trains up to town uncomfortably crowded these days. At whatever hour of the day I venture into some streets, such as Oxford Street or Kensington High Street, I can hardly move along, so dense is the crowd. If I wish to go to a theatre, either all the seats are booked for weeks ahead or there is nothing left but some seat at the end of a back row. Even in the afternoon the places are full. My only chance of dropping into a comfortable seat at a theatre at the last moment, it would seem, will have to depend on my writing a play myself and getting it produced. No matter what hotel I stay at, there is hardly ever any choice of rooms, and the lounge is always uncomfortably crowded from breakfast time to midnight. Lunch is a scramble for a table and a disheartening

tale of dishes that are "off." There is not even a
glimpse of solitude and quiet at tea-time. Dinner is
another adventure more reminiscent of race-meetings
and cup-ties than the serene and noble hour of refreshment. A late supper is not to be thought of, for
by this time one has not heart to push and jostle in
the chattering, gaping, elbowing mob. Even if, suddenly sick of it all, I decide to rush away and catch
the very next train home, there is not a taxi to be had
to take me to the station. And the trains that carry
me back to the country are still uncomfortably
crowded. It is as if everybody had decided to leave
the place the same moment that I had, and yet
when I return again, they are all back, determined to
crowd into the same streets, to fill the theatre or
restaurant before I arrive, and equally determined not
to miss anything, not to dine and spend the evening
at home, not to go to bed. Where do they come from?
Who are they? Why do they not go and do some
work, or visit a sick friend, or take a holiday in the
Sudan? Why is it that there are more and more of
them every time I visit the city?

As soon as I am back in the country, the newspapers
inform me that everybody has left town or that there
is a "slump," and that theatrical managers and restau-
rateurs are complaining, but there are never any signs
of anybody having left or of these "slumps" the next
time I arrive in town. And I have never been a lover
of crowds, and now find myself disliking them more
and more. If my pleasure depends upon my pushing

and jostling and snatching and grabbing among a
crowd, I would rather go pleasureless. If I found
Paradise itself crowded, with long queues waiting for
wings and harps, I should ask to be turned out; but
they will surely order things better up there, and will
reserve their crowding for the other region. I could
devise a very pretty hell for myself. It would be one
long Oxford Street without any side-roads whatever,
and everybody would be compelled to keep moving,
except certain fiends, assuming the shape of stout
middle-aged women, all umbrellas and elbows, who
would be for ever wheeling round and standing and
staring. All food and drink would have to be procured
at cheap tea-shops, gigantic establishments deplorably
understaffed and steaming with humanity. Enormous
crowds would be pushing their way in and out of these
horrors all day, and anybody who did not join them,
pressing in, elbowing a way from floor to floor, standing about for a seat, then banging a bell for hours,
would have to go without bite or sup. There would be
no homes at all to go to, but just this endless crowded
street, and at night the doomed soul, which would be
attached, of course, to a weary carcass, would have to
seek accommodation in an hotel. There would be
thousands of these, huge, cheap, nasty places, and nine
out of ten would always be full, so that the wretched
creature would be compelled to trail from one to another, encountering the sneers and hollow laughter of
demons in the form of reception clerks and night
porters. The rooms, when secured at last, would

always prove to be tiny garrets, and either distressingly hot or insufferably cold. In all the crowds there would never be a familiar face; day-long the faces would go jumbling by, sickening masses of them, pale faces, pink faces, long faces, short faces, whiskered faces, smooth faces, faces with beaks, faces with snouts; but never a familiar face, never a friendly glance, an answering smile. This, I flatter myself, would be a most ingenious and devilish touch. But here is another. It is obvious that after a few weeks of this, most men would be so crowd-sick that they would suddenly begin screaming their hate of the throng about them, and would hurl themselves in the thick of it, determined to kill or be killed, or preferably both. They would want to batter in some of these idiotic faces, have one glorious bare-sark moment, and then, the infuriated mob retaliating, find happy oblivion. But, of course, they would not be able to do this. Their screams of rage would attract no attention, and their blows would not be noticed by the passers-by, being nothing but a kind of shadow play. Nothing would stop the procession of faces, the pushing and the jostling, the swarming crowd. I fancy that the Hell of Too Many People would occupy a respectable place in the hierarchy of infernal regions.

Houses

I HAVE been wondering if most of those 217,000 new houses are like the ones that have been built just down the road. They are very ugly indeed, square little boxes that look as if they had been nailed on to the landscape, and so ugly that even time will never beautify them. As the years pass and sun and rain come to tint the walls and roofs and the creepers climb to the eaves, these houses will mellow a little but they will never be beautiful. Down here, of course, we cry out at their hideous aspect. Our own houses have great charm, for either they are old farmhouses or cottages adapted to our needs or they are mansions designed by artists, and so we take tea together on our trimmed lawns or under our old oak beams and are all very indignant or superior about the ugly little houses that stare at us as we go by, not unlike rather pugnacious poor relations who have been invited for once to a grand party. But there are other people here—people we do not ask to tea, of course—who are happy and excited about those houses. They sit up at night wondering if they can afford to live in one of them. For years now, you see, they have been living with the wife's father or the husband's brother, crowded into a couple of tiny rooms, perhaps, and it has all been very uncomfortable and there have been little quarrels and they have not been able to ask their friends when

they would have liked to, and when the husband was
down with the 'flu or the wife was having another baby
it was so bad that life hardly seemed worth living. And
now they may be able to have a place of their own, a
lovely place with a proper sink and a sort of bath in
the kitchen, if it will only run to it. So they go and
look over those new houses, seeing them as a kind of
signpost pointing to a sunlit main road of life; while
the rest of us, fortunate or cunning enough to have in-
stalled ourselves snugly and picturesquely, hurry past
the ugly little brick boxes to ask the Vicar's wife or
Major Brown if it really is not too bad and if something cannot be done about it.

Even a local builder, you will notice, can suddenly
turn our minds into a battlefield, where a desire for
beauty wars with our common human sympathy. A
few more of these houses and this place will no longer
charm the eye; a great many more of them and it will
be hideous; but on the other hand a number of people
will have the chance at last of living decently and in
comfort. The thorough-going æsthete, who admits to
caring for nothing but his own exquisite sensations,
would have the landscape unspoilt though the remaining cottages should be crammed with wretched
fellow-creatures. The rest of us, not being made of
such hard glittering stuff, cannot help feeling that
people should come first, that their chunks of happiness or misery are more important than certain delicate satisfactions of our own; and it seems to us that
the other way of thinking is like refusing to save a

man's life because he has a detestably ugly face. We
should be content to make the whole country hideous
if we knew for certain that by doing so we could also
make all the people in it moderately happy. Yet we
know too that if the country were thus absolutely shut
off from beauty, in the long run nobody would be
really happy, for some part of the good life would be
lost for ever. Thus once more we find ourselves faced
not with a problem but an apparently insoluble puzzle
which traps the mind into circular paths. (There are
so many of these that I for one have ceased to have
any opinions at all of any importance; and sometimes
I feel that we shall be compelled to start thinking all
over again, in a new way.) We are left crying out upon
the age that bore us. O cursèd spite!

But let us return to the ugly new houses. Is it
possible that there is compromise between leaving
people without a roof of their own and ruining the
landscape? Is it necessary that most of these houses
should look so unpleasant? I leave the answer to the
town planners, the architects and the builders. All I
can say is that I do not understand why there is such
a general passion now for building semi-detached or
detached little houses. Do people refuse to live in any
other kind? If they do, then I refuse to sentimentalize
over them any longer. Let them stay with their husband's father or wife's brother. I am convinced that
it is this detachment that is responsible for a great
deal of the ugliness. This it is that peppers the countryside with little brick boxes. Even those more lordly

suburbs that are filled with detached villas, not neces-
sarily ugly in themselves, always depress me, if only
because they have such a higgledy-piggledy appearance, no order or dignity about them. Moreover, they
eat up miles of good countryside, of meadow and heath
and woodland, making the town go straggling on and
on in the dreariest fashion. I like town and I like
country, but I must confess that I do not like this half-
and-half stuff, neither one nor the other, these hillsides
crazily dotted with villas, each bearing a meaningless
name. What is wrong with little terraces and crescents
and the like? They must be easier to build, and they
are certainly better to look at. Most of us have lived
in one of them at some time or other and found there
was nothing wrong with houses built on this plan.
Indeed, I am told they have certain advantages, being
easier to warm and so forth. I believe that the best
small houses built since the war, the model dwellings,
were devised on this plan, arranged in short terraces
or round three sides of a square. That is how civilized
people should live, and not be camped each in his own
detached bit of ugliness. Does not this, then, suggest
a possible compromise between overcrowding and a
countryside peppered with brick boxes? I ask the
question out of my ignorance, wistfully.

Here is another. How is it that we are not for ever
talking about houses and housing? Is it because those
of us who do so much of the talking about things
happen to be fairly comfortably and conveniently
housed ourselves? I am not going to say how large

my own family is, nor how many rooms we use, but I
will say that if the number of those rooms was halved,
my life would soon be very different and so, I suspect,
would my point of view. It means that I should never
be able to escape from the other members of my
family nor they from me, that there would be little or
no chance for quiet thinking or even talking, that if I
remained at home my temper would be always on
edge, that after a time I should neither stay in myself
nor ask other people in to see me. In the country, one
might manage in a tiny cottage because a good deal
of time would be spent in the open. But in a large
town, life in a very small house, of three or four little
rooms, would be horrible. Either every sense would
have to be blunted or existence would be a misery. In
the West Riding town that I used to live in—and there
are hundreds like it in the industrial North and Midlands—there were districts locally known as "back o'
the mill," and in these districts there were rows and
rows of what are called "passage houses," erected on
a plan that enabled the contractor to build four houses
in the space usually occupied, in slightly more civilized
regions, by two small houses. Thus each of these
dwellings, back to back as they are, has only one door,
and not as a rule more than three rooms, a living-
room and two bedrooms. These houses have not been
demolished, they are there still, all over the North and
the Midlands, I fancy. The children who attend the
Council schools, where they are taught to sing or even
to read the poetry of Shelley, live in such houses.

When they leave school, they continue to live in them.
Only a few are able to escape.

One of the objects of primary education, I believe,
is to refine its small pupils, to make them more sensitive. This seems rather a dirty trick when we consider
that the children have to return to those houses. It is
very difficult to go on reading the works of Shelley in
a room that has to be shared with all the rest of the
family and its various and frequently noisy concerns.
It is hard to live the sensitive life when you are never
alone. I think if most of us lived in such places with
a growing family, we should let many things go if we
were women, and get out as soon as we could and look
for beer if we were men. Certainly we should either
cease being sensitive or become embittered. I suspect
that the absence of two or three rooms, in which a
young man or woman might sit quietly and read or
dream, has gone to make many a revolutionary just
as it has gone far to make many a sot. There are some
learned gentlemen, who sit in quiet studies thirty feet
long by fifteen broad and consider the discontents of
the lower classes, I should like to take by the hand
and lead into one of these three-roomed houses, bid-
ding them share the place with a noisy family for a
month. A month would do, I think. At the end of
that time they would be no nearer settling any of their
problems than they were before, but there would be
some things that they would understand. "And all
man's energies seem very brave," says Mr. Squire, in
his beautiful poem on a house. Well, they might even
come to that conclusion too.

The Flower Show

IT is our annual flower, fruit, and vegetable show, and a great event. It may not look to you like a great event—for you can only see two marquees in a field—but you ask Quince, our gardener. He has been thinking and talking about nothing else these past four weeks. You will find him in one of the marquees, looking strangely clean (and somehow smaller) in a new suit. We—that is, Quince and our garden—have won nine prizes, including the first prize for onions. Quince is radiant. He has been after that onion prize from the first, partly because it had been won for seventeen years by the same man, Mr. Snug, who lives near the station, and partly, I suspect, because he must have talked expansively about his onions one night at the "Duck and Drake" and have been chaffed about them. So he set to work to grow some Ailsa Craigs (for that's our heroine's name) that would smash this seventeen years' record. "Oi don't care what happens, sur," he has said to me more than once, "so long as Oi gets the proize for them thar onions." He has spent whole days tending them and, latterly, gloating over them. After great deliberation, he chose nine of the largest, made a little stand for them, cutting a hole in the wood for each onion to rest in, so that they made a very fine show indeed, though I must confess that they looked to me like some new garden game, dis-

tantly connected with bowls. But there they are now,
with the red label on them that dethrones Mr. Snug,
who must be content with a blue label and the second
prize. Quince cannot keep away from his onions;
sometimes he takes a look at the apples (Second
Prize) or the tomatoes (Second Prize); but he soon
returns to the onions. It is really nothing to him that
we had no award for our mixed vegetables (though
they were as good as Snug's, which were given a First),
that our carrots have not had a look in, that our roses
only managed a Third. He has won nine prizes in all,
and a First for onions: his ship is in harbour.

Now you can hear the Plumborough Brass Band.
They are here in all the bravery of blue and silver
uniforms and peaked caps, though it cannot be said
they look quite at home in them. There are certain
kinds of faces and figures—soldiers and policemen have
them—that seem to belong to uniforms, and these
honest fellows from Plumborough have not acquired
such faces and figures, so look sheepish in their blue
and silver. Moreover, a brass band should be loud
and careless, made up of men who believe that this is
the best of all possible worlds and that life can be
generously saluted by brazen sounds in waltz time and
the clashing of flagons; but the Plumborough Band
seems too earnest, thoughtful, scrupulous, and picks
out the notes as if it were not certain they ought to be
touched, like visitors fingering bric-à-brac. They are
telling us now that two for tea and tea for two is their
ideal, but they are so uncertain and doubtful that we

feel that this view of life is too shallow for Plumborough. We will leave them and visit the man who is dressed in a jockey's cap and silk vest. He is a stout, middle-aged man, and looks ridiculous in this shimmering red and black; and what is more, he is the only man in the field in fancy dress; but he does not care, and has evidently long outgrown self-consciousness. He offers us three darts for twopence—there are prizes for the highest scores of the day—and we all throw darts, and some of them hit the board and some of them do not; but one of us, knowing no more of darts than the rest, makes 107, the highest score of the day so far. Such are darts, and such is life.

We are asked to guess the weight of a pig, and when we go to look at it, we find that it is a mere pigling, no bigger than a fox-terrier. Like most of the pigs in this part of the world, it is mottled, brown and black, and therefore—to my mind—quite unreal. That is probably why I find it impossible to imagine what its weight will be, and anyhow, it is eating all the time, and may be any size before the show is over. We try bowling at skittles, and I do very badly and laugh with the rest, but find myself pointing out that the ground is very uneven and that the bowls themselves are absurdly misshapen. The man we see dodging in and out of the little coal office at the station, a man who looks like a troll, asks us to pay sixpence each and put a stake, with one's name written on it, into a circle of ground where treasure is buried. (This must be a coalman's idea of life.) When we have done this, we are all weighed by the jovial gentleman-farmer in whose field the show is always held. This is something of an ordeal. There is nothing in being weighed if you step on to one of those automatic machines that send a pointer briskly round to a figure on a dial. But when you are weighed by a leisurely human being, who slowly puts one chunk of metal after another into the scale and then carefully announces the final result, it is quite a different matter. I am rather ashamed of my thirteen stone and five pounds, not because I really feel there is anything disgraceful in being a little heavier than most people, but because there is such a thing as the pressure of public opinion, and the world, which gets sillier, is now given over to banting and to people made out of cheese-parings after supper. We have a word with the retired schoolmaster who is one of the officials of the show. He is going about putting down names and figures in a notebook, and is quite happy, feeling that he is back again in harness. Schoolmasters never really retire; there is always, at the back of their minds, an unconquered, never-to-be-surrendered fortress of pedagogy.

We must try the other marquee. The cook, who entered the meat pie and the cake (to cost less than two shillings) competitions, has not won a prize. She did not trouble about the third competition, which is for the best dish of boiled potatoes. They are all here, these dishes, and very unappetizing they look too in the middle of the afternoon—unlike the meat pies and the cakes. You have to be hungry to appreciate a potato, and this is a fact that historians ought to remember. Whenever or wherever the potato is much talked of, hunger is stalking abroad. Opposite the meat pies and the cakes are the exhibits from the school, for the most part pages from copybooks and mats and tiny dolls made of crinkled paper and raffia, the kind of dolls that children prefer to the expensive and eyelashed beauties from the toyshops. On the table that runs down the centre are more fruit and vegetables, and an old man is measuring beans with a piece of string. I am surprised, and rather aggrieved, to discover that George, our giant pumpkin, is here. There is no mistaking him. What he is doing here, I cannot imagine, for there is no prize for which he could compete. Indeed, he serves no common uses, and was grown neither for the kitchen nor the drawing-room. He is to the garden what Falstaff is to the drama of "Henry IV." He is its comic poetry, and he has given me more pleasure than any other vegetable or fruit, not excepting those rounded maidens, Rubens creatures, that are the darlings of Quince's heart, the Ailsa Craigs. If ever I visited the kitchen garden, it was to see George the pumpkin, to mark his ever-increasing girth, to admire his golden and rotund magnificence, to give him an affectionate slap. Can you wonder that such a one figures in a fairy tale? Quince must have brought him down here because he felt obscurely that the garden should be also represented by its great comic character. Let us give pumpkin George a farewell slap.

Quince is still in the first marquee, trying—for he
is a good modest fellow—not to look too like a man
who has broken a long record for the onion prize.
But he cannot disguise the fact that he is the happiest
man at the show. His father is with him now, a very
ancient retired gardener, who looks as if he had grown
out of the earth, like a grand old tree. He puffs at his
short pipe and pretends to philosophic calm, but you
can see that he too is rejoicing over the great onion
victory. Quince's brother is here too, the signalman,
very brisk and natty in a blue serge suit, and seeming
to belong to a later (and perhaps less enduring) civilization than the other Quinces. He tries to make fun
of the whole thing, this man of machines, but I know
that he was helping Quince all morning and really
has the cause at heart. The small son and the smaller
daughter of Quince are also here (one got a prize for
a mat and the other for a copybook page—it has been
a great day), and keep pushing their apple cheeks,
which ought to have had prizes too, as close as they
can to their father's sleeve. I am positive that Quince
will not leave this marquee until the end of the day,
that he will be the last man in it. Here is the scene of
his triumphs, and here he remains. I congratulate him
again on the onion victory. "They shouldn't ha'
talked at me," he says; and I foresee his having a
triumphant pint or two to-night at the "Duck and
Drake," where they thought he could not grow Ailsa
Craigs. There is nothing more for us to do now. The
fifteen men from Plumborough are proclaiming,

through their instruments, that they are "Less than the du-ust beneath (pom-pom) his chariot whee-eel," but they do not proclaim it with much conviction, except the drummer, who is coming into his own in this riot of Oriental passion. As we wander down the road we can still hear him tom-tomming, and we leave the day to him and Quince.

The Inn of the Six Anglers

THIS morning, for the first time in my life, I wished that I was an angler, a real angler, not one of those fellows (as the fat man said last night) "who'll fish for an hour and then want to go and pick black-berries." As we rode away from the inn and left the lake idly lapping behind, with all six anglers happy on its bosom, I told myself that I had missed my chance of happiness in old age by not fishing steadily through all my youth. Perhaps, however, it was really the inn that did it, the inn and the lake to-gether. There is no resisting an inn that is small and quaint and good, a place that is shelter and fire and food and drink and a fantastic journey's end all in one. Nor is there anything in nature more enchanting than a lake. Rivers I have loved, and with them the restless sea, so magical and yet so melancholy, perhaps because it seems the symbol of our desires; but it is those lovely lapping sheets of water, neither seas nor rivers yet having the charm of both with something added, some touch of quiet, peace, soul's ease, that really possess my heart. You travel over leagues of hulking and stubborn land, then suddenly turn a corner and find a space where there is no earth but only a delicate mirroring of the sky and that faintest rise and fall of waters, the lap-lap-lap along the little curving shore. Where else can you find such exquisite beauty and tranquillity? May I end my days by a lake, one of earth's little windows, where blue daylight and cloud and setting suns and stars go drifting by to the tiny tune of the water. There is no mention of a lake in Wordsworth's strangely magical lines:

> The silence that is in the starry sky
> The sleep that is among the lonely hills,

but I will wager that they were written by some lake-side, for there is in them the lake spirit, the quiet enchantment, the heart's ease.

It may, then, have been the inn and the lake that made me wistful of angling. All yesterday we were travelling north through Central Wales, a lovely country, filled with an antique simplicity and kindness, that few people seem to know. I had heard of this lake and was determined to go there and, if possible, spend the night by its side. It is the one virtue of a motor-car that it can gratify such whims. We rushed north, then, and saw the hills grow in majesty and the sky darken over our heads. Where we stopped for tea there was some talk of a landslide, a road washed away by a recent storm, along the way we wished to travel, but by this time we were determined to see our lake or perish. (It is this spirit alone that saves the soul of the motorist, who would otherwise be a mere beast.) We discovered some kind of road on the map and were very soon bumping along it. The next two or three hours were Homeric.

I was at the wheel and, you may be sure, innumerable smoking-rooms will find me at that wheel again, will have to travel with me down that road. I have now a story that is a fit companion for that other story of mine, that account of how I once changed down to low gear with a screwdriver, when everything began to break in the middle of a Buckinghamshire hill.

The road dwindled to a mere tattered length of tape threading itself through the hills. There were great holes everywhere, and at times the steering-wheel was nothing better than a rattling useless ring of metal. The hills piled themselves all round us, great screens of slaty rock threatened to overwhelm our trumpery shivering craft, and the narrow bitten track went twisting this way and that, offering steeper gradients every five minutes. And now the mere drizzle, which had accompanied us for the last hour or two, darkened into a torrential downpour, blotting out everything but the next few yards of road. I had to open the windscreen because it was impossible to see through it. Big drops would hit me in the eye, so that at times I saw nothing at all. The track got worse, the rain fell more heavily, the car rattled and roared and leaped and bumped, and we laughed and shouted to one another, being now in that state of curious and half-sickening exaltation which visits us when sudden death is apparently just round the corner. But as the nightmare track lengthened out and the rain still fell in sheets, completely drenching us, smashing through hood and cap and coat, we settled down to the grim business of getting anywhere at all. At last there came a long descent and a slackening of the rain. We swerved down through a misty fissure into a grey and ghostly place, where we heard, once the car had achieved its easy hum again, the faint noise of water. We were in a hollow in the mountains, a hollow almost entirely filled with the dim grey sheen of water. Here then was the lake. Another ten minutes of twisting and turning and we were shaking ourselves, like dogs from a pool, in front of a low building that seemed nothing more than three brown cottages joined together. This was the inn.

There never was a better journey's end. A Pimlico boarding-house would have seemed Paradisal after that shattering ride, but here was a place in a million. We seemed to have rattled and bumped our way clean through this modern world into another and more lovable age, where "they fleet the time carelessly." It was not long before we were snug and dry, sipping sherry in front of the fire. We caught vague glimpses of elderly men, anglers apparently, for the place was full of rods and baskets of trout. Then came dinner in a low lamplit room. There was no nonsense about little tables and simpering maids handing round snippets of food. We found ourselves at a long table with all the other guests, and all the other guests were six jovial old anglers, the oldest and most jovial at the head of the table. The dishes, vast tureens of soup and joints of mutton, were placed in front of these two, who cut and carved and cracked their jokes. The dinner was good, made up of clean, honest, abundant food, and the company was even better. I have not had such a strange and satisfying meal for years. It was just as if one had somehow contrived to merge the *Compleat Angler* and *Pickwick Papers*. Outside, mist gathered on the lake, so remote that it might have been in the heart of another continent, and darkness fell on the hills. Inside, in the kindly and mellow lamplight, we sat snug, and ate and drank and listened, still half-dazed, still with the rain and wind in our ears, like people in a dream.

I saw it all in the clear light of morning, a morning of thinning mist and faint sunlight on the lake, when the mouth watered for the fried trout and bacon that the two oldest anglers handed round. It was only this morning. Yet, as I look back upon last night, it still seems like a dream. The journey, the place itself, the inn, the six old anglers—the whole experience is more like the memory of some happy chapter in a leisurely old-fashioned tale than a piece of reality. I can hardly believe that that valley and lake are on the map, that in some directory of hotels that inn may be found. It seems as if that remote place had slipped through some little crack in time, so that the years had rushed by without avail, leaving it brimmed with its old-fashioned spirit of leisure and courtesy and kindness. Its guests, the six old anglers, were not quite of this world. They were, or had been, I believe, schoolmasters, doctors, musicians, but one could only see them as anglers, living for ever at this inn, for ever strolling down to the boats in the morning and returning with their trout in the evening to carve the mutton and exchange their long and leisurely stories (like those that hold up our older novels for whole chapters) round that lamplit board. One of them, the one who mastered the joint, had been going there for at least forty years, and the others seemed to remember the place twenty or thirty years ago. Not that they did not know other places too, for they exchanged reminiscences about them, remote little lochs in Scotland, unknown Irish rivers, wherever there were trout and salmon to be had. They always gave one another all the facts, precise directions for finding places, the names of all the inns and innkeepers and gillies, and talked on as if life lasted a thousand years, kindly years of sunlight and mist and lapping water and leaping fish and golden hours about the dinner-table. They showed me, in the jazz pattern of our years, this silver thread of peaceful and quiet days that old Isaac Walton knew so long ago; so that I too would be an angler at last, and find my way again to that inn, this time to be one of their confraternity, and then perhaps I too could quietly angle my way out of time altogether. Yet even now it is all so unreal that I have a feeling that I could not find that lake and that inn again, and I am sure that by the time I am old and grey they will have vanished for ever.

The Toy Farm

ANGELA, at the house where I am staying, has just celebrated a birthday, her seventh, and is now the breathless mistress of a toy farm. You never saw such a farm. It has barns, haystacks, sties, hurdles, gates, trees (which must be looked at only from the front), and a yellow tumbril with scarlet wheels. There are fat brown horses, cows that stand up and cows that sit down, black pigs and pink pigs, sheep with their lambs, a goat, two dogs (one staring fiercely out of a kennel), and a coloured host of turkeys, ducks, hens and chicks. There are even people on this farm, five of them, and very fine people they are too. A man in his shirt-sleeves perpetually pushes a crimson wheelbarrow; and two carters, wearing white smocks, brown gaiters, red scarves, and little round hats, for ever stride forward, whips in hand, whistling tunes that we shall never catch. Then there is the farmer himself, bluff, whiskered, in all his bravery of scarlet waistcoat, white cravat, and green breeches, who grasps his stout stick and stares at things from under his hard brown hat. His wife, neat and buxom in a blue bonnet, a pink gown, and snowy apron, with a basket in one hand and a large green umbrella in the other, is setting out upon some never-to-be-accomplished errand. All these people, labourers, master, mistress, though

not more than two inches high and only made of
painted tin, stand there for ever confident, ruddy,
smiling in perpetual sunshine; they seem to stare at
us out of a lost Arcadia.

Perhaps that is why poor Angela has not so far
had that farm to herself, being compelled to share it
with a number of shameless adults. It is, of course,
an engaging toy, and there is not one of us here, I
am thankful to say, so old and wicked, so desiccated,
as to have lost all delight in toys, particularly those
that present something huge and elaborate, such as
a fort crammed with soldiers, a battleship, a railway
station, a farm, on a tiny scale and in brighter hues
than Nature ever knew. These toys transform you
at a stroke into a god, and a happier god than any
who look down upon our sad muddle. It is, of course,
the more poetical of our activities that are chosen as
subjects for these bright miniatures of the nursery,
yet there is so much poetry in the toys themselves
that even if they mirrored in little even the most
prosaic things, they would still be satisfying. I
remember that when I was a child, the boy next door
was given a tiny printing machine, a gasping, wheezing affair that would print nothing but the blurred
image of three ducks. He and I, however, collecting
all the paper we could lay our hands on, would spend
hours, hours full to the brim, printing ducks, thousands and thousands of ducks, and while we were
engaged in producing this monotonous sequence of
dim fowls we asked nothing more from life beyond

the promise of suety meals at odd intervals.

Yet so far, nobody, not even in America, I imagine, has produced a toy miniature of business life, the Limited Company complete in box from ten shillings upwards. What Angela and her like would think of such a toy I do not know, though their sense of wonder is sufficiently strong for them to find entertainment in anything; but I do know that I should be tempted to buy one this very morning. You would have a building, with the front wall removed as it is in the best doll's-houses, so that you could arrange the people and the furniture just as you pleased. There would be tiny stenographers and clerks and cashiers; typewriters, calculating machines, ledgers and files no bigger than your finger-nail; telephones that you could just see and never hear; and all manner of things, chairs and tables and desks, to be shifted from one room to another, from the Counting House to the Foreign Department, and so forth. There would be a Board Room with four or five directors, fat little chaps in shiny black, with the neatest, tiniest spats imaginable, all sitting round a table some six inches long. In the best sets you would be given a Chairman, quarter of an inch taller than the others and costing perhaps a penny more, who might be so contrived that he stood perpetually at the head of the table addressing his fellow directors. If I had him I should call him Sir Glossy Tinman. Then, if you wanted to do the thing properly, you would be able to buy Debenture Holders at two shillings or half-a-crown the dozen, complete with an interrupter who was rising to his feet and holding up an arm, the very image, in tin and varnish, of a retired Colonel of the Indian Army. Nor would you stop there; the possibilities are almost endless; and I promise to outline some of them to any enterprising manufacturer of toys who should consider putting the complete Limited Company on the market.

It may be, though, that there are special reasons why we should all be finding the toy farm so enchanting. Its little people, as I have said, seem to stare at us out of a lost Arcadia. Behind them, and their bright paraphernalia of beasts and belongings, is the Idea, dominating the imagination. This farmer and his wife are the happy epitome of all farmers and their wives, but they are unmistakably idealized. These white-smocked carters, for ever soundlessly whistling among the clover, are not the countrymen we know in miniature, but are images from an old dream of the countryside. Looking at these trees, or at least looking at them from the front, we might cry with Keats:

Ah, happy, happy bough! that cannot shed
    Your leaves, nor ever bid the Spring adieu.

Here is the bright epitome, not of the country we can find where the tram-lines come to an end and the street lamps fade out, but of the country that has always existed in our imagination, so clean, trim, lavishly coloured. None of us here, I venture to say, has any passion for agriculture as a pursuit, for real farms, with their actual lumbering beasts, their mud and manure, their clumsy and endless obstetrics, their mortgages and loans and market prices, their long days of wet fields and dirty straw. We may regard the farmer as an excellent solid fellow or as a grasping ruffian, but certainly he never seems to us a poetical figure whose existence is passed in a golden atmosphere. Yet there is such a farmer somewhere at the back of our minds, a farmer in a picture-book, and this piece of painted, moulded tin is his portrait. If we could only find him in this actual life, not all the pleasures of the town would keep us from living in his shadow all the rest of our days, for we know that his world is one long dreamed of, that countryside where there are no ugly downpours, no sodden fields and lanes choked with mud, where only the gentlest shower of rain breaks through the sunshine, where everything is as clean as a new pin and fresh from the paint-box, where men and women are innocent and gay and the very beasts are old friends, where sin and suffering and death are not even a distant rumour. Is not this the Arcadia that men lost long ago and have never found again?

How long this dream has lasted no man can say. It shines through all literature, from the poets and novelists of yesterday to Virgil and Theocritus. It is the burden of more than one half of our old songs, with all their "Hawthorne buds, and swete Eglan-

tine, and girlonds of roses, and Sopps in wine," their
Corydons and neat-handed Phyllises, their hay-
makers, rakers, reapers, and mowers waiting on
their Summer Queen, their hey-down-derry of
shepherd lovers in the shade. And always this lovely
time

> When Tom came home from labour
>   Or Cis to milking rose,
> Then merrily went their tabor,
>   And nimbly went their toes

had just passed away. Nobody ever saw this countryside, but it was always somewhere round the
corner; a turn at the end of a long road, a descent
from some strange hill, and there it might be, shining
in the sun. It is not the perfervid vision of towns-
men, longing for the fields in their wilderness of bricks
and mortar, a revolt against the ugly mechanical
things of to-day, but a dream that would appear to
be as old as civilized man himself, touching men's
imagination when towns were little more than specks
in the green countryside. Poets who lived in the
country, who passed all their days among real shepherds and dairymaids, could sing of this other
country where there was nothing ugly nor any pain
and sorrow, knowing full well that this was not the
land that stretched itself beyond their gates but a
land they had never seen. It is one of the more
homely manifestations of that ideal of unchanging

beauty which haunts the mind of man everywhere and in every age, and from which there is no escape except into brutishness. Its shadow can fall even upon a number of little pieces of painted tin newly come from the toy-shop.

On the Moors

IF you go from Bradford to Bingley, from Bingley to
Eldwick, then up the hill from Eldwick, you arrive
at Dick Hudson's. Mr. Hudson will not be there to
greet you, because he has been dead this long time.
But the old grey inn that stands on the edge of the
moors is called by his name and by no other. Even the
little bus that runs up there now has "Dick Hudson's" boldly painted on its signboard. And there's a
pleasant little immortality for you. "We'll go," they
say to one another in Bradford, and have said as long
as I can remember—"we'll go as far as Dick Hudson's." If you start from the other end, climbing the
moorland track from Ilkley, you will inevitably come
to Dick Hudson's when you finally drop down from
the high moor, and if the hour is right, you will inevitably have a pint of bitter at Dick's. That is what
I did, the other day. I returned, after years of
southern exile, to the moors, and began by having
two pints at Dick's. And I was mightily relieved to
find it still there, the same old grey building, the same
cool interior, still smelling of good beer and fried
ham; for at any moment now, they may begin mon-
keying with the old place, turning it into an ice-cream
parlour or some such horror.

If you live in Bradford, Shipley, Keighley, you
kindle at the sound of Dick Hudson's. That is not

merely because you have been so often refreshed
there, but chiefly because you know it is the most
familiar gateway to the moors. The moors to the
West Riding folk are something more than a picnic
place, a pretty bit of local countryside. They are the
grand escape. In the West Riding towns you have
something to escape from, for industrial mankind has
done its worst there. But the moors are always waiting for you, and you have only to leave the towns for
an hour or two, climbing the hills, to see them dwindle
into a vague smoulder and a sheen of glass roofs in
the valleys, then vanish, and perhaps be forgotten.
The moors are there, miles and miles of countryside
that has not changed for centuries, and you have only
to squeeze through the little hole in the wall, just
beyond Dick Hudson's, to take your fill of them. It
does not matter who you are, for they are yours while
you are there, and the richest wool man in the town
can claim no more right in them than you can. Once
through that hole in the wall, you have escaped miraculously; and if you were a favoured lad in a fairy
tale you could have no better luck, no more elaborate
transformation worked for you, for one afternoon. So
if you are a stranger to those parts and should visit
them, do not let the black streets, the monotonous
rows of little houses almost set on end, the trams that
drone away between factories, the whole grim paraphernalia of old-fashioned industrialism, depress you
too much, but please remember that the winds that
suddenly swoop down on the sooty slates have come

over leagues of moorland and still have the queer salty tang in them.

Well, I had my pints at Dick Hudson's, went through the little hole in the wall, and climbed on to the moor, as I had so many times before and yet had not done for many a year. It was a weekday and very quiet. The sun was hot and seemed to smite these uplands, bruising every blade and blossom so that they sent out sharp odours. Once more I seemed to be walking on the roof of England. The singing larks only rose a little way from the ground, as if they were high enough now. The winds came sliding or shooting over the top, at no more than shoulder height, and there was in them the old magical scent, earthy enough and yet with always something of the sea in it, that strange saltiness. Against the brown hillsides I saw the tender green of the young bracken. There, once more, were the tumbled rocks, floating in and out of the great cloud shadows; the ruined byres and the mysterious stone walls; the granite dust of the moorland path glittering in the sunlight. I heard again the baa-ing of the moorland sheep, like complaining voices coming from great hollows. Everything there was as it had always been.

Down in the valleys, among the streets I once knew so well, they were putting up new buildings and tearing down old ones, they were going into bankruptcy or starting afresh, old men were dying and young men were marrying, and nothing was standing still. The life of the town was hurrying away from the

life that I once knew, and down there, among the
stalwarts that had so suddenly and strangely grown
bent, grey and old, and the babies that had so suddenly and strangely shot up into young men and
women, I was rapidly becoming a man from another
place, a stranger. But up there, on the moors, there
were no changes at all. I saw what I had always
seen, and there was no sense that did not receive the
same old benediction.

Yet it was not the same. I sat down on the smooth
springy grass, with my back against a rock, and as I
smoked my pipe in that high lonely place, I tried to
disentangle it all. I was happy to be there again, and
not a sight, a sound, an odour, that returned to me
failed to give me pleasure, and yet in this happiness
there was the strangest melancholy. It was as if
there was between me and these dear and familiar
sights and sounds a sheet of glass. I felt as if I had
only to pluck the ling and heather at my side for it to
wither and crumble in my hand. I might have been
a man on parole for one golden afternoon from some
distant internment camp. There were no tears in my
eyes but I will swear my mind knew the salt glitter of
them. If I had spoken to a fellow-traveller then, he
would have concluded that I was a man who had
once known great happiness in these parts and had
then gone into some sad exile. And he would have
been wrong. I am happier now than ever I was when
I used to come to these moors week in and week out,
when I was on the easiest and friendliest terms with

them, and every rock and clump of heather spoke to me in my own language. When I walked these moors then, or stretched myself on the grassy carpet in the sun, hour after hour, I spent my time dreaming of the happiness that would be mine when I should be as I actually am now. I do not say that I was really unhappy in those days, for I was a healthy youngster with plenty of things to do and with many good friends, but I was certainly restless and dissatisfied and apt to be sulkily despondent in a world that did not appear to appreciate my unique merit. I thought I was a fine fellow then, but nevertheless I had not acquired that armour of conceit which begins to protect our self-esteem later in life, that armour which compels some elderly members of my profession to move so ponderously. I could be snubbed then, could retire in haste, all hot and pricking, from many a company. There is no doubt whatever that I am happier now.

What hocus-pocus, what sentimental attitudinising, was it then that made me feel so melancholy, the other afternoon on the moors? I was not an exile at all. If I want to live near the moors and visit them every day, there is nothing to prevent me. I could go there, and stay there, to-morrow, if I really wanted to. I know very well that I don't want to, that I would much rather live where I do live. I am well aware of the fact that the moors would bore me very soon and that I get more out of them by visiting them now and again than I ever would by living near them.

Like most people, I have lost several persons very dear to me, but, there again, to be honest, I must confess that there is nobody who is associated with the moors in my mind who is now lost to me. The only possible person is that other, younger self, who had trod these very paths so often; but then, I do not mourn him. Let the young cub perish. First youth has gone, it is true, but I do not see that there is anything specially admirable in early youth. I have strength and vigour, a sense of fun and a sense of wonder, still with me, and I have not the slightest desire to be nineteen again. All this I pointed out to myself, as I sat against that rock and watched the great purple cloud shadows drift across the moorland, but that feeling of melancholy remained and would not budge. It was like one horn, amid the happy tumult of a full orchestra, ceaselessly sounding a little theme of despair. If the moors were real, then I was a ghost. If I was real, then all this sober richness of bracken and heather and tumbled rock and blue sky was a mirage, a bubble landscape that one determined forefinger could prick so that it gave a wink and then vanished for ever. I returned, a man in a puzzling dream, but also a hot and thirsty man, to Dick Hudson's.

A Road To Oneself

SOMETIMES, on one of these sunny autumn mornings, when I turn my back on the town and take to the high-way, I seem to have the world to myself. I walk forward, as it were, into a great sunlit emptiness. Once I am a little way out of the town it is as if the world has been swept clean of men. I pass a few young mothers, who are proudly ushering their round-eyed solemn babies into the presence of the morning sun, a lumbering cart or two, and maybe a knot of labourers, who look up from their task with humorous resignation in their faces; these and others I overtake and pass by, and then there is often an end of my fellows. I alone keep a lounging tryst with the sun, himself, I fancy, a mighty, genial idler and the father of all dreamers and idlers among men.

A light mist covers the neighbouring hills, which are almost imperceptible, their shapes and colours showing but faintly, so that they seem to stand aloof —things of dream. As I go further along the shining road I seem to be lounging into a vast empty room. There are sights and sounds in plenty; cows looking over the walls with their great, mournful eyes; here and there a thin blue column of smoke; the cawing of rooks about the decaying woods; and distantly sounding, the creak of a cart, a casual shout or two, a vague hammering, and, more distant still, the noise of the town, now the faint murmur of a hive. Yet to me, coming from the crowded, tumultuous streets, it seems empty because I meet no one by the way. The road, for all its thick drift of leaves, deep gold and brown, at either side, seems to lie naked in the sunshine, and I drink in this unexpected solitude as eagerly as a dusty traveller takes his ale. For a time, it comes as a delectable and quickening draught, and though outwardly a sober, meditative, almost melancholy pedestrian, I hold high festival in the spirit, drink deep, and revel with the younger gods.

One of the greatest dangers of living in large towns is that we have too many neighbours and human fellowship is too cheap. We are apt to become wearied of humanity; a solitary green tree sometimes seems dearer to us than an odd thousand of our fellow-citizens. Unless we are hardened, the millions of eyes begin to madden us; and forever pushed and jostled by crowds we begin to take more kindly to Malthus, and are even willing to think better of Herod and other wholesale depopulators. We begin to hate the sight of men who would appear as gods to us if we met them in Turkestan or Patagonia. When we have become thoroughly crowd-sick, we feel that the continued presence of these thousands of other men and women will soon crush, stamp, or press our unique, miraculous individuality into some vile pattern of the streets; we feel that the spirit will perish for want of room to expand in: and we gasp for air untainted by crowded humanity.

Some such thoughts as these came to me, at first, in my curious little glimpse of solitude. I am possessed by an ampler mood than men commonly know, and feel that I can fashion the world about me to my changing whims; my spirit overflows, and seems to fill the quiet drooping countryside with sudden light and laughter; the empty road and vacant fields, the golden atmosphere and blue spaces are my kingdom, and I can people them at will with my fancies. Beautiful snatches of poetry come into my head, and I repeat a few words, or even only one word, aloud and with passionate emphasis, as if to impress their significance and beauty upon a listening host. Sometimes I break into violent little gusts of laughter, for my own good pleasure. At other times I sing, loudly and with abandon: to a petrified audience of one cow and three trees I protest melodiously that Phyllis has such charming graces that I could love her till I die, and I believe it, too, at the time. I brag to myself, and applaud and flatter myself. I even indulge in one or two of those swaggering day-dreams of boyhood in which one finds oneself suddenly raised to some extraordinary eminence, the idol of millions, a demi-god among men, from which height one looks down with kindly scorn on those myopic persons who did not know' true greatness when they saw it, sarcastic schoolmasters and jeering relatives for the most part.

Only by such heightened images, seemingly more applicable to centuries of riotous life than half an hour's sauntering, can I suggest in stubborn words the swelling mood that first comes to me with this sudden, unexpected seclusion.

But as the morning wears away, the jubilation arising from this new expansion of oneself dwindles and perishes; the spirit wearies of its play. The road stretches out its vacant length, a few last leaves come fluttering down, and the sun grows stronger, sharpening the outline of the hills. The day is lovelier than ever. But I met no one by the way, and even the distant sounds of men's travail and sport have died down. After a time the empty road and silent valley become vaguely disquieting, like a great room spread for a feast, blazing with lights, opulent in crimson and gold, and yet all deserted and quiet as the grave. I ask myself if all men have been mewed up in offices and underground warehouses, by some ghastly edict, unknown to me, which has come into force this very morning. Have I alone escaped? Or I wonder if the Last Day has dawned, and been made plain to men not by sound of trump, but by some sign in the sky that I have overlooked; a vast hand may have beckoned to all men or the heavens may have opened while I was busy lighting my pipe. Have all but one of the weary children of earth been gathered to their long rest? I walk in loneliness.

Suddenly, I see a tiny moving figure on the road before me, and immediately it focuses my attention. What are walls, fields, trees, and cows compared with this miraculous thing, a fellow human being, played upon by the same desires and passions, his head stuffed with the same dreams and fluttering thoughts? In one of the world's greatest romances is not the most breathless moment concerned with the discovery of a human footprint in the sand? Does not the world's story begin with one human being meeting another? As I keep my eyes fixed on the nearing figure the last of my vague fancies and egotistical imaginings are blown away; my mind is engrossed by the solidly romantic possibilities of the encounter. Just as I was glad to escape from the sight and sound of men, so I am eager now to break my solitude: the circle is complete. And as we come up together, the stranger and I, I give him a loud greeting, and he, a little startled, returns the salute; and so we pass on, fellow-travellers and nameless companions in a great adventure, knowing no more of each other than the brief sight of a face, the sound of a voice can tell us. We only cry out a Hail and Farewell through the mist, yet I think we go on our way a little heartened.

The Pessimists

THEY burst in upon me last Sunday morning, these two young men—we will call them A. and B. They came striding through the clear sunlight, in which there was already a faint suggestion of autumn, a touch of her cool forefinger, and descended upon me like the demigods or heroes they are, dusty and roaring and red-faced and clamourous for beer. Within a second or two my cottage was crowded with their sprawling legs and gesticulating arms. I had been spending the morning, laying down one after another of its exquisite pale gold pieces, in meditating a few pages of fine writing, something spun out of a reverie over that first autumnal whisper. It was already taking shape in my mind, a whimsical, melancholy, deckle-edged affair, the very matter for numbered and signed copies. There is something curiously depressing about late August, when the world is dusty and blown and fretful. Summer has gone, dragging her roses off the stage, and there is an interval of waiting, during which we yawn over our programmes, before the lights turn golden and misty for the pomp of autumn. I was beginning to feel depressed myself and that was why I decided to attempt some fine writing, there being no better cure for this malady, itself mostly a literary affair, than a whole-hearted literary debauch, in which armfuls of gorgeous adjectives are scattered like largesse. But the entrance of my two young friends put an end to that, and what with the cares of hospitality and the roaring sea of their companionship, on which I soon found myself adrift, I said good-bye to my tender melancholy and fine phrases.

I call these guests "my two young friends" as if there were whole generations between us, whereas a really elderly person, casually surveying us, would lump us all together as contemporaries. We are not, however, and the difference is significant. They are post-war (one of them is still up at his university and the other has not been down long) and I am not, and very often they contrive to make me feel as old as I frequently try to appear in my more responsible compositions. Last Sunday they were in magnificent form. They had been walking all Saturday, and had managed to cover an odd ten or twelve miles that very morning. They bellowed their news and stretched themselves in my sitting-room, sang and splashed in the bathroom, and then came down to put away the lunch of six. My bottled beer went winking down their throats. My coffee disappeared between two epigrams. They filled their youthful and aggressive pipes, blew out great blue clouds of old matured Virginia and young raw satisfaction, and then accompanied me into the garden, where we lounged and smoked through the afternoon. We watched the sunlight fall upon the ripening pears. Across the lawn, the seven-foot hollyhocks stood like girlish grenadiers. The poppies blazed among the distant weeds. From somewhere close but mysterious there came a murmuring of doves, and far away an old bell jangled faintly. The afternoon went rustling by in blue and white. Well-fed, glowing, their strong young limbs out-stretched, my guests leaned back, and after smoking idly for some time with half-closed eyes, at last began to talk. The moment was ripe for a symposium, and Epicurus himself would not have disdained the situation. Naturally enough, they grew philosophical.

Objecting to some timid remark of mine, A. pointed out that all our efforts are probably futile. His companion loudly and cheerfully agreed, and together, with raised voices, they hunted down man's foolish strivings and little sentimentalisms, hallooing as they went. Their sparkling eyes saw inward visions of this life as a desert, marked only by the whitening bones of wasted effort. They roared together over our pitiful illusions. Politics and art and religion and love were whirled away on gusts of laughter. Our whole civilization might perish at any moment, if, indeed, it was not perishing already. Gleefully, their faces alight, they pointed out to one another the unmistakable signs of this collapse, and upon me they rained evidence. They kicked out in ecstasy as flaw after flaw was discovered in this structure of ours. But now there arrived a difference of opinion between them, which resulted in the jolliest argument imaginable and all the pointing with pipe stems and the frequent striking of matches that accompany such jolly arguments. B. emphatically declared that the sooner this civilization was nothing more than a memory, the better it would be for all of us. A. was positive that it was doomed, but thought we had probably made a mistake in letting it go, if only because our next state would be immeasurably worse. For this he was heartily chaffed by B., who said that he would not have suspected his friend of such obvious sentimentalism. Then they both began to examine the situation more closely, making fewer concessions to mere human weakness and broadening the base of the discussion, so that by the time we had sat down to tea they were in full flight.

"The fact is, of course," cried A., dealing heartily with his fifth sandwich, "the universe is entirely indifferent to any of our concerns. A minor planet goes rotten and begins to breed all kinds of queer creatures, and after a time these creatures have the impudence to imagine that their affairs are important, that what they want is what the universe wants. As a matter of fact, though, that's wrong because the universe doesn't want anything. It will just grind away till it stops, and we might as well recognize the fact. We can make up our minds that the whole show will be blotted out sooner or later—and, on the whole, a jolly good thing, too! What do you say, B.?" And he beamed at us, and passed his cup for the third time. "I don't mind how weak it is," he remarked. "I'm still thirsty enough for anything."

B. cut himself a hearty chunk of cake and patted it lovingly. "I don't agree with you," he began. "You're nothing but an old materialist. You're years out of date, you and your mechanical universe! I don't mind telling you, too, that you're a jolly sight too optimistic. The universe is alive all right and knows what's going on here. But why?—" And here he paused and A. reached out for a cigarette. "To make an unholy mess of it, of course. The old idea was right all the time. We're just a droll spectacle for the gods. If there's a supreme deity, then you may depend upon it, he's probably a sadist."

A. considered this view and clearly found it attractive, but was compelled, perhaps a trifle reluctantly, to reject it. He went on to draw a picture of man, doomed to perish with all his little notions of beauty and goodness, standing erect, his head lifted to the pitiless stars; and so warmed to the task that he quite forgot to finish his tea and keep his cigarette alight. Dancing with impatience, B. finally cut in with his own view of things, and showed us this life of ours as a tragedy of marionettes, with a dominating principle of evil, a malicious and omnipotent power, pulling the strings. We were allowed to develop so that our capacity for suffering might be increased. His companion declared that this view was far more rosy and sentimental than his, because "people would rather have an evil spirit than none at all." B., on his side, humorously incensed at the notion that he was at the old trick of pandering to human weakness in his revelation of truth, waved away what he called "this pleasant little idea of the machine universe," and added more crimson and black to his own picture of things. The cottage resounded with the flushed and eager pair of them, but the talk had gone little further before it was time for them to be off, for they were catching the 6.25 back to town, to end their happy week-end jaunt with a pleasant little dinner somewhere.

I was genuinely sorry when they departed, roaring down the road in farewell, for bereft of their high spirits the cottage seemed vacant, lifeless. It is really these evenings in late August that make the season, or brief interlude between seasons, so depressing. The long daylight has dwindled, but yet it is too early to light lamps and draw curtains. Fires are not to be thought of, yet there is a chill in the air. It is the drear little interval between the two magics of summer and autumn. Its long pallid face stares in at the casement, whispering that something is ending for ever. The sky looks like the window of an empty house. In this light, dimming to a dusk without warmth and kindness, Tchehov's people chatter quietly and break their hearts. By the time the owls were hooting round the eaves and the room was ghostly with moths, I was more depressed than usual at such an hour and was sorry that I had not pressed my friends to stay or gone up to town with them, laughing and chattering away, on the 6.25. I saw them, in a wistful vision, sitting down to that pleasant little dinner, rubbing their hands, ruddy and bright of eye, preparing to round off the day and then march happily on towards the new morning.

These Our Actors

I CROSSED Piccadilly Circus and then walked into another world. I did this by meeting a man I know, a man whose brother helps to run an agency for film actors. We began by threading our way through that little tangle of streets behind Regent Street and climbing some narrow stairs. At the top of those stairs was a small, noisy, smoky, and friendly club, used by people connected with the film industry, especially actors. These were not the people who go on with the crowd at a guinea a day, nor were they, for the most part, the stars. They were mostly character actors. We ate our cold silverside of beef and salad, surrounded by characters, who all ate, drank, smoked, talked, and gesticulated with such gusto that you would have sworn the whole scene was being taken down on celluloid. In the other room—the bar, lounge, or smoking-room—roistering companionship was being registered magnificently. Tall heavies, with colossal eyebrows and chins, roared "Hello, ol' man!" to family solicitors, doctors, and mild father parts, and slapped them on the back. Heroic young men with waved hair shook hands as if they had just encountered one another in the Brazilian jungle. Whiskies and beers were tossed down as if it was the young squire's twenty-first birthday and the Old Hall was ringing with the cheers of the assembled tenants.

"How's it going, ol' man?" they asked one another, and to see them looking so intently at one another, eyebrows raised, hand outstretched, you would have sworn that the plot was thickening every second.

From this club we went to the office of the film agency. This office was mostly waiting-room. It was obviously a place where you waited and waited and waited. Photographs of that waiting-room ought to be supplied to anxious parents whose daughters have announced their intention of becoming film actresses. "You imagine," those parents ought to say to their daughters, "that in a very short time you will be at Elstree, on the 'lot,' playing the part of the beautiful Lady Helen, possibly extending your be-diamonded arms towards the handsome Jameson Thomas. You are wrong. You will be spending nearly all your waking hours in that waiting-room, hoping against hope that there is 'something for you,' that something being the chance of falling into a duckpond or jumping out of a car, at one guinea per day." We marched into the private office, which was full of photographs of noble profiles, signed by their delighted owners. A call came through the telephone, demanding the crew of a destroyer. Word was sent out at once that imitation sailors were in demand, and after a little interval, batch after batch of men were admitted, all neat and smiling, though it must have been weeks since some of them had earned even a guinea.

The two agents looked at them, very quickly. "Sorry, you're not tall enough," they would say to one man. "Sorry, too old," would dismiss another. And the men who were thus dismissed still smiled, and I think Drake or Nelson, seeing those smiles, would have signed them on, for their courage. This film agency business is no job for me; I should be too soft for the work, never finding it possible to turn one of these smiling waiting men away. They all deserve medals—to say nothing of guineas—for the way in which they keep themselves so trim, turning out every day with clean collars, creased trousers, and carefully brushed coats. I should like to have heard all their stories, and if I were a powerful producer, I should scrap the silly story on which I was engaged, and demand to make a film out of the lives of these hangers-on, beginning with a "shot" of one of them creasing his trousers in some distant and dingy little lodging before he set out to smile and wait, wait and smile.

A lady sailed in, very large, very dignified, the image of a duchess if duchesses really contrived to look the part. She leaned over the office table, superbly confidential. "Anything else for me, my dear?" she began. I gathered she was not too well pleased with the crowd work on which she was engaged. After a few sentences that I could not catch, she continued: "Mind you, my dear, I don't mind fighting with the Lascars at all. It's fun, so long as they're sober. But when they get filled with black beer, it's too much, really it is, too much. I'm black and blue," she concluded, smiling graciously. You would have thought

she was opening a charity bazaar. "You do understand, don't you, my dear? That's right. If there is
anything you know, just—er——" and, dropping the
most condescending smiles all round, she departed.

She was followed by a confident young man with
side whiskers. Was there anything for him? "Can
you drop the side-boards?" he was asked. He shook
his head. "Sorry, I can't," he said. "I'm on con-
tinuity with 'em." And so they left us, all three of
them, the two whiskers and the young man they sup-
ported. There is in this queer film world a sort of
hirsute gardening. An important producer can set
beards and whiskers in motion for miles around.
Apparently, the more fastidious producers will not
tolerate false beards and whiskers: they must have
the real thing. One of these gentlemen undertook to
do a mid-Victorian film, a short time ago, and could
not get a proper caste together at first, among so
many shaven cheeks and chins. Within a month, however, those little streets running behind Regent Street
or off Shaftesbury Avenue were bristling with full
beards and Dundreary whiskers. The word had gone
forth that hairy faces were wanted, and immediately
all razors were put away. They have just been
brought out again for the destroyer crew.

I was then taken round to the place where the
humbler sort of film actors and actresses amuse themselves. I think it was once a night club, and its walls
still bear traces of that determined jollity which is so
depressing in night clubs. There is a good long room,

with a dancing floor, little tables scattered about, and a refreshment bar. There are hardly any real people in that place; they are all types. Monocled dude drinks beer there with picturesque old artist type. Detective partners humorous landlady at bridge against middle-aged aristocrat and refined girl. Vamps and innocent girls fresh from Peroxideshire share a pot of tea and a great deal of chat. Rustics borrow matches and tobacco from East Enders (male). The Dear Little Mother explains to Sinister Hag just what she really did say to the assistant producer. In fact, there can be seen in that room all the faces you notice in any crowd scene on the films. Several of them deliberately registered things at me, being under the impression that I was a new producer, for they had never seen me before and I was there in the company of well-known agents.

I believe that all manner of film folk occasionally use this Guild club room, but obviously most of the people there were simply supers, on the guinea-a-day basis. Some of them, it was clear, were both young and ambitious, and hoped to rise in their strange shadowy profession. Others were not strictly actors at all, but men and women who had discovered that there was a market, some occasional demand, for their squint or broken noses or goatee beards or dignified appearance. Others again were old hands, who had once been on the Halls or the "Legit.," and were now taking an occasional toll of twenty-one shillings from the new thing that had closed so many theatres over their heads. I caught sight of one broken old man who had once topped the bill on the Halls, but now was lucky to get an odd day's work as a tramp or outcast of the slums in a crowd scene. I was told that between jobs he slept on the Embankment. You may see his ruined face, for five seconds, the next time you visit a picture theatre.

Mad Make-Believe

I STOOD on the boat-deck of a liner that was motion-less under the midnight sky. Our nearest neighbour, an Orient liner, looked like a factory working over-time. Beyond, the lights of the docks and more dis-tant ships glimmered faintly. The air stirred uneasily, as it always does above the wide river. All round me were the passengers and the crew. Some of the passengers were in dressing-gowns and pyjamas; some were in evening clothes; some in a motley assortment of garments. There were distinguished-looking old gentlemen, pretty girls, gaping negroes, anxious middle-aged women, smart youths, nurses, roughs, all in a huddle and muddle. In front of the first lifeboat a space had been cleared, and suddenly this space was dazzlingly, cruelly illuminated. A ring of great arc lamps poured down a quivering purply-white flood of light. It was horrible, unearthly, like high noon on some crazy planet at the other side of the universe. For a minute, nothing happened but the sizzling of the huge lamps. Then a whistle sounded.

Out came, pell-mell, a little crowd of passengers, hurling themselves across the deck to get to the boat. They screamed; they fought. The sailors on the rails grabbed hold of the women and swung them into the lifeboat. The male passengers struggled fiercely, fight-ing one another and the sailors. I could see the

shining black face of a negro, his eyes rolling white
despair, on the far side, where he had climbed up the
davit but could not reach the boat. Other agonized
faces flashed up for a second, then disappeared into
the churning mass. The whistle sounded again, and
now the boat sank slowly down, leaving the men still
fighting at the rails. A woman's face, a chalk mask
of tragedy, caught the light in the descending boat for
one moment, then vanished. A hand or two, waving
last farewells, were flung out of the group of strug-
gling men left on deck. And now the whistle went
once more, and everybody suddenly relaxed.

A burst of talk came from a knot of men standing
or crouching in the second lifeboat. Something was
said about "another shot." But most of them jumped
down on to the deck. There was the chief camera man,
a pale, thick-set American, dressed in one of those
queer coat-waistcoats that some golfers wear. There
was the assistant producer, a little harassed man, who
was perpetually bawling through his megaphone. And
there was the great man himself, the producer, a man
who really had a touch of genius. He had a fleshy
parrot-face, brutal, intelligent, very German; he wore
a check cap the wrong way round, a muffler over his
coat, flannel trousers and slippers; and all the time
he pulled sulkily at a long briar pipe. He did not talk
much, and never addressed the crowd; he merely
stared out of his clever little eyes, and now and then
dropped a remark in guttural English to one of his
assistants.

This was the third night that little army of supers had been fighting for the boats, and they would be doing it for another week. They had to be there early in the evening, and it was nearly broad daylight when they left. The scenes had to be "shot" over and over again, not merely because they were not performed to the producer's satisfaction the first time, but also because they had to be taken from all manner of queer angles. About a hundred and fifty yards away there was a line of barges, and these had huge lights on them so that the whole ship's side could be flooded. It was enchanting to see the water in this sudden radiance. Indeed, these crazy hours were filled with enchanting glimpses, the most astonishing alternations of fierce light and the soft midsummer darkness, lovely flashes of colour in the mysterious night; and the irony of it was that nothing of this would appear in the few minutes of film that would be the flower and fruit of these evenings. Nor have you far to look for a further irony, for the story itself that had set all these people in motion was a pitiable thing compared with the thousand-and-one stories that you could pluck out of this thronged deck. The shivering elderly women who clutched the tickets that would admit them to the saloon below, where hot coffee and sandwiches were waiting for them; the doll-like young girls, with round eyes, painted mouths, and shrill Cockney voices, who jazzed and flirted in dim corners, during the long spells between the miming; the lascars and negroes in whose eyes there lurked a darkness that this river had never known; the carefully correct ex-officers, the yawning old "pros," the dozens of men whose past could not be imagined; had they not all brought stories too? In what picture theatre, in what shadow show flickered across the ether, would those stories appear?

An Indian philosopher would have felt at ease on that daft liner. "If the red slayer think he slays," he could have murmured to himself, "or if the slain think he is slain." Here was a dream within a dream, shadow show inside a shadow show. To begin with, it is easy to lose your grasp upon reality if you are taken to a strange place just as dusk is falling. That is what had happened to me that night. I had been taken in a fast car through a part of London I had never seen before, and then we had left the streets behind and had raced along a wide road, broad and dark as a river in twilight, that was raised above mysterious hollow fields. I remember a fine new bridge, with great arches at each end, and its stone looked almost luminous in the queer light. It might have been admitting us into Nineveh, that bridge. Then a vague tangle of dock roads, with policemen shadowy at the gates, and after that a ship's ladder-gangway mounting to the sky, with this crowded boat-deck our final goal. All this was unreal, a little over the edges of ordinary experience, and there, awaiting us at the end of it all, was this huge traffic in unreality.

I saw a group of ship's officers at one end of the deck, and I thought how amused they must be to see these familiar decks turned into a stage for melo-

L

drama. I caught a word or two, and, puzzled, went nearer, only to discover that they were all made-up a little and were indeed members of the film company. A few minutes afterwards I saw some more actors playing the part of ship's officers but then discovered that they were not made-up and were real ship's officers. As for the sailors, I never did find out which was which, though I know that both kinds were on board. After a time, my sense of reality was so treacherous that I began to feel uneasy as these scenes of frantic shipwreck were repeated. The liner made no movement, was there, safe in dock. When these people screamed and fought to get into the boats, I too made no movement, but looked on complacently, smoking a pipe. But suppose, I thought—and it was now well after midnight—things just slip out of control, for these people are so persistent with their shipwreck that they may make reality swing round in their direction. So far, I who had stood there looking on at a piece of make-believe, had been in the right, for the ships and the docks kept rigidly in their places, and all these others, for all their fervour, their writhing limbs and agonized looks, had been in the wrong. But would it last? What if, the next time they did it, they were in the right and I was in the wrong? Again, it was possible that neither party was right or wrong, that what I was seeing was both a shipwreck *and* a piece of make-believe. I do not say that I seriously debated these questions with myself, but as I wandered about in this place of crazy shadows and crazier lights, such questions stirred a little somewhere at the back of my mind.

When we left, they were all still at it, shipwrecking away, with another six or seven nights more of it in front of them. If not that night, perhaps the night after or the one after that, things might have begun to edge over towards their make-believe, reality might have quietly slipped its moorings, together with the liner. I do not know that it would really surprise me to learn that all those film people have never been heard of since, that they can be seen in picture theatres, as screen appearances, but never again in streets and pubs, having sailed away in open boats, perhaps towards those South Sea islands that do not exist in this world but only in films.

Before Opening

WE pushed open the swing-door, let it close behind us, and thus quietly annihilated Shaftesbury Avenue. The vestibule or lobby or foyer or whatever it is called was deserted. We marched across it and opened other swing-doors. My companion had a right to be there, and I, being with him, shared this right, so that if anybody had stopped us and demanded our business, it would not have mattered. But nobody did stop us. I do not suppose anybody ever does stop anybody entering a theatre when rehearsals are going on. In future, if I find myself in the neighbourhood of Shaftesbury Avenue on a wet afternoon, I shall march boldly into the nearest theatre that is closed for rehearsals. A modern production has so many persons concerned in it that it must be impossible to decide who has a right to walk in and who has not. You have, of course, to be a bit of a simpleton to enjoy this sort of thing; but then I write chiefly for simpletons. We all understand one another's foolishness.

We made our way to the stalls, down corridors and stairs more deserted than any I have trodden this year. When a theatre is empty it is incredibly empty. We found the auditorium all shrouded, and peered up at ghostly circles and galleries. Then we turned our attention to the stage. It seemed to be illuminated chiefly by an absurd row of electric bulbs suspended in mid-air. Most of it was a very charming old-fashioned panelled room. Through one window I caught a glimpse of an equally old-fashioned street, basking in lost sunlight. Another window, however, showed me a dirty white-washed wall, broken only by one dismal light above the word "Exit." This was very odd and attractive, and I was sorry when three men in their shirt sleeves began pulling red and gold curtains up and down these windows, shutting out the view.

At this point we found ourselves joined in the shrouded stalls by no less a person than the dramatist himself, who was looking very worried and smoking in a detached sort of way, as if the cigarette had really nothing to do with him. It seemed we had come either too late or too early to see a rehearsal. They had been rehearsing that morning, and at seven there was to be a dress rehearsal. This, being the middle of the afternoon, was neither one nor the other. Some members of the company were trying on their clothes, and others were being photographed. The "set" was demanding attention too, and somebody or other—I cannot remember his name, though I heard it often enough—was busy with "the electrics." All this seemed to me very fine, and when the dramatist began telling us that this particular "set" would do or would not do for the something theatre in New York, it seemed to me still finer. I told myself once more that plays are the thing. I would be a dramatist too, and worry splendidly in the deserted stalls in the middle of the afternoon (a time of day when there is never much to do), and talk about "electrics" and "sets" for New York. If you are an author, nothing happens but a specimen page and then some miserable proofs. The dramatist's wife was there too, examining costumes and carrying a notebook and borrowing pencils and hurrying from the stalls to the stage and then back to the stalls again, thoroughly enjoying herself. An author's wife has no fun and fuss of this kind. All she can do is to sit at home, trying to work out the royalty payable on a sale of 1,754 copies, thirteen reckoned as twelve, and including 135 sold to the Colonies; in other words, virtually given away.

The three men in shirt sleeves decided that they had played long enough with the red and gold window curtains, took them away, and returned with some grey and purple ones. Immediately a young man whom I had hardly noticed at all burst into speech from the row in front of us. He was a young man with a noble forehead and a very short pipe, and he was almost passionate on the subject of pelmets. The three men in shirt sleeves never even looked up from their curtains, but a man with eyeglasses, who had been bustling vaguely about the stage for some time, stopped for a moment and nodded. The young man with the very short pipe then sank back into his seat again, and, I trust, forgot about pelmets.

Then a row of little black boxes came wobbling into view at the top of the stage. They seemed to be very uncertain things. First they came down several feet, then rose a foot or two, changed their minds and shakily descended, stopped, then finally lowered themselves creakily almost to the floor. A fattish man strolled on and gazed dreamily at these boxes, after which he went off, only to return with another and thinner man and a cloth or two. The pair of them then unscrewed some lenses from the boxes and polished them in a meditative fashion. One of the men in shirt sleeves arrived now with a picture, which he held up against the wall for a moment and then apparently conjured into thin air, for I never saw it again. By this time, however, a pretty girl in a riding costume was claiming our attention. She was standing in the centre, crying, "But, darling, it's *terrible!*" and turning round and round. A very dignified woman with *pince-nez*, who was my idea of a dowager in a Mrs. Humphrey Ward novel, though actually I believe she was the wardrobe mistress, came forward and looked at the riding costume in despair. She was joined by a little man of an Hebraic cast, who pointed and shrugged and wriggled and talked to everybody at once, including the man with eyeglasses, who was, however, still bustling vaguely and nodding here and there.

A moving tape caught my eye. One end of it was held by a youth standing in the corner of the dress circle. The other end was being carried round the opposite side of the dress circle by another youth. I watched these two and their tape for several minutes, and they all seemed to be very busy, very important, gravely happy, but I never understood what they were doing. There was, indeed, a Wonderlandish look about them. Perhaps they were measuring the theatre for a croquet party, to be given by the Queen of Hearts. And now a flash of flame colour on the stage announced the presence of a lady in old-fashioned evening clothes and full make-up. I do not know whether she was saying that it was "terrible, darling" too, because I could not hear her. All I could hear was the hammering of the two remaining men in shirt sleeves, and constant cries of "Where's So-and-So?"

Almost everybody there wanted to know where somebody was, and so far as I could see, nobody ever supplied an answer. Something was said about "fifteen men and a black out," as if a new version of the pirate song were being prepared, but it did not seem to mean anything to anybody. Finally, a very handsome young actor strolled on, most sumptuously arrayed, and he was immediately asked where So-and-so was, and the dramatist's wife rushed on again with her notebook and tried to borrow a pencil, and the man with the eyeglasses dodged here and there and nodded away for all he was worth. After that, nothing at all happened. There appeared to be about thirty people present, and not one of them looked as if he or she would ever be able to go home again, but nothing happened.

"It's the hanging about," my companion told me, "that would bore me in this theatrical business. Amazing—the way they hang about!" And as I agreed, I began to wonder whether I really did want to write a play. Undoubtedly a play does not take long to write. But what is the mere writing of the thing? It is the—well, I do not know what to call it, but whatever it was we saw going on in there—that takes the time.

A Mad Shepherd

THE world is at once saner and yet more given to
lunacy than it used to be, for the people outside
asylums are saner than their grandfathers were, yet
there are greater numbers under some sort of treat-
ment, or at least under lock and key, for madness. I
do not know whether it is because there is increasing
harbourage for lunatics in our time, or because it is
merely becoming more difficult, every year, in the face
of specialists whose own sanity is never questioned, to
prove that one is not yet ready for the madhouse;
but it is clear that the eccentrics and half-wits who
chuckled and grimaced in our older literature, through
the long tales of our grandparents, are fast disappear-
ing. A host of notable figures in Shakespeare, from
Hamlet to Petruchio, would not be suffered to walk
abroad these days unless they piped in a lower key.
It is a great pity that all the crack-brained, whimsical
fellows are leaving us; we need a little variety in our
experiments with existence, for there is a danger that
we are all crazed and have only decided for unanimity,
that we are Mad Hatters who will not suffer a March
Hare; and these others, extravagant but harmless,
have their own visions of life and we cannot prove
them wrong, but can only point to the majority—a
trick unworthy of us.

These bold experiments, the crack-brained, are now

so few and so precious, that I travel with one eye open
for them; for a man is as well, if not better, occupied
collecting eccentric essays in life, as he is casting about
for ancient coins or earthenware. Remote towns or
villages make the most promising hunting-grounds,
and only a short time ago, my search was well rewarded in a certain small market town. I had been in
the place several days, and had come to know most
of its prominent figures well by sight, when one fellow,
whom I was always seeing, here, there, and everywhere, began to excite my curiosity. He was an oldish
man, with a close-shaven, tanned face, and always
dressed in gaiters and what seemed to be a long
smock, with a curiously-shaped cap, of the same
material as his smock, pressed down upon his head.
These and other particulars I noted with interest, but
what intrigued me most was a long pole, roughly
shaped like a shepherd's crook, which he always
carried in his hand, and which seemed to be some implement of his trade. But what his trade was, I could
not guess; I never saw him employed in any way,
never caught him piloting beasts towards the market
or making any kind of use of the mysterious pole. Yet
whenever I ran across him, which I did frequently, he
always seemed to be fully occupied, neither rushing
heedlessly nor yet loitering, but resolutely pressing
forward to some important piece of business—a sober
man of affairs. Even in a little market town, there are
many ways of earning bread and beer that fall outside
the scope of a stranger's knowledge, tiny trades that

are commonplaces in one shire and unknown in the next, and I might easily have contented myself with assuming that my man was thus engaged. But the archaic costume and the quaintly fashioned pole, now so familiar, were too provocative, and led me to question my landlady, whose talk was fluent and full of good matter, though rather obscure. I had scarcely begun my description of the man before she had snatched the subject from me and panted forth the whole tale.

In spite of his quaint figure, I had set my man down as a sober busy citizen, engaged in some obscure little trade of his own. He was even more fantastic than his clothes, more mysterious than his own strange implement. For it appeared that this fellow was nothing more nor less than a crack-brained idler, one who had —in my landlady's words—"gone soft in the head." Up to a few years ago a lonely, quiet man, expecting nothing from the world, he had suddenly come into a fortune, and the surprise and joy that followed this stroke of luck had turned his brain; thenceforward he blossomed madly and ran to amazing whims and crotchets, harmless enough, but strangely odd and diverting. His greatest and most delectable fantasy was this, that he took upon himself, from time to time, the duty of acting in a definite character, usually one of the ancient trades of the world; he would dress himself for the part, and, so far as it was possible, take over the habits, the interests, the mode of speech of the particular type he copied. Thus, he would be a

sailor for some time, then a fisherman, and after that
maybe a gamekeeper or forester; always dressing himself accordingly and keeping strictly to the type, and
not declining to the actual indistinguishable characters
of our own day, but presenting in his attire, as it were,
the ideal sailor or forester; and so, tricked out in such
homely yet symbolic vestments, perhaps thinking to
take a place with the poet "in the calm and proud
procession of eternal things."

When I saw him, he was a shepherd; indeed a shepherd appeared to be his favourite character, for he
had maintained the part for some time, and, according
to report, showed no signs of changing. There are few
shepherds in that part of the country, and the few
there are do not wear smocks or carry a crook as he
did. But he followed his usual practice, looked back
to a simpler, smaller and more clearly defined world,
and dressed the part to mark it off from all other
trades. It was the least he could do, seeing that he did
no actual work and devoted all his energies to the
masquerade. His apparent busyness was all moonshine. The sheep he herded could not be driven to any
mart in this world, for they were nothing but drifting
phantoms. When he walked the sunlit streets, his
grotesque shadow pursued by laughter, he hurried to
mythical appointments, moved in shadowy markets,
and trafficked in thin air. At the end of the day, after
being urged here and there by his lively fancy, doubtless he returned home as tired and as well content with
his day's unsubstantial labour as any sober man of

business; sometimes maybe he would return elated, at others mortified, for there must be triumphs and grievous losses even in this matter of pursuing phantoms. Then, in the evening, his crook laid aside, perhaps he would make plans for the next day; but what such plans could be, no man can imagine, for they must be dreams within a dream and shadows of a shadow. So he would pass his time, hurting no man, his life, like that of all such quaint fellows, only marred by loneliness. Nor would he lack a companion, supposing his present whimsy holds, if I had my way; for somewhere in a large and dirty city there is a sheepdog that I once knew, a dog that had never known the life it was meant to lead, never seen the hills with the sheep scattered upon them, and yet, in the yard of a warehouse, it spent its days herding invisible sheep, running round bales and barking furiously at barrels. Were that dog mine, the crazy shepherd should have him, so that the two might walk the streets together, happily pursuing their mythical flocks and otherwise busying themselves in their dream-pastures.

The maggots of the brain are not to be enumerated and labelled: what led this harmless fellow to such fantasies, no man can know. Perhaps after the sudden stroke of fortune sent his wits wandering he had been mastered by some old thought, some half-forgotten protest against the drab formlessness of labour in our day, against the absence of any marks of distinction between men of one trade and men of another; he had reverted to a more ordered clear-cut time, when every man was stamped with the sign of one or other of the ancient industries. Only in some such way, one can attempt to explain this strange masquerade of his. He has his own vision of life, his own idea of that poetry which transfigures the mechanism of blood and bone; and I trust that he will be left to himself to go his own way, for when he is weary of a shepherd's life, there are still many time-old tradesmen, from tinker to tailor, that he can personate. Nor will it be long before I see him again, caring little whether he is still a shepherd or metamorphosed into a fisherman or cobbler, so long as he is still with us, going his own fantastic gait.

The Eternal Cheap-Jack

THE war has not changed him. But then all the tumults and long wars of centuries have not changed him. Like the pedant, the demagogue, or the place-hunter, the cheap-jack is an ever-enduring figure. Boccaccio's Frate Cipolla and Chaucer's Pardoner were his first cousins; from Shakespeare to O. Henry (to adopt the popular termini), he has chaffered and cozened his way through literature. And he is with us yet in the flesh, for I saw him only last week. I was visiting the weekly fair in a pleasant little town, and had joined the crowd of country folks drifting about the stalls in the market square, when, suddenly, a mighty voice burst from the centre of a group of persons huddled in a far corner. In the country, where the long days are filled with the sight and sound of the lower creatures, there is no resisting this eruptive clamour of a human voice for an audience, and, along with others, I hurried to join the thickening press of folk in the corner. There, after many years, I found him, as of old.

There was the same indefinable air of something like bravado about his whole figure. His hard face still bore that curious trace of the Jew, mingled with something a great deal worse than the Jew. His clothes, which were new and smart, still seemed to proclaim that they had been made for someone else; and the various trinkets about his person still confessed their inability to inspire confidence. In front was the same old stall, laden with innumerable, mysterious packages, all thickly wrapped in tissue paper; and by the side of the stall stood the inevitable assistant, silent, dejected, unshaven, looking like a rough and shabbier copy of his master, or perhaps a poor relation. Nothing had changed. The great man still flourished the sign of his office, a wooden mallet with a ponderous head, with which he hammered upon the stall from time to time as a sort of dramatic punctuation.

Best of all, his voice, that one talent which removed him from common men, was there in all its pristine fullness. He spoke in the manner of his kind; in that accent which owns no shire, city, or clan, and yet is heard in all the marketplaces in the land. His very whispered confidences were enough to stir the old bones in the neighbouring churchyard. The crowd, trying to appear sophisticated, was held and mastered by the voice that was trumpeting, cajoling, mocking, within the space of one mighty breath, and yet still went sounding on, dropping manna by the way. Unknowingly he was a passionate votary of the art that has now nearly forsaken the pulpit and the council chamber. We, his audience, stifled all doubts, and waited, promise-crammed.

There was little or no alteration in his methods. Whether they have been designed, once for all, by some Master Psychologist of cheap-jacks, or are the result of accumulated experience, a secret tradition

M

passed from generation to generation of genial trick-
sters, I cannot say; but these methods, like the human
nature on which they are based, do not change much.
As before, he had not come among us to make money.
With passionate emphasis, he declared that he was
not a profiteer (a new note, this), but had been sent
down here by the well-known firm of Mumble-
Mumble to smash profiteering. He would teach us
the meaning of the word Lib-er-al-ity—that is how
he mouthed it, with splendid significance. And then
he proceeded in the time-old fashion.

From some half-a-dozen persons nearest the stall,
he borrowed a few coppers, promising to return the
loan with the addition of a "small present." These
people, becoming sharers in the business, naturally do
not care to go away, and thus, by this simple trick
whatever may happen he has about him at least the
nucleus of a crowd. Then, flourishing several mysterious packages before our eyes, he asked us to bid
for them. "Any gentleman got the pluck," he demanded, with the dispassionate earnestness of a god,
"Any gentleman got the courage to offer me a Silver
Shilling for this?" Any gentleman showing the necessary public spirit was given the article in question,
and his money, his Silver Shilling, was handed back
to him. Nor did our friend spoil his acts of munifi-
cence by the manner of giving; every package was
divested of its numerous wrappings before it was
handed over to the lucky man; the contents were ex-
posed to the public view, and described in a style that

"Ouida" would have envied. Our minds reeled before
this riotous splendour of gold and jewels. Sometimes in
a frenzy of reckless generosity, he would pile up a heap
of articles, and with a magnificent sense of the dramatic, would cry; "Here's number One! And here's
number Two! And here's another one, making number Three! And another one, making number Four!"
—working up to a climax that left us gasping. Then,
after being extraordinarily bountiful to one person, he
would pretend to answer a perfectly imaginary charge
of confederacy from some member of the crowd, looking all the while very sternly at no one in particular.
"One of a click (*i.e.*, clique) is 'e?" he would roar.
"One of the click! Do I know yer, Mister? Never
seen yer before. I'll show yer whether 'e's one of the
click! I'll show yer!" And being apparently stung
by this vile taunt, he would lash himself into a fury,
and proceed to squander his glittering wares even still
more wildly. I left him with the sweat running
down his face, his hair all rumpled and his collar
a wreck; yet he was still undaunted, giving away
gold watches with the magnificent air of an Eastern
Emperor.

I, for one, welcome the cheap-jack because his
presence in our midst proves that there is still a little
poetry left in the race. For all his machinations are
based on a certain notion which the experience of this
world proves to be a fallacy, and which is yet as old
as the hills and as little to be despised. It is the fine
old notion that it is possible, somehow or other, to get

something for nothing; and it was not born of this world. When we have entirely forsaken the idea, then we are lost indeed, for it comes from the depths of our primal innocence, and has about it the last lingering scent of the Garden of Eden.

Strange Encounter

YESTERDAY, the people in the bungalow below took us to Hartland in their car. We went through Stratton, whose oldest inn has a notice that reminds you that the battle of Stamford Hill was fought just round the corner. And there are such perils, such hairbreadth escapes, in Stratton's narrow and twisting street, where gigantic buses miss you by an inch, that all the battles of that Civil War seem part of an idyll, old and happy, far-off things. We went, through Kilkhampton, where I saw nothing of interest except one of those queer families, those monstrous collections of odd humans, that you never see except when you are travelling. It is impossible to imagine them at home. We climbed to the top of a rustling moor, and then crossed it in happy solitude. We ran down steep and narrow lanes, and at last came to the headland where there is a crazy hotel and the ruins of Hartland Quay. A green sea shook itself now and again and then went creaming over the rocks. It was far below the shattered brickwork of the old quay, but you felt it was giving a glance in that direction every now and then, and muttering, "Just try building another breakwater, that's all! Just try it!" Lundy, that familiar speck, was now a big fat rock of an island, almost absurdly melodramatic. I spent a dreamy half-hour—and every scribbler will know how pleasant it was—vaguely

planning a thriller that would have a Lundy chapter
or two in it. The others, I believe, were trying to
decide whether the blackbird fluttering about the face
of the cliff really was a raven. Perhaps it was, as we
shall see, and was trying to cry "Nevermore."

We walked to the top of the cliff, and watched
some great buzzard hawks go wheeling up into the
blue. There were sweet smells, an old intoxication,
in the air. To have the heather about your feet and
to look out to sea is to be happy, so happy that you
feel it is incredible that you will not live for ever. But
the shadow of mortality soon fell upon us. We arrived
at Stoke Church. This church is miles from anywhere, except from the rocks and foam and the ruined
quay, the gulls and ravens and hawks, yet it lifts a
great tower to the sky, just as if the bustling plains
of Flanders were beneath it. There are a few white-
washed cottages, a few gnarled trees, and this church
with its enormous tower. We wandered about the
churchyard, in which a whole host has been buried,
so that mounds and stones almost jostle one another.
There you may meet generations of Chopes and
Prusts and Okes, whole centuries of them. Their
stones show a grim appreciation of the fact of death.
our ancestors may have had their weaknesses, but
sentimentality about death was not one of them. They
lived round the churchyard. Not a single passing coffin escaped their eyes. When they died themselves, they pointed out, in clear inch lettering in
granite, that you would soon be dead too. The Shrop-

shire Lad himself had not a better eye for all the
signs of mortality, but they did not make the same
fuss about it. Here was the older Western Front and
all was quiet upon it, but decency and reticence had
been given a turn too. In the lovely old interior of the
church was a tablet to a local gentleman, and he was
described, simply and superbly, as "a plain good
man." I do not think that I am a plain good man, but
I felt that here was a community in which I could
have lived without frequently suspecting that we were
all mad together.

And it was here, in this remote western corner, this
place of foam and heather and great wild birds,
among the unknown Chopes and Okes and Prusts,
that I discovered my old publisher—John Lane. He
lies in this very churchyard, and in the church itself
there is a memorial tablet to him. It was the queerest,
the most startling encounter. I knew that he came
from some little place in Devonshire, but I had forgotten—if I ever knew—that it was Hartland, and
that he was buried in Stoke Church. I stared and
stared at his name. The memory of the man himself
returned to me, very vividly. I only knew him during
his last years. He was my first London publisher, and
for several years I was his "reader." He used to give
me lunch at his clubs, the Reform and the Cocoa Tree,
and dinner down at Lancaster Gate. I saw again his
short figure, his bearded face, his peering vague eyes.
I heard again his curiously characteristic tones, at
once a little hoarse and squeaky. It seemed only a

month or two ago since we were sitting in some corner, heavy with cigar smoke, and I was listening to his rambling good talk about some portrait he had picked up or the idiosyncracies of one of his older poets. He was one of those men—and I mean only the men with whom one has business relations—of whom it might be said that they cannot be approved of or recommended and yet cannot be disliked. He was one of the old school of publishers, a sort of genial literary brigand, who believed quite sincerely that authors should not have any money, and so whittled down your terms to nearly nothing, but at the same time poured champagne and liqueur brandy down your throat and pressed upon you the largest cigars. He would give you anything so long as it was not a matter of percentages. The idea of an author who had an agent and a decent bank account and artful notions about dramatic rights shocked him. Authors to him were either people in society with incomes or wild geniuses who simply needed a good lunch or dinner now and again to keep them going. He always seemed to know about books, though I can never believe he ever read any. He was a character, and I liked him enormously.

Devon boys have roamed about these heathery Hartland cliffs, gone out into the world and, after many Odysseys, have returned to this remote place to die. But few of them, for all the epics of Moorish galleys, sacked towns, and sunken gold, can have had a queerer history than this of John Lane. Only the day

before I had been reading an advance copy of Miss
Viola Meynell's delightful life of her mother, Alice
Meynell, and John Lane had popped up there. He
pops up everywhere in the 'nineties. He was himself
an intensely respectable man, a solid bourgeois, but
as a publisher he had a flair and knew when the
moment had arrived for naughtiness and fine writing
and devil take the suburbs. As I strolled away from
that churchyard, where cavalier's man, eighteenth-
century farmhand, and Victorian coastguard all lie
so peacefully together, and their times seem all one
under that wide gull-haunted sky, I thought about
the queer adventures of this wandering Devonian.
How far away, how odd, seemed all the old activities
of that Bodley Head! The "nest of singing birds."
The "decadents." Beardsley and Harland and the
Yellow Book. "I have been true to thee, Cynara, in
my fashion." John Davidson, with his ballads and
eclogues. Max Beerbohm's *Works*. Le Gallienne's
Quest of the Golden Girl. The *Keynotes* Series. And
the little man with the peaked beard and the near-
sighted eyes threaded his way through these things,
smoked his cigar at the Reform and the Cocoa Tree,
surveyed his first editions and portraits at Lancaster
Gate, conjured Anatole France into yellow-coloured
English volumes, and then left what was mortal of
him under the shadow of these Hartland Cliffs.

These Novels

I WILL admit that I, too, in my time, have grumbled about the number of new novels that come out in these days. I grumbled, however, as a reviewer, a fellow who heard his table groaning beneath the weight of unread books. A reviewer has a right to grumble, and no doubt booksellers and librarians have a right to grumble too. But I cannot see why ordinary members of the public, people who are not reviewers, publishers, booksellers, or librarians, should so often complain about the number of new novels. What harm does this mass of print and paper do them? The public is not compelled to read all these new novels. It need not spend a penny of its money or waste a moment of its time on them. To hear some people talk, you would imagine that their lives were somehow endangered by the swollen lists of the publishers. After all, it is very easy to ignore the existence of a new novel, for the thing does not follow you about, snapping at your heels.

If instead of grumbling about new novels, people grumbled about new motor-cars, there would be some sense in the complaint. Cars are useless unless they are running up and down the public thoroughfares, and the more cars there are, the more crowded and dangerous, smelly and uncomfortable, noisy and obscene, the roads become. Very soon it will be im-

possible to move about in London and equally impossible to get out of London, simply because so
many new cars are published every month. One
motor-cycle can make a bigger nuisance of itself than
ten thousand bad books. A novel, even a very bad
one, comes into the world quietly, allows itself to be
put on a shelf or thrown into a dustbin, and never
makes a sound. It does not snarl at you and try to
crush your leg. The house next door may have been
invaded by a hundred new novels, and yet you may
not know they are there. They do not insist upon
your noticing them, as new radio sets and gramo-
phones do. And men do not stand outside bookshops
trying to entice you in to buy new novels. No hawkers
pester you at the door with them. You have only to
keep away from lending libraries, the interiors of
bookshops, publishers' offices, and the advertisement
pages of the literary weeklies, to be completely oblivi-
ous of the fact that these novels are arriving in the
world at all.

A great many people must be engaged now in
writing fiction. But what of that? In such a world as
this, writing fiction is a comparatively innocent occupation, its worst results being nothing more than a
certain curtailing of exercise and a certain increase
of irritation and vanity. On the whole, writing novels
will do a man less harm than going to the races,
standing in bars drinking double whiskies, falling in
love with the wrong women, murdering animals and
birds, sitting at bridge tables, or dining too expen-

sively and heavily. It is only on very rare occasions that doctors have to warn their patients not to write any more novels. Now that all kinds of mischief are open to young girls, they are probably better employed sitting quietly in the little spare room upstairs writing fiction than in doing almost anything else they would like to do. When a girl appears in a police court and is charged with being the author of a certain novel, the event is so rare that the newspapers make a tremendous fuss about it. No doubt, members of both sexes would be more sensibly occupied if they took to gardening, but then you cannot be always out of doors, and authorship provides you with one of the pleasantest and safest indoor recreations.

We are told that very few of these new novelists can possibly make much money out of their work. But what of that? They have had their fun. If they do not make much money, then they will be kept away from the miseries of professional authorship; for most of these novelists are enthusiastic amateurs and you may depend upon it that they will not turn professional unless they see that their fiction is about to be very profitable. But whether they make a lot of money or none at all, it is their affair and it does not concern any member of the outside public. If you regard fiction as one of our industries, there is a good deal to be said for it. For example, as Mr. Guedalla has pointed out, it forms one of our very few successful export trades, triumphantly surviving all slumps. Proportionately, we scribblers do a better

trade with America than almost anybody else. The
time may come when England will be thought of as
the great fiction-producing country. As it is, our
exports of mystery and detective stories to all parts
of Europe are very considerable.

On the other hand, if you prefer to regard the
creation of novels as a hobby, then why should you
or anyone else be so bitter about it? I hear people
say, "Oh, everybody writes novels now," and when
they say this they add to it a sort of hollow sneering
laugh, very unpleasant in the ear. And why? What
is the matter with them What harm have the novels
done them? It is all very mysterious. If you went
to some distant country and a man said, "Oh, everybody here plays in string quartets," and then brought
out this horrid laugh, you would stare at him in
amazement.

It may be true that publishers are losing money by
bringing out so much new fiction. If you are a share-
holder in such a concern, then you have a right to
complain; but if you have nothing to do with the
business, it cannot matter much to you. Obviously, a
publisher who loses money year after year will arrive
at a point where it will not be possible for him to
publish any novels at all. Meanwhile, it can be
said that the publishing of fiction, like the writing of
fiction, is one of our more innocent employments. A
man might persist in publishing stacks of new novels
each spring and autumn season, and yet remain a
fairly decent citizen, a devoted husband, a kind father,

a good friend. No, I don't think we need worry about the publishers.

I have proved that this flood of fiction does no real harm to the public (which is at liberty to ignore it), to the authors, and to the publishers. What have we left? Very little; only what might be called the Age. These fellows who grumble about all the new novels seem to think that our Age will be laughed at because it has produced all this foolish fiction. They are clearly under the impression that the bad novel is a new thing, almost a typical product of the twentieth century. Apparently they imagine that all the novels of the Regency were written by Jane Austen and Scott, that only Dickens, Thackeray, the Brontës, George Eliot, and a few others wrote novels for the Victorians; and that forty or fifty years ago Hardy and Meredith divided the spring and autumn seasons between them. They should examine any book of the last century that has some pages of the publisher's advertisements at the back, and there they will discover a number of novels they never heard of before and most of these will not be ordinary unsuccessful novels but what publishers now call "winners." They should buy a batch of "old novels" from a secondhand bookshop, genuine unknown works of fiction from the 'thirties, the 'fifties, the 'seventies, and then they will quickly discover that we have no monopoly of bad fiction. The truth is, of course, that ever since there have been novels at all, there have been stacks of them, new novels all over the place, and some people have pounced on them and read them, and other people have said, "Can't understand why they bring out all these silly novels." Old gentlemen were saying that in Bath one hundred and forty years ago. There are, of course, more new novels now, but then there are millions and millions more people to read them. I suspect that in proportion to the number of literate persons, there are fewer novels brought out now than there were in 1800.

Let us have done with this new novel complaint. I call it a waste of a grumble, now that there are so many things that should be grumbled at good and hard. If you must complain, why don't you complain about—but no, I must stop. I am ending an article, not beginning a series of volumes.

On Cartomancy

A SHORT time ago, in a strange town, evil chance confined me in a dingy room overlooking a dismal little
street and then, having done this, left me to my own
devices, without company and with few books. A
grey tide of boredom and depression was already
threatening and would have soon engulfed me, had I
not come across a little volume in a corner of the
bookshelf. It was—to set forth the full title—*Cartomancy, or Occult Divination by Cards*. The identity
of the writer was not revealed; he or she was
shrouded in true oracular fashion. I had heard of
fortune-telling by cards; indeed, I had vague
memories of having my destiny unfolded, in the dim
past, by elderly ladies who tapped the assembled
cards impressively and talked of letters, journeys
by land, and dark ladies. But I had no idea such
occult knowledge could be gleaned from books. If I
had thought about the matter at all (which is doubtful), I had probably imagined that the art of Cartomancy was preserved by oral tradition, handed down
through generations of maiden aunts; or that the clue
to its mysteries was the inalienable property of a
League of Decayed Gentlewomen. But no, here it was
in a trumpery little volume, sold everywhere for a
shilling. Truly, this is an age of books.

So I lost no time in making myself acquainted with

the art, and boredom fled. Nor could I have found a better preceptor, for in this little book all was revealed; with fitting gravity and wealth of detail, it set forth the meaning of the cards and the various methods of laying them out. Each card had a distinct meaning, which was modified by the presence of other cards. All this was made clear, but the instructions were delightfully free from pedantry: "If intuition leads you to give a different meaning, do so," was the advice it tendered—and what could be better? There was good reason attached to the meaning of some few of the cards, which had a very pretty symbolism. What else could the Queen of Hearts be but a fair woman? What could be a better symbol of death than the Ace of Spades reversed? Never again shall I see that innocent piece of pasteboard without feeling a sudden chill. But the symbolism of most of the cards was not so obvious. Why—it might be asked—should the eight of diamonds represent a roadway journey, the nine of spades disappointment and tears, the ace of clubs a letter of good news? These are mysteries, and not to be lightly compre-hended. All the cards, however, are alike in this: they stand for the life that the centuries leave unchanged, the eternal verities of human existence, the things that are significant alike to the emperor and the clown; they do not adapt themselves to any pale, half-hearted way of living, but are downright and talk boldly of birth, death, and marriage, of jealousy, love and anger, of quarrels, accidents, and sudden endings. As to the various methods of shuffling, cutting and laying out the cards, the little book dealt with all these matters with high seriousness and at some length; and no sooner was I acquainted with one or two of the methods than I began to put them into practice. "These coloured scraps of pasteboard," I said to myself, as I ranged the cards, "shall be the tiny windows through which I will stare at the past, and peer wonderingly into the future. And I shall be as a god."

As no other person was near, I decided to read my own fortunes, past, present, and future. I learned from the book that this was a difficult thing to do, and so I found it. True it is that through the medium of the cards, "the gay triumph-assuring scarlets—the contrasting deadly killing sables"—as Lamb called them, my fortunes appeared to take on richer hues, to run to more passionate extremes than I had imagined; and in the vague mass, both my past and future took on the aspect of a riotous, crowded pageant of love and intrigue, of tremendous sins and strange virtues. All this was heart-stirring enough, but there were difficulties waiting upon any sort of direct interpretation. Though I lived splendidly, and appeared to swagger through an existence crowded with incident, the whole fifty-two, hearts and all, seemed to combine to make me out a rascal, whose mind must have been corroded with the "motiveless malignity" of an Iago. Why, for example, should I rejoice at the death of a dark boy in a railway accident? Why should I

hound a white-haired old gentleman to his grave?
And why—for there were numerous other incidents
of this kind foreshadowed—should my villainy
always take this vile form? Was I this kind of man,
I asked myself and the cards, after each new instance
of my calculated knavery, and if not, at what precise
moment in the near future were all the forces of evil
to take command of my soul. So I abandoned the
attempt to discover my own fortunes, and, turning to
the book, found that if one "thought strongly of one's
absent friends" it was possible to dip into their past
and future.

For some little time I shrank from this course.
To pry into their past was bad enough, but to attempt
to look into their future, which even Time has the
decency to keep covered for a while, seemed posi-
tively immoral, an action compared with which the
publication of a man's love-letters was a mark of
friendship. It was not long, however, before I had
stifled this feeling by some sophistry about warning
them of dangers and so forth; and so I proceeded to
satisfy my curiosity. As I shuffled and laid out the
cards, I saw myself as the sinister magician of lurid
fiction, and relished the part. I had only to take up
the cards and the stage was set for great dramas,
bravely tricked out in crimson and sable for one
secret spectator. If this is not puissance, then where
is it to be found among men? What were books when
one could spell out the narrative of the cards, and
make each friend in turn the hero or heroine of the

pictured story. Or if books were to continue, what magnificent plots could be evolved from these strange combinations of coloured pasteboard. But if, through the cards, my own existence had assumed brave proportions, though everywhere smirched by villainy, that of my friends was no less highly-coloured and crowded with incident. As I ranged the cards, and spied into the secret life, past and future, of one friend after another, I was dumbfounded, aghast at my former ignorance. Men who had been hidden away, for the last twenty years, in college rooms and lecture halls, whose outward existence had appeared as smooth and unruffled as the immemorial lawns outside their windows, now seemed to be moving in a violent Elizabethan drama. They made love to dark ladies, and were in turn adored by fair ones; they lost and gained great sums of money, aroused the jealousy of dark men, wrecked innumerable homes, and lived in a constant whirl of good and evil tidings, sea voyages, railway journeys, and strong passions. Here was a set of men who had been living like this (and were to go on doing so) for years, and yet I, who counted myself one of their friends, had been kept in ignorance. What consummate actors!—to present an unruffled front to the world, and even to their friends, and yet all the while to know, in secret, a life that resembled nothing so much as a thunderstorm. Could such things be? In truth, I came, in the end, to doubt the cards.

But though I have forsworn Cartomancy, and hold

such occult practices in abhorrence, I will say to every man who has suddenly found that life is one long piece of boredom, dull grey in warp and weft: Go to the cards, and see existence woven madly in black and crimson. The life they present knows nothing of boredom, for no card in all the pack stands for such a thing—Go read the cards! As for myself, I have but one confession to make: I dare not play at cards now, for they are fraught with such significance to me that I could not trifle with them in a mere game. I cannot rid them of their meanings, and while others are thinking of nothing but winning tricks, I see myself, and my unconscious colleagues, playing havoc with the destinies of dark ladies and fair men. I cannot trump an opponent's Queen, but what I feel that I am probably bringing misfortune upon some unknown innocent woman. If I fling down the Ace of Spades upon the King, it is not unlikely that I am consigning some dark man—a good fellow probably —to his grave. This would be murder, and an odd trick is not worth it. So there is nothing for it but to leave the cards alone.

On a New Kind of Fiction

THE literary year books and reference books do not make very cheerful reading these days, but there is a certain note in one of them that should not be allowed to remain in obscurity. It is contributed by the editor of an American journal, *Ambition,* who informs all writers and would-be writers that he and his paper are prepared to accept:

> Stories, 4,000–4,500 (words), in which the hero advances in position and earnings through study of a trade or profession by means of a correspondence course (preferred occupations indicated by Editor on application).

One can only hope that this passage has not met the eye of any reader of *Ambition,* one who has urged himself along the steep, narrow way, and found sustenance in such heartening tales, for he might become disillusioned, lag in his course (if only a correspondence course), and turn cynic or communist. Our editor, with true occidental ruthlessness, takes us behind the scenes with a vengeance; he strips each wretched player and spares us neither paint nor plaster-and-lath; had we any illusions on the matter, any roseate dreams of "advancing in position and earnings," which we have not, how rudely we should have been awakened. But one would have thought that the readers of *Ambition*, grimly practical fellows, every one of them essentially "a man of this world," were above the mere trifling of the storyteller, that they were ready, nay, eager, to face the stern facts, the naked issues of life, without calling in the writer of fiction to beguile and comfort them with his cunning old tricks. But no, even in this bleak and forbidding region, the storyteller is welcomed; the ancient craft is not allowed to perish even in these high altitudes. But while so much is conceded to frail human nature, the earnest young people who read *Ambition* cannot have their minds stuffed with any glittering nonsense, love stories, tales of piracy, and the like; if there is to be fiction, it must be of one kind only. The hero must not be some absurd swash-buckler, the prey of we know not what romantic whims and fancies; he must be a good solid young fellow "who advances in position and earnings through study of a trade or profession by means of a correspondence course." Well told, the story of such an enterprising youth must be worth any man's reading.

But while we are thus to some extent restricted—and, after all, does not art imply restriction?—yet within these bounds there is ample freedom. The writer is at liberty to choose the hero's name, we take it, and may even let his fancy wander somewhat in his description of the fellow, making him tall or short, fat or thin, dark or fair, according to the author's taste in these matters. For example, he may relate how Joe Brown, short, fat, and fair, advances in position and earnings by taking a correspondence course of steeplejackery (or whatever it is that makes a steeplejack); or, again, he may show how Marmaduke Grubstock-Datterville not only advances in position, but retrieves the family fortunes by applying himself to a course (entirely by correspondence) of wholesale grocery. This, surely, is something. Moreover, the rate of advance in the hero's position and the extent of his earnings are matters that are probably left to the author's discretion, and he is no true penman who cannot make something of humour and pathos out of such material.

The type of story being thus fixed, it is clear that the most important point left is the hero's trade or profession. If the storyteller is free to give his hero any trade or profession he pleases, he has no right to complain of undue restriction. If, on the other hand, the trade or profession used in each story is determined beforehand by the authorities, then we may say that perhaps our editor is pressing a little too heavily upon his contributors. The remark in parenthesis, coming at the end of the editor's note as if it were a sudden inspiration or a kindly afterthought, settles the question: "Preferred occupations indicated by Editor on application." It is compromise, and, we think a very sensible one; neither author nor editor is enthroned or fettered; there is a possibility of mutual help and, we trust, sympathy. Note the advantages of such an arrangement. In the first place, as the readers of *Ambition* are men who have their eye on the labour market, men who know what is what, it will not do to put before them any sort of trade or profession and to talk wildly about it. Writers of fiction may be very tricksy fellows, but it is quite clear that it would not be wise to leave them entirely to themselves when they are choosing trades for their 4,000–4,500 word heroes; without expert guidance there is no telling into what gimcrack, monstrous jobs they would thrust the creatures of their fancy. It is easy to see that one would have to be circumspect in this matter of a trade; in this, as in other things, there must be judgment; an apt choice is requisite. It would, for example, be quite useless scribbling down four thousand words about a young ambitious crossbowman or alchemist; we may be sure that our editor would not have his confiding readers dealt with so anachronously; he would not suffer them to be led by desires that are several centuries beyond fruition.

Again, there are many trades that are not in the best of taste—swindling, forgery, sandbagging, and so forth; an occasional story using one of these might do little harm, and even some good, inasmuch as it might enlarge the scope of one or two readers, but a journal that began to show favour to such doubtful, and even unpopular, industries would soon lose its hold. Other occupations, while free from the objections urged above, must be regarded as useless for our purpose, because they do not appear to offer sufficient room for a really determined hero; they are cramped, confined, and show no tempting horizons; the trade of ferryman, programme-seller, of liftman, to name only a few, must be passed over for this reason. Moreover, the selected trade or profession must be the subject of a correspondence course or the hero can make no headway; a correspondence course is essential. Now, although our correspondence schools are daily quickened by the spirit of enterprise, there are still many occupations that they have left untouched; most of the trades we have already dismissed would have to be rejected again on this count, while there are many others, such as that of torturer, milkman, astrologer, or acrobat, that we imagine to be still without correspondence courses. It is clear then that the choice of a suitable trade has difficulties, and that a mere writer of fiction should be glad to accept the proffered advice of the expert, his editor. There is, however, another reason that more than justifies the editor's wisdom in offering to indicate "preferred trades or professions." Some authors, knowing more about such things than most of their fellows, might very well choose entirely suitable trades even if they were left to themselves; but there is more in the question than this mere choice, for each story must not only be acceptable in itself, but it must also be good when it is considered in its relation to the other stories that it follows or precedes. As we have seen, the tales themselves have unity, but within that unity there must be variety. The cunning arrangement of literary matter so that one item contrasts with another, the effect of both thus being heightened, is the very mark of good editing. Are the readers of *Ambition*, any more than any other readers, to be denied this variety, this beguiling blend of light and shadow, this dazzling counterpoint of literature? By no means. Our editor very wisely makes use of variety and contrast by apportioning out the trades and professions himself. Otherwise, there is no telling what would happen. Four consecutive numbers of the journal might each contain the life story of a successful young gasfitter, and there would probably be some grumbling and even a falling off in circulation. As it is, our editor can make the most of his material; one number, we will say, gives us the history of a young man who learns accountancy by correspondence, a brainy occupation, but perhaps a trifle prosaic and needing an indoor setting; in the very next number the balance is restored by a tale of a smart young correspondence school pupil who turns beekeeper, which brings in a flavour of the open air and sunlit gardens, and is not without a touch of poetry; while in the following number we return once more to the city, with all its romantic bustle, and breathlessly follow the swelling fortunes of a square-jawed young plumber; and so it goes on.

By such means our editor has taken care to achieve both unity and variety in the stories at his disposal. What we thought at first restrictions pressing some-

what heavily upon the storyteller are now seen to be
hints for his guidance, aids without which he cannot
expect to be successful in this kind of fiction. If there
are men of more than ordinary talent, born story-
tellers, among us waiting for an opening, let them
take leave of the stuff they have been writing, worn-
out romance and so forth, all tears and tatters or
mere coloured foppery, let them keep pace with the
times, for here in the pages of *Ambition* is opportunity indeed. While they are pushing hero after
hero along the road to success they can surely make
shift to advance themselves "in position and
earnings."

A Beetonian Reverie

THERE are only three books in the room. *The Foundling* by Mrs. Porcherson. *The Magazine of Domestic Economy* for 1848, and *Mrs. Beeton's Cookery Book*. I am for Mrs. Beeton. *The Foundling* is one of that poisonous brood of little evangelical stories for children which appeared, I fancy, during the 'seventies; it has a frontispiece, a gloomy drawing, depicting an enormous bearded policeman staring down at a ragged little boy; if I remember rightly all these stories had frontispieces of bearded policemen and little ragged boys under dismal gasjets. Such drawings are strangely depressing, and the stories themselves are even worse. *The Magazine of Domestic Economy* appears to have been a signally unattractive publication (at least in 1848), and so I put it aside at once for Mrs. Beeton. Not that I can read Mrs. Beeton, for her solemn counsels fall a little heavily upon my ear, but I can look at her bright pictures and dream over her. She is not very well represented, though, in this volume, published in 1909, for it appears to be only an abstract or abridgment of the great original, intended, I believe, to meet "the requirements of smaller households than those in which such a very comprehensive volume as *Mrs. Beeton's Household Management* is a necessity." No doubt, no doubt; these parsimonious smaller households must be catered for; but I must say that I do not admire such cutting and carving of Mrs. Beeton, though she herself was such a cutter and carver, nor do I admire the persons, however small their households might be, for whose benefit such a transformation has been brought about. They lack poetry, a feeling for atmosphere, to be thus willing to accept in place of the great original work, that cosy and luscious epic, a mere dry abridgment, Mrs. Beeton, as it were, as a cook's mate and not as a great lady. I am disappointed indeed to discover that this is not the massive *Book of Household Management*, for it was that volume which we had at home in the old days (though we were a small enough household), and it was that volume over which I used to pore for hours when I was a small boy. By turning these pages I had hoped to recover some fleeting emotions of my childhood, but I am afraid that the difference between the two versions, between the Mrs. Beeton I once knew and this shadow of her old self, is too marked. At best, I can only titillate my memory and perhaps evoke the ghosts of my former emotions.

There was something, I remember, about the appearance of our old copy of Mrs. Beeton as it stood on the bookshelves (for we kept it among our books, Shakespeare, Scott and the rest, and did not exile it into the kitchen) that always attracted my attention, as I stood on tiptoe before our tall bookcase. It was easily the fattest book on its shelf, as indeed it ought to have been, and still handsome in the crimson and

gilt of its binding, it had a look of fatness and richness, an air of opulence, that inevitably won my regard. Reaching up, a little dangerously, I would
clutch at the top of the book and swing it rather than
take it down, to pass a solitary hour or so lying out-
stretched and face downward on the rug like the
young savage I was, turning its pages and dreaming
over its brightly coloured plates. Occasionally, no
doubt, I read a few lines of letterpress, but the
pictures were my joy. Unless my memory deceives
me, this present volume I have in my hand has nothing like the number of coloured pictures that our
old book had, and the few that it has do not seem so
bright, so ideal, but seem to have come to terms with
sad reality, showing us the pudding as it is and not
as it ought to be. The best picture this later book can
offer me is that of the cheeses, the twenty great
cheeses, and very fine it is, too, nobly coloured, with
great golden hulks of Double Gloucester and
Cheshire flanked by the exotic Parmesan and the
sinister Schabzieger. But our old volume had a score
of plates infinitely richer in colouring and grander in
composition; it spread for the mind a feast that was
opulent beyond Roman dreams and yet not too gross
for the most delicate appetite, a feast that left one
not a well-filled animal but a dazed and wondering
poet; it laid the world in ruins and rebuilt it in
entrées, garnishes and creams. In the days when I
brooded over such things, I was, be it understood, a
well-nourished child, allowed to risk a third or even

a fourth helping of suet pudding; but nevertheless, in the company of Mrs. Beeton and her enthusiastic artists and lithographers, I discovered a new world. Page after page revealed the most enchanting confections, coloured like a May morning and luscious even in their printer's ink; there would be Pyramid Cream, I fancy, and certainly there was Gâteau à la Ceylon, in white and crimson, and Rose Meringue, a most delicate and harmonious invention, and Imperial Tipsy Cake, dark, flushed, and imperial indeed, the very sweet for bull-necked Cæsars, and after them a riot of gâteaux, trifles and pastries; and then perhaps best of all, for its flawless image floats triumphantly into the port of memory, a raised pigeon pie, massive and golden, raised in very truth above time and mutability, a pie that never was on land or sea. And when I had done with these bright comestibles, having feasted upon them as Ariel might have done, was there not a fine coloured picture of a dinner-table, a gorgeous perspective of napery and cutlery and carefully ordered flowers, that for all its tameness had something in it to awaken a child's wonder?

I am much too lazy to inquire into these things, but I trust that there really was once a Mrs. Beeton, a super-housewife who sat down some sixty or so years ago to tell us everything, and that we have not been fobbed off with a crafty publisher's invention, a name merely covering a synod of cooks. I like to think that there was a Mrs. Beeton, and that therefore there was too a Mr. Beeton. If there was, he

would probably play the G. H. Lewes to her George
Eliot, that is, he would look after her affairs, arrange
her salon, and shield her from adverse criticism. That
he would live in a splendid whirl of sweetbreads in
aspic and iced pudding and never know a dish that
contained less than ten eggs and a pint of cream, as
some people have imagined, seems to me very doubtful, for you cannot compile a gigantic volume on
housekeeping and keep house at the same time. I
should not be at all surprised to learn that all the time
his wife was writing her book, Beeton himself was
living a spare life on bottled porter and half-cooked
chops. Perhaps he starved that we might feast: life
is like that. I can see him, a little wistful man, with
something of the visionary's look stamped upon his
partially emaciated features, rising, with a half-sup-
pressed sigh, from his cold mutton and lumpy potatoes to visit his wife in her study and to inquire, a
little timidly, how she is progressing. I can see the
light in his eyes when she answers, her natural dignity
tempered by the exuberance of the author who has
done some work, and tells him that she is already
half-way through the chapter on Poultry and has indeed just finished her notes on Mayonnaise of
Chicken. And as he goes tiptoeing away, perhaps to
finish up the cold rice pudding, little Beeton seems to
me at once a touching and a noble figure, to be
honoured by posterity.

It is, however, the lady herself, the authoress, who
commands our attention. Her book, at least in its

o

old form, is something more than a collection of re-
cipes and notes on marketing, kitchen utensils and
table decoration; it is a social document, a glimpse of
a vanished world; it has an atmosphere, a flavour, of
its own. Not merely on account of what they put in,
but also on account of what they leave out, all such
big books composed strictly in one key, have their
own particular atmosphere, something upon which it
is difficult to lay a finger, something not to be found
in this chapter or that, but which pervades the whole,
which calls up to the wandering and sensitive mind
associations enough to form the material of a whole
world. And our pleasure arises from the recognition
of this peculiar atmosphere, this suggested world that
lies behind the book itself; although such an atmosphere or world may not be particularly pleasing to
us in itself. To give such pleasure, however, the book
must be quite useless to us, so that our æsthetic sense
is set free, just as Mrs. Beeton's book is useless to me.
Thus, her famous prodigality, her habit of "taking"
scores of eggs, pints of cream, and the roes of strange
fish, and so forth, in order to make even a fairly
simple dish, is irritating to women, who really go to
her for advice; but to me, who ask for no advice, such
prodigality is simply delightful, and I would not have
the grand old lady deprived of a single egg. We may
look back upon this great work of hers, with its
chapters on the dignity and worth of housekeeping,
its multifarious marketing, its solemn pages on the
management of servants, its diagrams of table deco-

ration and napkin-folding, and discover that a whole
age, idealized, it is true, but still recognizable, has
been suggested to our mind. The enchantress has only
to wave her salad bowl or touch our eyes with one
of her folded table-napkins, and lo!—time has rolled
back, and once more we are all cosy and superbly
fed, all intent upon small social matters, and beyond
the torment of ideas; Victoria, that comfortable-look-
ing one of the middle period, is on the throne; Darwin
has been heard of but is not believed, and we are still
specially created, brought into the world to occupy
our stations, to demolish Salmi of Duckling and
Almond Pudding, and do good to the poor; none of
the 'isms have yet arrived and would not be tolerated
if they had; and father is in the counting-house
counting out his money; and sister is in the drawing-
room reading *The Idylls of the King;* and the Rector
is coming to lunch, so mother and cook are in the
kitchen, Mrs. Beeton in hand, "taking" twenty-four
eggs and a quart of cream.

An Apology for Bad Pianists

IGNORING those musical labourers who are paid so much per hour, at cinemas and dance-halls, to make some sort of rhythmical sound, all pianists, I think, may be divided into four classes. There are, first, the great soloists, the masters, Paderewski, Pachmann, and the rest, who would seem to have conquered all difficulties. With them the piano, a dead thing of wires and hammers, becomes a delicately responsive organism; its hammers are extra muscles, and its strings added nerves, running and leaping to obey every fleeting impulse; their playing is as saturated with personality as their gait or speech. Not so with the members of the second class, which is, to my mind, a dubious fraternity. They may be called the serious amateurs. Very often they take expensive lessons from some professor, who undertakes to "finish them off." But they never are finished off. The sign and mark of the serious amateur is that he practises assiduously some piece of music, maybe a Chopin study or a Brahms sonato, until he has it by heart; after which he assembles a number of friends (or more often, new acquaintances), squashes their attempts at conversation, and amid a tense silence, begins to play—or, as he would say, "interpret"—his laboured solo. The fourth class consists of odd strummers, vampers and thumpers; young ladies who

play waltzes and old ladies who play hymns; cigar-
ette-in-mouth youths with a bang-and-rattle style of
performance; all inexorable, tormenting noise-makers,
from those who persist in riveting—rather than playing—Rachmaninoff's C sharp minor Prelude to those
who buy Sunday newspapers in order that they may
pick out with one finger the tune of a comic song. All
such are enemies of peace and harmony, and as they
cannot be ignored in any other place, here they can
be quickly dismissed with all the more pleasure.

It remains now to say something of the third class
of pianists, which, if it were reduced to such straits,
could count me among its members. To write at some
length of one's class after perfunctorily dismissing
others may seem to savour of egotism, but the truth
is, we—I speak fraternally—have been so much
maligned and misunderstood up to now, we have
endured so many taunts in silence, that we have a
right to be heard before we are finally and irrevoc-
ably condemned.

It is only on the score of technique, the mere rule
of thumb business, that we stand below the serious
amateurs; we belong to a higher order of beings and
have grander souls; in spirit we come nearer to the
great masters. The motives of the serious amateur
are not above suspicion. In his assiduous practice, his
limited repertoire, his semi-public style of performance, is there not a suggestion of vanity? Is his conscious parade of skill, taken along with his fear of
unknown works, the mark of a selfless devotion to

music, and music alone? I doubt it.

But our motives are certainly above suspicion. Music has no servants more disinterested, for not only do we gather no garlands in her service, but daily, for her sake, we risk making a fool of ourselves, than which there can be no greater test of pure devotion. We, too, are the desperate venturers among pianists; every time that we seat ourselves at the keyboard we are leading a forlorn hope; and, whether we fall by the way or chance to come through unscathed, the only reward we can hope for is a kindly glance from the goddess of harmony.

It is hardly necessary to dwell on the fact that our execution is faulty, that we are humanly liable to make mistakes, seeing that our weaknesses have been for years the butt of musical pedants and small souls. In the dim past we received some sort of instruction, perhaps a few years' lessons, but being bright children with wills of our own we saw no use in labouring at scales and arpeggios, at the tepid compositions of Czerny, when there were balls to throw, stones to kick, and penny dreadfuls to be devoured. An unlocked door or an open window—and we escaped from the wretched drudgery, thus showing early that eager zest of life which still marks our clan.

Now, it is enthusiasm alone that carries us through. Our performance of any "piece of average difficulty" (as the publishers say) is nothing short of a series of miracles. As we peer at the music and urge our fingers to scurry over the keys, horrid gulfs yawn before us, great rocks come crashing down, the thick undergrowth is full of pitfalls and mantraps, but we are not to be deterred. Though we do not know what notes are coming next, or what fingers we shall use, if the music says presto, then presto it must be; the spirit of the tune must be set free, however its flesh may be lacerated. So we swing up the dizzy arpeggios as a hunted mountaineer might leap from crag to crag; we come down a run of demi-semi-quavers with the blind confidence of men trying to shoot the rapids of Niagara. Only the stout-hearted and great of soul can undertake these perilous but magnificent ventures.

Unlike the serious amateurs, we do not pick and choose among pieces until we have found one to which we can give the cold glitter of an impeccable rendering. We attend concerts (for, above all, we are the concert-goers and dreamers of dreams, as O'Shaughnessy might have said) and come reeling out, intoxicated with sound; for days we are haunted by a lovely theme or an amazing climax, until we can bear it no longer; we rush off to the music shops to see if it is possible to capture this new lovely thing and keep it for ever; more often than not we return home in triumph, hardly giving ourselves time to flatten out the music before plunging into the opening bars. Nothing that has been arranged for the piano or that can be played in some sort of fashion on the instrument comes amiss if it has once aroused our enthusiasm; symphonies, opera, tone-poems, string-quartets

are all welcome. Nay, we often prefer the arrangements of orchestral things, for we do not think of the
piano merely as a solo instrument; to us it is the
shining ivory and ebony gateway to the land of music.
As our fingers wander over the keys our great dream-
orchestra wakens to life.

I believe that at the very end, when the depths of
our folly and ignorance are fully revealed, when all
our false notes have been cast up into one awful total
by the recording angel of music, it will be found that
we, the bad pianists, have been misjudged among men,
that we, too, have loved and laboured for the divine art.
When we file into Elysium, forlorn, scared, a shabby
little band, and come within sight of Beethoven,
whom we have murdered so many times, I believe
that a smile will break through the thunder-cloud of
his face. "Ach! Come you in, children," he will roar,
"bad players, eh? . . . I have heard. . . . Very bad
players. . . . But there have been worse among you.
. . . The spirit was in you, and you have listened well.
. . . Come in. . . . I have composed one hundred and
fifty more symphonies and sonatas, and you shall
hear them all."

Polish Interlude

POLAND may be said to have begun for us within hailing distance of Tower Bridge. There, distressingly small at first sight, lay our ship, of some two thousand odd tons, and she belonged to the Polish-British Steamship Company. Her interior was Polish, and was decorated with notices in that mysterious language, which appears to have been invented merely in order to be foreign, as if for theatrical purposes. At the sight of our cabin our hearts sank. True, there were four berths in it, and only two of us, but what berths!—what a distance from fresh air!—what an atmosphere! We told one another that the voyage would only last three or four days, but there was a gloomy languor about our unpacking. In our dreams as prospective guests of a Government, we had seen no such cabins as these, which had the air of being oubliettes in a cheese factory. But our spirits revived when we climbed to the deck and the oxygen heights again, and the Thames sparkled at us. It was, we pointed out, an adventure; and then we prowled about the decks and secretly took stock of the other members of the party, who were busy taking stock of us and vainly imagining they were doing it secretly. By the time the ship passed under Tower Bridge, we were all convinced we detested one another.

Long before we left the Thames Estuary, however, we were all friends. This was because we had all marched into a foreign country together. We did this at dinner-time. This was when Poland really began, when we were all seated round the dining-table, with the large smiling captain at the head of it; and the stewards, Poles to the last astonishing consonant, set before us colossal stacks of *hors d'œuvres* and liqueur glasses filled with neat whisky. In Poland, you begin a meal by tossing off a few little glasses of neat spirits, and the stewards imagined that we should prefer whisky. I may say that the nearer we drew to Poland, the more mountainous these *hors d'œuvres* became and the wilder the choice of spirits. These stewards had a passion for opening bottles and filling glasses. Long before we reached the Baltic coast, I noticed the Professor complacently drinking cherry brandy with his sardines and eggs, and such gentlemen as Trade Papers and Economic Expert could be seen swigging vodka like Dostoieffsky characters. All these countries round the Baltic seem to have adopted the same principle in dining, which is to fill you up, leaving you either dazed or hilarious, before you have even reached the soup. The remaining courses you eat in a vague dream of conviviality.

The next day, Saturday, remains in my memory as a day of bitter strife, my opponent being the Polish Cigar, which had made its appearance, out of sinisterly brilliant boxes, late the night before. As a cigar, the Polish has its charms. Given the Thames Estuary, the Kiel Canal, or any other calm stretch of water,

the Polish Cigar is a welcome companion, a friend.
But on that Saturday we were crossing the North
Sea; it was very cold and rough; and the boat, lightly
loaded, pitched abominably. I always call myself a
fairly good sailor, and so I am under ordinary conditions; but I had never sailed before with the Polish
Cigar. No matter what corner of the three decks I
found, there, within a few minutes, Trade Papers
would arrive, bringing with him the Polish Cigar in
full blast. Three of us, a faint smile on our green
faces, tried to make out a sort of handicap list of our
opponents, beginning with the whiff that floated out
of the galley from time to time. Even while we were
doing this, the heavy tread of Trade Papers was
heard, bringing with it the inevitable blue cloud, and
we groaned in chorus: "The Polish Cigar—game and
set!" and reeled away.

The first thing we heard, the next morning, was the
blare of a band and some cheering. We looked out
and saw green banks on each side. We were in the
Kiel Canal. The band and the cheers were from a
passing boatload of German excursionists. We were
all the morning ambling down this street of water; the
sun came out; the Polish Cigar was tolerated, even
welcomed; and now the voyage took on that spacious
air which properly belongs to a journey by sea. Time
broadened, allowing us to exchange long reminiscences of travel and the sudden confidences of the
boat deck. The Baltic was merely a pleasing back-
cloth, against which we ate largely, told stories, and

drank toasts. The stewards—especially the bullet-headed, smiling one with the gold tooth—opened bottles like mad. The captain, who had sailed the Black Sea for twenty-five years and seemed to have popped out of one of Tchehov's more cheerful stories, stroked his long fair moustache and made jokes in the odds and ends of six languages. It would take pages and pages of artful sentences to capture the unique flavour of this expedition, its fantastic conviviality, its genial idiocy.

At last we found ourselves in the mouth of a river, and I was thrilled to learn that this was no other than the Vistula. After that, no matter in what part of Poland we were—and we travelled hundreds and hundreds of miles—wherever there was a river, it was the Vistula. There was no escaping that stream, sluggish though it seemed; you could go East one day, two hundred miles or so, then as far from your original starting point towards the West the next day, but the Vistula went with you. Yet when I remember that first thrill, I forgive the Vistula its ubiquity. It brought us first to Danzig, a city that pleased me immensely, if only because it is full of curly buildings, Gothic vistas, old wood and beer. Given a steady supply of English tobacco, I could write a book in Danzig.

Our first show place, however, was not Danzig but the neighbouring port of Gdynia, where we were taken to the town hall in a body and solemnly addressed in several languages. We were then put

into a bus, taken out and put into a tug, put into a
bus again, and shown the docks. The Poles are very
proud of Gdynia, and they have every right to be.
Only a few years ago, it was nothing but a fishing
village. Now it is a real port, to say nothing of its
being a seaside resort, almost entirely filled with
young men wearing comic hats. It has grown nearly
as fast as those famous Klondyke towns. It is growing now. All the officials we met there were extremely
energetic, voluble, and proud, and I am sure they are
all happy men. They are creating something, seeing
the thing grow, and not hanging about, reading
Spengler. It was good to see a port coming into existence, after seeing so many ports sinking into a decline.
Even when those Poles insisted on my examining
their methods of cleaning rice or storing tinned apri-
cots, and it was one of those hot, tiring days, I still
admired them.

They had put the same energy and exuberance into
the official lunch they gave us, a lunch that offered
one enough food and drink and speechifying for two
or three wedding breakfasts and a conference. It
ended about four, and then, pleased but dazed, we
were put into a large launch or a small steamer, only
to find that its saloon was crammed with more food
and drink the very sight of which sent us reeling back,
affrighted. Dimly I remember that launch or
steamer, that shadowy vessel, making its way back to
Danzig, where an optimistic young man in a raincoat
tried to explain to us something about the docks,

little knowing that we were all moving about in the
haziest of dreams. If you imagine from this that we
were unappreciative visitors, you are wrong. The
fact is, that when you have lunched until four on a
hot day, after a morning's hard sight-seeing, and have
drunk all the toasts proposed to you, it is almost impossible, to give a coal shoot the attention it deserves,
say, at about half-past five. We were nothing but a
party of somnambulists.

Early that same evening, we caught a train that
was due to land us in Poznán (once Posen) in the
small hours. It went roaring across an enormous
plain, and then we shut out the night, told stories,
sang songs, and did conjuring tricks with pennies.
Curiously enough, none of us was sleepy by this time,
though we all felt we had been up and awake for at
least several days. It was rather like being back in
the war again, or in the pleasant part of it. By eleven
or so we began to feel hungry, and then discovered
there was no dining-car on the train. Something had
been arranged, however, we were told, and quite
suddenly, in the middle of the night, at some mysterious halt, that something happened. A number of
white-coated men suddenly swarmed into the corridor
of our coach, and they carried plates of steaming
Wiener-schnitzel and fried potatoes, bottles of beer and
glasses, dishes of wild strawberries and cream, nap-
kins and cutlery. There was our supper, done to a
turn, miraculously arriving out of the unknown darkness. In a few minutes, not a white-coated man was

to be seen, the train was rattling on again, and we were eating and drinking away, enjoying the strangest picnic. Could anything so pleasant ever happen to visitors to this country? I doubt it. I arrived at Poznán, prepared to enjoy the great exhibition that was being staged there, and with my opinion of Poland soaring; and this was largely the work of the kindly thought that flashed along the telegraph wires and brought those magical white coats out of the night.

Oberammergau

LET me admit, at once, that I was in no fit state to see a play, not even a quick-fire crook play. We are staying in the Bavarian Hills, but a good many miles from Oberammergau, and in order to get there in time for the play we had to leave this place at half-past five in the morning. That meant that we had to be called about quarter to five. I went to bed early the night before, and fell asleep almost at once. I woke up to hear a clock strike two, and then I remained awake, thinking the most dismal of thoughts. Instead of growling at the porter's knock, I welcomed it, and by the time I had shaved and had some coffee I felt wide-awake and comparatively fresh. I felt like that for exactly one hour, and then for the rest of the day—and such a long, long day—I felt as if I had been nursing somebody day and night for several weeks. My eyelids weighed seventeen pounds; my head kept falling down; no seat was comfortable; I was perpetually hungry and yet I disliked all the food I tasted; and altogether I was in no condition to be the happy spectator of a Passion Play eight solid hours long. That much I will admit. But even then. . . .

The ride there in the car, two hours of it, from the chill-washed five-thirty to the blue and sunlit seven-thirty, was very pleasant, even to me. Against a sky

of the palest blue silk, the snowy heights of the great
Zugspitze, clear in the sunlight, with every crevice
and wrinkle sharply etched, would have raised the
spirits of a man who had not been able to sleep for a
week. There was a grand climb up to the plateau
of the Passion *spielers,* with the road curving magnificently above dwindling green mists of larch and fir.
We were not, of course, the only people on that road.
People were pouring into Oberammergau, in every
kind of conveyance. It was very pleasant and rather
exciting to arrive at the village itself, to notice that
every second man there had the long hair and beard
of an apostle or chief priest, and though the place was
so full that it was not easy getting a cup of coffee
before the play began, it had a fine stimulating Derby
Day atmosphere. We went to the theatre (and you
have only to imagine Olympia sawn into two to see
it) in good time; our seats were in the middle and just
the right distance from the stage; and, in short, everything was in splendid trim. I felt rather tired, a trifle
drowsy, but felt sure that I should be alert once that
tremendous stage, all built of solid stone and about
the size of four Drury Lane stages, was brilliant and
thunderous with the clamouring crowds of ancient
Jerusalem.

As you probably know already, the morning session
of the Play lasts four hours. It seemed to me (and once
again, I beg to remind you of my condition) to last
several weeks. It was like being back in school again
and spending a morning composed of the very dreariest

periods. You remember how you longed, how you ached, in those days, for the time to pass, and how the minutes dragged out, until at last you were not merely bored, but suffering in an agony and a fury of tedium. That is what I felt. There were some scenes representing meetings of the Grand Council of Jerusalem, scenes in which every character had a lengthy speech to make and made it with grim deliberation, that seemed to me a closer approach to some devilish eternity than anything I have ever known apart from the front-line trenches during the winter of 1915–1916.

It was not the actual scenes that did the mischief, but the prologues and the singing. Before each scene, there entered, in a slow solemn procession, the speaker of the prologue (the famous Anton Lang) and a choir of forty-eight men and women who were supposed to be guardian spirits. Considered as a village choir, these singers were unusually good, but they were certainly not good enough to be given such scope, for before we had done we must have had four hours of them, and four hours of mediocre singers going rather tamely through a great deal of mediocre music are too much for any man. Moreover, these guardian spirits went through the same slow ritual of entrance and exit before each scene, and, as you can imagine, there are a great many scenes. The first two or three times they did it, I was quite pleased to see them, but after that their entrance either irritated or depressed me, and long before I had seen the last of them, I think

that if the man sitting next to me (he spent all his
time either yawning or dropping sandwiches) had
turned a machine-gun on them, I should not have put
out a restraining hand. Oh, how I came to hate those
guardian spirits!

The lunch interval came as a pleasant relief, but I
cannot say we enjoyed it. To begin with, our lunch
was such a bad one that we could not eat it, and we
ended by sitting on a bank outside the village and
eating chocolate, and by this time it was hot and
rather dusty and the chocolate was soggy. The village is, of course, unique, filled as it is with crucifixes
and Cooks' agents, apostles and the American Express, but somehow its uniqueness did not please us.
Perhaps it was too hot, dusty, crowded, and fussy,
but certainly it did not seem to us a very charming
village. There are too many shop windows filled with
crucifixes, saints and martyrs, all at special Passion
Play prices. I told myself—no doubt because I was
sleepy and cross—that this village was a durned sight
too quaint and pious and old-worldly for my taste:
it might have been invented by a tourist agency. I
returned to face the guardian angels again in the
lowest spirits, knowing that they would parade in and
out in the same way a good many more times between
two o'clock and six. And they did; though I must
confess that the afternoon session was much better
than the morning one, and that at times, such as in
the scene before Pilate's house and the scene of the
last terrible march through Jerusalem, the Play

leaped into drama, terror and beauty. Nevertheless, I was glad when it was six o'clock and I could get out into the air again and totter to the car.

You cannot say of things of this kind that they are good or bad unless you refer them to some particular background and some standard of judgment. Now, considered as a performance by a number of wood-carvers, potters, artisans and workmen, in a remote Bavarian village, the Passion Play, attempting as it does to put on the stage, with every semblance of reality, the most famous scenes in the world's history or legend, is an astounding achievement. If you came across it, by accident, you would never stop talking about it, just as the fortunate travellers who wandered into these parts a hundred years ago could not stop talking about it. Unfortunately, it has been talked about, written about, pictured and photographed, too often, and now, when it is an international event, with a vast Press, you have the right to judge it from a very different standpoint. Judged then as one of the great events of 1930, an affair that has diverted tourist traffic all the way from San Francisco, has called out special trains, airplanes, buses, ships, the most talked-of, written-up play of the year, performed in a theatre that holds over five thousand people and demands the equivalent of a pound for most of its seats, judged from this standpoint, I say, it is not good enough. It has ceased to be an affair of a few unsophisticated peasants acting in order to fulfil a vow, and on the other hand, it is not a first-

rate theatrical performance. To begin with, the music
is not good enough. They need far better singers, or
none at all, and preferably none at all, for then the
Play would not last so long. It needs cutting even in
the actual scenes. The acting, with one or two ex-
ceptions, is not good enough. A first-class producer
would make a tremendous difference.

I shall be told that I have no right to criticise what
is virtually a religious festival in this way. But even
if it is still a religious festival, it is a religious festival
on such a scale, with such an audience, that it should
be performed in the best possible manner. Great
cathedrals, famous for their music, offer their visitors,
who have presumably come to worship and are not
asked twenty marks for a seat, the best possible
singers. I suggest that a few people like Rheinhardt
and Bruno Walter have a hand in the production of
the next Passion Play. After all, Oberammergau can
hardly be considered the simple village of the vow
any longer now that all the tourist agencies have offices
there and all the actors are photographed and inter-
viewed, and there are reporters waiting outside the
meetings of the Passion Play Committee so that all
the world may know at once who is to play the next
Jesus. Many a Hollywood publicity man's mouth
must have watered when he saw the Press this Play
could command.

It has been pointed out, with truth, I believe, that
the villagers themselves not only do not make money,
but so far have actually lost it, on the Play, though

undoubtedly this year will pay for all. But indirectly, of course, the village lives on its Play, selling its sculpture, pottery, and wood-carving a great deal more briskly than ever it would have done if Oberammergau had been merely an ordinary upland place in Bavaria. For the 1940 Play, I have no doubt that special airships from the United States will be sailing down into Oberammergau, and that all the seats will be taken even if 100 and 200 marks are charged for them. So I suggest that they make a shorter and much better show of it, with all Germany lending a hand. If they don't, it is all the same to me. I shall not be there.

Lilac in the Rain

WHEN we went out, after our first lunch in Heidelberg, the gentle drizzle suddenly became a downpour, so we took refuge in a motor-coach that promised to spend the next hour or so wandering round the town. The only other passengers were four sad American women. In a few minutes the guide arrived, first to salute us and then to beam upon us. He was a spectacled, long-haired fellow in the inevitable peaked cap, and he looked like an unsuccessful student of metaphysics. His English was fluent but fantastic, and appeared to have been learned entirely from books. It sounded more foreign than German itself. Listening to him, you could never quite believe that this guide was a serious, real person and not an actor playing a foreigner in an old-fashioned farce. No sooner had the motor-coach started than he began bombarding us with queer syllables. "Aboaf, vere you see now, zat eez 'Oly 'Ill, ven ze Chairman Beoples vairst begin." This is how he opened his performance, and the American women, who—poor things—had been conducted and guided out of their senses, looked at him and at the Holy Hill in dumb despair.

I liked that guide. He was a man of temperament. Sometimes for a mile or two he would not say anything, but would simply sit there looking at the rain

223

and no doubt pondering over the problem of the world as Will. Then, perhaps, after catching the eye of an American passenger, he would begin guiding us again. He would explain everything, the blossom on the trees, the very stones in the road. He might have been conducting us through a new solar system. Glistening with sweat and with his eyes flashing through his glasses, he would grow wilder and wilder in his English, every word of which, by this time, would be wearing spectacles and a peaked cap. "Yaiz, yaiz," he would cry, pointing, "in zat building zere, ze vater of Cöln, ze shmelling vater of Cöln, makes zere—ze bedst shmelling vater—you know id?" And he looked imploringly at the American women; but they only stared blankly back at him, not being able to translate his fine phrases into eau-de-Cologne. To the end, they never understood his "rococo," for which he had an enormous enthusiasm. We left him, saluting and still sweating, under the towering and be-candled chestnuts near the Castle, where the rain made a pretty music among the leaves.

When, after the Day of Judgment, the earth is remade and all the things that have disillusioned us are hurled into the fiery pit, Heidelberg, I trust, will remain as it is now and have its place in that smaller world. Heidelberg is dead right. The moment I set eyes on it, a little bell rang in my mind. It is what I have always imagined an old German town would be. When they sing about a town in the *lieder*, they mean a place like Heidelberg. It is the right lovable mixture

of the beautiful, the heavy grotesque, and the absurd.
That vast, dark, strawberry-coloured ruin, the Castle,
could not have been better devised. At one minute,
when the mists blow across it like smoke from a
cauldron and the wooded hills above are conjured into
remote mountains, it is at once elfish and grim, a Nibe-
lungen fastness, set to the thunder of Wagnerian trom-
bones. The next minute, however, when the mist has
vanished before the sun and there is a lovely blue
beyond the tender green of the firs above, the place
wears the look of an operetta back-cloth, is electoral,
eighteenth-century, charming and ridiculous, and could
be introduced with propriety into that piece by old
Johann Strauss we saw last night at the Stadt Theater.
The town is as perfectly German, as say, Wells or
Oxford is English.

When you remember the sentimentality of the German, the further sentimentality of nearly all graduates,
and the loveliness of Heidelberg in spring, it must,
you will agree, be a terrific business for an old Heidelbergian to re-visit the place. This morning I saw an
old gentleman totter towards his waiting car, and he
was wearing one of those fantastic hats of the students'
unions. He must have been nearly bursting. What a
town to be goldenly young and foolish in! Even I,
who had never been in the town before, felt like an
old Heidelbergian. I could have gone about the enchanted steets crying over my lost youth. It is not
the situation of the place that works the magic,
though its situation is almost miraculous; it is not the

river, the Castle, the woods above, not the old buildings near the Rathaus and the Kornmarkt, though no
doubt all these play their part; it is the blossom and
the atmosphere. Here is a town smiling out of a
garden in a wood. The chestnuts are bright with
pink or white candles; the hawthorns are all in flower;
the magnolia and laburnum are neighbours down
every street; the villas of the professors are overhung
with wistaria; and everywhere the rain is sweetening
the lilac. I do not know what Heidelberg is like at
any other season, but now it is a place filled with wet
lilac. The Neckar winds smoothly between its steep,
green hills; the mists, liks puffs from a giant's cigarette, swirl about the red castle hanging above the
town; and there, between them, are the little streets
of wet lilac. I hope that among these students with
the comic hats, which they are for ever raising, there
are some poets, some good old-fashioned rhymesters,
so that the purple and white blossom shall not go
unsung. Let them raise their hats to the rain-
drenched lilac.

I nearly burned my passport and my boats this
morning. We had sauntered along the Leopoldstrasse,
which is entirely filled with bright little shops, the
greenest of green leaves, and this multitude of blossom, and as we walked along the rain shrank to a few
glittering drops. We turned down and found ourselves in a little street just behind the Stadt Theater.
A few people were hanging about, and they were
listening to a good round baritone voice that was sing-

ing a jovial air and being excellently accompanied by
a piano. It came, this voice, from the upper window
of a villa, an oldish, slightly dilapidated but altogether
delightful villa that had the spring itself blossoming
in its courtyard. The jovial voice came rolling out
above the shining leaves and the blossom. Obviously
it belonged to a member of the Stadt Theater troupe,
who was practising next week's operetta. There is
nothing in all this, I admit; and yet, for a moment,
there was everything in it. I said to myself: I will
stay here for ever, for this is the town I have dreamt
about when I have awakened to find myself miserable
in my own world; I will wander along the Philoso-
phen Weg across the Neckar and watch the mists
above the Castle; I will eat my share of ragout of
calf and fillet of swine's flesh at the Ritter and drink
my Niersteiner and Goldberg at the Silver Harp; I
will sleep in a bed that has everything on top, and
will, if necessary, wear a comic hat and peer through
spectacles at Gothic newspapers; and no doubt many
pleasant things will be *verboten;* but here, in this
enchanting town of mists and wet lilac and learning
and operetta, I will stay. Probably I would have been
bored in a fortnight, but nevertheless it was a great
moment, and I believe I shall remain in spirit an old
Heidelbergian.

The people are unusually pleasant, smiling, and
attentive, but of course they do not live up to their
town. Indeed, to be brutally frank, they are a plain
lot and might have been plucked out of the streets and

offices of Düsseldorf or Essen. This will not do. Germany ought to look to this. These people ought to have a picturesque, slightly fantastic air, with a suggestion of the romantic Eighteen-Thirties about it, something of the poetical-philosophical-mysterious-handsome-stranger-with-cloak-and-staff line of business. These streets should be filled with beautiful, tender maidens ready at any moment to go into a decline, and with men whose minds are fixed on Truth, Beauty, Goodness, Love, Tobacco, Drink, and nothing else. The place ought to have a Jean Paul Richter and early Carlyle flavour. The Eternal Yea —whatever that is—ought to be easily obtainable in the town. The place itself has this atmosphere, but not the citizens, who are making an all too successful attempt to look like all the other Germans. Only the students, magnificent and happy in their yellow, green and scarlet hats, keep it up.

I do not know what *drang* is on in Germany now. The famous *Drang nach Osten* came to an unpleasant conclusion a few years ago, and if anything has taken its place, I do not know what it is. But I suggest—with all the usual apologies of the ignorant and interfering outsider—a new one, a *Drang nach Heidelberg,* that is, *nach* misty castles and rococo mansions and little steamers setting out pompously for nowhere and small towns where everybody knows the chief tenor and metaphysicians lost in the fumes of tobacco from huge untidy packets and solemn little societies with coloured hats and tender songs in the moonlight and sausage and beer and fireworks and waltz tunes in the woods. It can't be done, I suppose, for now there must be world politics and rationalisation of industry and stunts in Persia and commercial campaigns in South America, together with large motor-cars and too much electricity and new buildings that look as if they were designed in Mars for a race of ambitious ants. The radio resounds through a host of steel and concrete electrified flats. This is a Germany one can respect. But give me the Germany I can smile at and love, with the Stadt baritone trolling above the wet lilac.

Rhine Legend

On Sunday afternoon I stood on the balcony of my bedroom and looked down into the streets of Coblenz. These streets were gay with bunting, for the town was celebrating some military festival, some reunion of old comrades of the War. Dozens of buses, blaring like *heldentenors,* were bringing in more old comrades every few minutes or so. There was a great deal of handshaking and back-slapping and marching and singing. Everybody below was full of beer or *Laubenheimer,* and the air was heavy with the reek of 10 *pf. stück* cigars, which, together with the mixed odour of fried onions wrapped in wool, make up the characteristic smell of Germany. There were thousands of peaked hats, which meant that thousands of men and boys there were happy, for I am convinced that there is some connection between peaked hats and happiness throughout Central Europe. If anybody in power in one of these states wishes to know how to avoid revolution, I suggest that he looks to the supply of peaked hats. What there was to see and hear, that afternoon, I saw and heard, but nevertheless, I was really busy on my balcony with thoughts that were a thousand miles away from the roaring old comrades. I began by trying to remember this town of Coblenz.

I had been there before, for in the glorious June of 1914 I had set out to glance at Holland and Belgium and walk down the Rhine. I remember many things about that trip, the last expedition I made in that ancient world. I remember the clothes I wore, the knapsack I carried, the books I read in the *Tauchnitz* edition, the large German pipe I bought and smoked and did not enjoy, the food I ate and the beer I drank, the piano I played; yes, I remember the very dust on my shoes. Yet the Rhine itself, and all its towns, big and little, I could not remember. Cologne seemed a strange place. So did Coblenz. So did the little towns. I suppose none of them would have seemed so strange as the boy who came walking this way in the summer heat and dust of 1914. I would have liked to have slipped down a side-road and met him, that boy with his patched tweed coat and baggy trousers, his precious ten sovereigns in a little purse, his large German pipe, his happy idiocy, innocence, and wonder. He took a Rhine away with him and set it flowing past enchanting ruined castles and little inns out of an idyll, and it ran on and on until at last it went flowing through this mind of mine, which is very different from the mind of that boy, and I must have brought it here with me, that other Rhine, to shame this huge dull stream. I remember *his* Coblenz quite well, and it was different from this one, where the old comrades meet (and why can't I meet my old comrade, that boy?); much better, a thousand times better. This other Coblenz bores me.

I do not know what I thought, sixteen years ago, about that monument at the junction of the Rhine and the Moselle called *Deutsches Eck,* but I know what I think about it now. I think it is a symbol, that monstrosity of a monument, with its thick emperor and thick horse and thick female and general howitzer-like decoration, of the Germany one cannot help disliking. It is a huge clumsy fat sham of a thing. And now I am afraid that my old friend, the Rhine, is its cousin. I wish I had never returned to visit it again. It would have been better to have kept my illusion, to have had a river of green enchantment for ever flowing through my mind. In 1914 I walked one way and then sailed the other way. The other day I sailed down it again, and it was all changed. I suppose the Rhine steamers of to-day are better vessels than those of sixteen years ago, but to me they seemed a great deal worse. Robbed of romance, they were simply large clean river-steamers with rather too much eating and drinking and map-reading going on in them. Every German on the boat, the other day, had his or her route-map in hand. I must confess, though, that the only English besides ourselves on board, went one better; for the large thin woman read Baedeker aloud to her husband, a large thin clergyman, the whole way down the river, and she cannot have seen anything but the printed word. But that may have been her wisdom, for the Rhine of the printed word is a good deal more exciting than the actual river. The Rhine of the last fifty years represents a triumph of the art of writing up, and the further art of manipulating mass sentiment. The poets, who can write anything up if they feel like it, began it all. How Heine would laugh if he saw steamer after steamer full of folk who shout with excitement and jump to their feet when they approach that dismal Lorelei rock! Even our two honeymooning wander-birds, who did not wear enough clothes and sat about all the time in one another's arms, unclasped when they saw the Lorelei.

Before we got to Mainz, I seemed to have been on that steamer several years. I knew every face on it off by heart. If there was an old comrades' association based on that voyage, I should feel compelled to join it. By the time every German woman aboard had in front of her a colossal slab of creamy cake, in the *Deutsches Eck* tradition of architecture, it began to rain. I looked through a grey drizzle at Bingen, where I had spent a golden night in 1914, and I saw nothing but a commonplace little German town, giving itself airs as a resort. It is strange, but I could not recognise the place at all. If it has not changed, then I must have changed out of all measure. It is true that I have very little sense of place. I can never find my way about places until I have stayed in them some time, and there cannot be many men in England who would make worse guides or chauffeurs than I would. But it annoyed me when I could not recognise Bingen. We never saw the sun again that day. It rained all the way down to Mainz, and we arrived there and ran to that hotel opposite the landing stage, in a downpour. It was a large hotel, but it was entirely filled by an American who seemed to have come from Sinclair Lewis's "Zenith." There were a good many public rooms there, but he contrived to be talking in all of them at once at the top of his voice. But they were very comfortable, even luxurious. We had arrived in that mood in which you demand the best room in the town, if necessary with several suites of furniture, two private baths, and telephones you cannot use all over the bedroom. We bathed and sprawled all over our luxurious apartment, drank a Martini that must have been made partly out of gold-dust, judging by the price, ate an excellent dinner, finished a bottle of capital Rhine wine, forgave the American, thought kindly of the river, and then, discovering that the rain had stopped, went wandering through the town.

It was very pleasant. The moon shone out of a clear sky, and it illuminated all that was medieval, Gothic, in the old city, and subdued the rest. This was Gutenberg's town, where he first set to work with his types and made possible all manner of subsequent beauties and idiocies. In this moonlight we first saw the cathedral, the wooden tower, the iron tower, and other gnarled old buildings, and we were under the spell of that ancient elfin Germany. It was delightful, too, to see the ghostly crimson of the massed tulips in the little squares, and to return at last to the *Rheinpromenade,* from which the river seemed a noble piece of silver. We explored the place again in the morning, when the sun shone as brightly

as the moon had done the night before, and made
pretty patterns of light and shade among the lime
trees by the river and lit up the front of the Electoral
Palace. We told one another, as we sauntered there,
with a good hour to spare for the train to Heidelberg,
that it was good to be in Germany and that the rain
had spoilt the Rhine for us.

Then at eleven-thirty this good-will was shattered.
I paid my bill. It was a monster, of Gothic height and
fantasy. And, to crown all, they charged me twenty
per cent. for service, because, they said, the French
were still in the town. Twenty per cent.! And on
that monstrous bill! Instantly, the sunlight faded
from the water-front, the Electoral Palace became a
stupid piece of eighteenth-century affectation, the
cathedral was nothing, and the Rhine was an over-
rated canal, a giant sham. We were overcharged for
the hotel bus to the station. The train to Heidelberg was full, and full of people who were too hot and
woolly. We could not have lunch (as we were told
we could have), because all the places had been taken
before we boarded the train. I said a bitter farewell
to that dirty streak in the distance, the Rhine, and
asked myself why I had been fool enough to come to
Germany. And all the time, at my elbow, there was
the ghost of a boy who had been this way before, a
happy fool, the dust on whose shoes I still remember.

The Shining Graces

A RECENT column in the paper succeeded in startling me twice over in the course of a few lines. It told me that Miss Marie Studholme, the former musical comedy actress, was dead, and then it also told me that she had been born and bred in a place not five miles from my old home. I had forgotten the existence of this actress, and never once have I set eyes on her, even on the stage, yet these two facts in the paragraph conjured me back immediately into my boyhood. Once more I saw those shining post-cards, of which Marie Studholme, forever flashing immaculate teeth, was perhaps the queen. The whole shining bevy of graces returned to memory, fresh and glossy from the wholesale photographer's: Marie Studholme, Gertie Millar, Gabrielle Ray, the Dares, Zena and Phyllis (and their brother—was he an engineer?— for such is fame, so great the power of beauty, that he was photographed, too). The post-card age lived again.

There are picture post-cards still, just as there are roller-skating rinks, grey toppers, whiskers and oyster bars, but they are little more than an article of commerce. Here and there, in faded provincial towns, people may still collect them, but their glory has departed. Many a stationer and fancy-goods man must sigh when he remembers the trade he did once in

albums for them, albums of every size and quality,
frivolous albums for the coloured comic ones, charming medium albums for the actresses, the kittens, the
puppies, the fishing fleets, the massive heavies for the
views of Notre Dame and the Bay of Naples. The
cards themselves blossomed in every other shop
window. Blackpool alone, which had a marked taste
for the low comic cards, boarders in night-shirts,
amorous fat women, and the seasick of every quality,
must have imported millions of them. In those days
a postman's life was worth living; he could entertain
himself and learn something about the world on his
rounds. On thousands and thousands of bamboo
tables in the corners of drawing-rooms, the albums
were piled up, ready for the next visitors. And in
these albums, on page after page, shining in best sepia
finish, the beautiful musical comedy actresses smiled
upon an adoring world. They could not vote; they
could not enter Parliament or sit upon the Bench;
their property was at the disposal of their husbands,
if they were married; they were still members of a
downtrodden sex; but nevertheless they smiled and
smiled, and not a tear dimmed their eyes and not a
curl was out of place.

I remember now that it was not the men who were
the enthusiastic collectors of these shining graces,
though the men were not above examining and comparing them. I seem to recollect that it was the girls,
the young women, the older sisters of my friends of
those days, who piled Studholmes on Rays and sought

frantically for yet more Dares, just as it is the girls
and women who line up, I believe, to applaud Miss
Tallulah Bankhead, and swarm to see the Greta
Garbos. Feminine beauty attracts a feminine
audience. All the girls in our provincial place lived
more richly because of Marie Studholme's teeth and
Gabrielle Ray's demure loveliness, and the dark good
looks of Zena and the bright good looks of Phyllis
Dare. No doubt thousands of girls, after a brief
interval of despair, became steadily prettier by simply
staring and staring at those post-cards; not beauty
"born of murmuring sound," as with Wordsworth's
heroine, but beauty born of best glossy finish.
These beauties of the post-cards had no such fame as
our contemporary film stars, whose very wrinkles and
eyelashes are familiar to millions, yet they had, I
think, a unique fame of their own, for they smiled
along every street that could boast of a few shops,
and in a hundred-thousand drawing-rooms and
parlours, wherever picture post-cards found their way.
What they got out of it, whether they enjoyed it, I
do not know. Their stage careers were a mystery to
me then, and I have never met one of them since.

Indeed, I only ever saw one of them on the stage,
and that was the youngest of those shining graces—
Miss Phyllis Dare. I stood at the back of the pit,
clutching my school-cap, in our old Theatre Royal,
and saw her play in *The Dairymaids,* the first
musical comedy I ever attended. That astonishing
world of pretty girls and dancing dudes and comic

uncles, now—alas!—wearing a very machine-made
look, burst upon me, to the sound of our Theatre
Royal augmented orchestra—oh! a Pisgah sight! The
stately Gibson girls were hardly my style, but there
was a comic sailor who pleased me—and there was
Miss Phyllis Dare, lovely, riotous, enchanting. I fell
in love with her at once. If there had been millions
more post-cards, they would have been more than
justified, though what post-card, what mere photograph, no matter how artfully posed and brilliantly
glossed, could do justice to that graceful and vivacious
creature, that fountain of high spirits? When the
interval came and everybody else went off to struggle
for bottles of Bass, I stayed where I was, leaning
against the wall, feverishly planning a career that
would turn me as soon as possible into a comic sailor.
That Miss Dare's brother (the engineer?) should be
photographed and post-carded surprised me no longer;
I would have had her uncles, cousins, second cousins,
all shrined on post-cards, for even the most distant
of them would have been touched with glamour. It
is astonishing to me now to think that this excellent
actress is actually a contemporary of mine, for to me
she dates from the era of legends. I have friends who
are acquainted with her, and no doubt if I pressed
them they would consent to introduce me; but it seems
to me incredible, even now. It would be like meeting
Rosalind out of Arden. I should shrink from it, and
would prefer to stand for ever, bewitched, my school-
cap screwed in a hot grasp, at the back of that pit.

I was, I admit, very susceptible in those days. (Curiously enough, later on, when I drew nearer the age when young men are supposed to haunt stage doors, this susceptibility vanished, and I have been a heart-free playgoer ever since.) I did not go to the theatre often then, but when I did, I promptly fell in love. Outside, I could be austere, and still sneer at the sex, but once in that thick warm atmosphere of gas, oranges and heated humans, I was the worshipper of some visiting goddess. There is an actress playing comedy parts in the West End now, who lighted a whole six weeks of winter for me, when I was at school and she was playing principal girl in our local pantomime. I stared down from the gallery at her white neck and glossy black ringlets until my eyes ached as well as my heart. It was thrilling merely to see her name in print. Almost suffocated with secret emotion, I would introduce that name into the talk. The "Last Two Weeks" on the bills meant the very end of everything, for I saw less and less opportunity of saving her life somehow just outside the theatre. She came, she went, and she never knew.

Why did the post-cards come and go so quickly, too? Why, for a few years, did everybody want to collect pearly teeth and curls and dimples, and then after that care no more about them? What was it that flared up, covered acres of card with bewitching smiles, and then died down? We know well enough that since then fame and rewards beyond the dreams of the young Miss Marie Studholme have been offered, by the film industry, to pretty girls; yet, in spite of that, it is difficult not to feel that when the post-cards went, something, a kind of astounded wonder at feminine prettiness, went with them. Before the post-cards came, people had lined the roads to see a famous beauty, had cheered and mobbed her; you read of it in one age after another, down to the beginning of our own time. The picture post-cards, I suspect, absorbed the last traces of that wondering and worshipping spirit. Since then, there have been beautiful women, pretty women, innumerable, more than ever probably, but no crowds, no cheering, no collecting and comparing. Now we mutter "sex appeal" and walk away. But then perhaps the common standard of feminine looks have been raised, and is still shooting up, so that whole bevies of typists and shop assistants and young matrons are on the picture post-card level of loveliness. What happens to the susceptible youths, I do not know. I do know that if somebody had talked to me about "sex appeal" in my early youth, I should have wanted to enter a monastery.

Our Bad

A FORTNIGHT ago, we had never heard of Bad Tölz, in the Bavarian Highlands. Now it will remain one of our happy memories, a little green place, forever there in our minds. It was not even a name before, but now, while our memories hold, we shall only have to say "Tölz" to one another and—behold—the little carriages will be clippety-cloppeting down the cobbled street and over the bridge, the stout visitors will be drinking *Löwenbrau* or *Kaffee Hag* under the lime trees, the pines will be rustling on the hills, the roads will be bright with unfading apple blossom, and in the rising meadows the gentians and wild pansies will bloom again.

We should never have come here at all if I had not picked up, in an idle moment at the hotel in Munich, a handful of booklets. A photograph or two stood out from the rest, and so we came to Bad Tölz, pleasantly remote among these Bavarian Hills and in the valley of the Isar, which rushes through the place like a flood of milk into which somebody has emptied a few casks of *Crème de Menthe*. We seem to be the only English in the town, and certainly we are the only people in this hotel (the Alpenkurhof Parkhotel, and very pleasant, too; and nothing is being taken off my bill because I am telling you so) who are not here to try the cure. We have paid the Kurtaxe, but have never been inside the Kurhaus yet and do not know exactly what the cure is. On the other hand, it is possible that we are being cured far more quickly and effectively than anybody else. We drink no waters and take no special baths, but we have found rest and refreshment in the leafy little town.

The season has begun, which means that all the hotels are filled with bobbing waitresses and chambermaids and their 'buses meet every train, and that Hans Much, of the *Bad Tölzer Personen Autovermietung,* is ready to take you to see all the neighbouring sights, *Die herrlichen Königsschlösser Hohenschwangau-Neuschwanstein, die Perle der Bergseen, der Königsee;* but actually hardly anything is happening here but *Mittagessen* and *Abendessen.* If you came here in search of frivolous entertainment, you would be provided with the most extraordinary Barmecide's feast you could possibly imagine. A stroll round the town and an examination of the various notices, set out in the boldest type, would give you the impression that the place was a constant carnival of pleasure. We are surrounded by notices of Grand Happy Viennese Evenings of Song and Dance, Great Symphony Concerts, and Festivals of Play and Song and Mirth, but on close examination these tremendous affairs all dwindle to a violinist and a pianist playing to twelve people who are sitting over cakes, coffee and beer. We have such evenings, which are advertised in the longest words and in the largest type, in this hotel, which has its own Viennese Kunstler-Duo. Very good these two are, both the violinist and the pianist, and they are prepared to play you anything. On festive nights (there is one to-night, in the Casino, that is, the room at the end with the six Chinese lanterns), they sing choruses too, very Viennese, I imagine, though unfortunately I can never understand the words. I am dying to know why everybody laughs at the chorus that begins "Auf Wiedersehen, Frau Doktor."

When we are not eating, drinking, or sleeping, we spend most of our time in this hotel greeting one another. Germany, as we all know, is a country in which everybody greets everybody else; and even among the Germans, these Bavarians are notorious greeters; and I imagine that this Bad must be the most famous greeting place in Bavaria. No better punishment for one of those very stiff and exclusive Englishmen could be devised than six months as assistant manager or head waiter in this hotel. He would discover to his horror that not only had he to say Good morning to all the guests when they first appeared, but that he had to keep on saying things to them every time he saw them. The rule here is, Never pass a guest without saying something. You must smile, and then say Good morning, Good evening, Good night, Good Appetite, God Bless You, To Our Next Seeing, Thank You, Please, Thank You Beautifully, Please Very Much.

The manager, a very busy little man who runs perpetually from room to room, cannot hold his head

upright any more, for he has to nod and smile so
many hundred times an hour that his neck is now
fixed in a little forward curve. The guests themselves
are expected to be equally polite. To leave the
dining-room or enter the lounge, if you intend to do
the thing properly, is a formidable business, like being
a member of a royal family. When polite guests intend to go for a walk or for a drive in one of the little
carriages, they seem to shake hands and say "Auf
Wiedersehen" all round. When they actually leave
the hotel for home, I suspect they do it very early in
the morning, otherwise the final greetings, which must
be on a colossal scale, would take up most of the day.
As it is, a conventional guest here, after taking the
waters in the mornings, need not worry about the rest
of the day, for he can pass the hours between meals
and naps simply exchanging the usual greetings. The
next time I stay at an English hotel, I shall probably
forget where I am, go round smiling and nodding and
greeting everybody, and be locked up as a lunatic.

It is not quite true to say that nothing ever happens
in this town. Last Sunday, there was the annual fair,
and we were fortunate to be here and see it. All the
peasants for miles around came in, mostly on bicycles,
and all the beer-rooms along the main street seemed to
be filled with trombone and euphonium players who
were emptying huge jugs. The fair itself was nothing
out of the ordinary, being the usual collection of little
merry-go-rounds and stalls, but the people attending
the fair hardly belonged to this world at all. Most of

them wore the local costume, with the result that one found oneself wandering through the opening chorus of an opera. I told myself, as I looked at the brown-faced fellows in feathered hats, embroidered waist-coats, and shorts, and the girls in their little flat black hats, short coats, and scarlet and green billowing skirts, that at any moment cardboard tankards would be given out, we should have to group ourselves, and then up would go the curtain. Not that there is any-thing ridiculous about these Bavarian peasant costumes. I hope they will go on wearing them for ever. These clothes make the men stalwart, pic-turesque, and manly, and they make the women look pretty, equally picturesque, and womanly. I never saw so many pretty girls in one small country town, and how pleasant it is to smoke a good long cigar on a fine Sunday morning in a fantastic foreign place and stare, in what I hope is a discreet gentlemanly fashion, at pretty girls who look as if they have just hopped out of a ballet! It was just as pleasant, though, to stand on the bridge and look down at the young men, scores and scores of them, who went flashing below in Rob Roy canoes, hurled along by the greeny-milky torrent of the Isar.

We are here, I suppose, at the magical time. A few weeks ago, the snow was thick everywhere. In a few weeks more, high summer will come and it will be all a dusty green. But now it is intoxicatingly lush and rich. To go a walk in any direction is to go reeling through a green paradise. The meadows here are crazily fertile, lifting whole armies of Ragged Robin towards the sky, showering the fine gold of butter-cups, kingcups, dandelions, and some nameless flower of a finer gold still and beautifully shaped, colouring the very horizon with orchis and gentians, madly scattering the wild pansies among the heartsease. It is the enchanted lunacy of spring. I think I never saw the commonest leaves of lime and chestnut so green, so rich, so happily tangled with the sunlight. There are little pictures by the thousand; a young larch, with its delicate tracery, against a white wall; a blossom-loaded branch of an apple tree reaching out towards a wooden balcony. Enough, enough, for I am sliding down towards the prose of the men who write the little books for the tourist agencies. We leave to-morrow by the 8.50. We have been happy here. We are not the same people who came here, for we carry away with us, secure in our humming skulls, the racing river and its bridge and the people of the *feste,* the hills of breathing pine and the snowy tops behind, the mad meadows, and the great jay that was so proud in the green and gold of the leaves. Yes, we have taken the cure. I could go from this Bad to verse. Little town, I greet you: Good morning, Good day, Good night, Good Appetite, God Bless You, *Auf Wiedersehen.*

The Other Christmas

I SEE them going back, dwindling and fading as they retreat in time, these Christmases that I have had, and as I strain my eyes, searching the dimming corridor of memory, I wonder which to choose, to recapture—for once it has been chosen I believe it can be recaptured. There was the year, now about a quarter of a century away, when I was given the football. That will do as well as any other. At first I can remember nothing but the football (I have always had a passion for footballs, and to this day cannot hear the *thud-thud* of one without a quickening of the heart), but gradually, other things return, one corner after another of the curtain is lifted, the light grows stronger, and the scene is vivid again. The football comes bouncing back, bringing with it a whole lost world.

On that Christmas morning, then, I awoke to find the grey light sneaking through my dormer window and the old magic at work, for at the foot of the bed was that delicious heaviness, that strange and enchanting bumpiness which only arrived once a year. My stockings, which were hanging over the bed-rail, for that was our custom, were filled, as usual, but I had got past the age when the most important gifts could be crammed inside stockings. These bulged with oranges and chocolate and the like. But I think the shirt was tucked away in one of the stockings. It was a football shirt, of a happy, triumphant colouring, red and white stripes. If you are wondering what use a football shirt is to a boy if there are not ten other boys with similar shirts to hand, then you have no imagination. I would have preferred to have had ten other boys, all in red and white stripes, for football company, but I was quite prepared to be happy as the single representative, the nucleus, of a red and white team. On the other hand, the shirt would not be a success, would, indeed, be merely tantalizing, without a football. But the football was there, blown up, taut, trim and ready—and, oh, the beauty of that firm but bouncing sphere, true symbol of our planetary life! I sat up in bed, the queer half-light of the December morning round me, caressing its leather sides, running my fingers up and down the seams. It was still very early, the house was hardly stirring yet, but very soon I would be bouncing it happily upon my bedroom floor. Meanwhile, I put it aside, very close to the shirt, and continued my treasure hunt.

There was, as usual, a book that year, and I can tell you what it was. It was *The Triple Alliance*, by Harold Avery; and if you imagine that this was some boy who wished to become acquainted with European policy, then you are wrong. It was a school story. I have just looked up Mr. Avery in a reference book (and how astonishing it is to find him there, this magician from the distant past, just like the rest of us, plain scribblers!) and discover that he has written

R

Play the Game, Firelock and Steel, True to His Nickname, and a great many other stories, but nothing is said about *The Triple Alliance.* But that was the name of my book, and he was its author. I was very fond of school stories in those days—Talbot Baines Reed was my man, though that was before I came to *The Captain* and its more sophisticated authors—and I can remember how surprised I was to find that the boy next door, who went away to school, never had any of these adventures with bullies and town roughs and comic French masters and that his school was, on the whole, rather dull, considerably duller than mine. I was so fond of school stories that I used to write them myself, or, at least, I used to begin them. And they all began in the same way, I remember: *"Hurrah!" cried Dick as the train came into the station. "Greyfriars at last!"* That was my opening formula or gambit, Dick to Greyfriars in one move. But that, I think, came a little later. Then I was still reading and not writing. I spent quite a considerable fraction of the holidays that year reading *The Triple Alliance,* whole afternoons with it. How we could spin out books in those days!

When at last the time came to descend to breakfast, that Christmas morning, I was wearing my red and white striped football shirt. If it had been raining hard or snowing, I believe I should have burst with vexation, but fortunately it was doing neither, so five minutes after I had swallowed my last mouthful of cocoa I was dashing towards the field at the back of

the house, carrying my football. No other boy was in
sight, but that did not matter. For an hour I played
football, leading a triumphant red and white team,
all by myself. The grass was long and very wet—and
now, as I write, I can see again the very glitter of
its beaded blades—and it was a raw morning, but I
was happy, and when at last another boy turned up,
I was happier still. (His name was Victor; he afterwards went to Australia; and now I do not know
whether he is alive or dead. Most of the boys I played
with are dead, and not a few of them all died on the
same day, July 1, 1916.) The pair of us chased the
soaking ball and happily booted the morning away.
When I returned, muddy, with a football shirt that
looked like a football shirt, to the house, it was already
full of turkey and plum pudding, to say nothing of
my aunts and my grandfather.

When my aunts and my grandfather came to the
house, they always filled it at once, because they
talked broad Yorkshire and talked it at the top of
their voices. When I went to see them, at the other
side of the town, I always sat in a corner, in a small
rocking-chair, and pored over *Nicholas Nickleby* and
David Copperfield, both of which seemed to me then,
I remember, books with a strange, dark, tragic
atmosphere of their own, peopled with mysterious,
sinister beings who crept in and out of the shadowy
scenery of a dream. It was, I think, the illustrations
and not the text, always a subordinate matter to a
child, that gave me this idea of them. One half of

my mind would be exploring fearfully this dream world of shadows and twisted faces, while the other half listened to the cheerful shouting of the adults. Some of my earliest memories are tangled up with the tall, bearded figure of my grandfather. I seem to have trotted miles by his side, hearing him talk to the other adults about house property, his favourite subject when out for a walk. "Nah, yon's a bit o' property that's just fetched nowt like what you'd ha' thowt it would," he would say, and I would go trotting along by his side, occasionally rewarded with a mint humbug, a kind of sweet to which we were extremely partial in Yorkshire. And I doubt if I remember anything earlier than his bringing me home once in a bus, one of the old horse buses. I fell asleep on his knee, for it was terribly late, terribly dark, but not before my mind seized hold of the little interior, the flickering oil lamps, the huge figures in two rows, and the straw on the floor, to keep it for ever, so that I have only to shut out this other world for a moment to see again, to smell again, the straw on the floor of that old horse bus.

After dinner, which we had in the middle of the day, I crept into a corner with *The Triple Alliance,* and no doubt spent the whole afternoon, enjoying every minute of it, with the first chapter or so. I know that it was considerably later in the afternoon, perhaps after tea, when I went next door, where there was a boy of my own age, not Victor, but another. His chief present had been a small engine, and this

engine, which worked with a kind of smelly fury, could
be made to print three ducks, three rather smudgy
ducks, but still quite recognizable ducks, on pieces of
paper about half the size of a post-card. This is all the
machine could do, but we asked for nothing better.
After collecting all the scrap paper in the house and
trimming it to the right size, the two of us sat at a
little table in the kitchen, set the engine going, and
printed ducks, hundreds and hundreds of ducks. Ah,
the grave ecstasies of boyhood and that enchanted
season when you can print ducks, the same three
ducks, by the hour and be happy!

It is strange how little has been lost. The football,
pressed between my rapturous hands, seems to be here
now; I remember the red stripes, the white stripes,
the very texture, the woolly fluffiness, of that shirt: I
catch again the glitter of the wet grass; Harold
Avery's story is only round the corner; my grandfather is shouting across the dinner-table; the kitchen
next door is being filled with smudgy ducks; and I am
a boy again, in another world.

Seven Gods

IT is open to the connoisseur to step forward and point out, with a smile of pity faintly spiced with contempt, that this little Japanese ivory is a recent product, a thing of commerce, hastily manufactured for the export market. "It's not too bad an imitation of the genuine old *netsuke*," he will probably say, taking it up between an exquisite finger and thumb, "but you can see the difference at once if you examine it closely. Look at that—and that—and there, you see——" I shan't see. I shan't care, either. When the connoisseur has gone (and I shan't press him to stay), I shall put the little ivory on my table again and stare at it once more with delight. It looks like a genuine old *netsuke*, for the two holes at the back look as if they have been used and the ivory itself, with its beautiful pale highlights and its fried-egg coloured shadows, seems to have known a good many years of travel and use; and, what is vastly more important, it gives me pleasure, and would still give me pleasure, even if I learned that the thing had been turned out last year in a Tokio factory. It is only three inches high and could be slipped into my trousers pocket, but, possessing it, I seem to hold the gorgeous East in fee. It is an East that hardly exists any longer, I imagine, now that Japan has taken to lawn-tennis, films, industrial psychology, machine-guns, and battle cruisers. Its tiny figures smile at me out of a lost world.

I gave a few pounds for this *netsuke,* and nobody, not even the most cynical expert, with his quotations of what such things cost by the gross f.o.b. Yokohama, can convince me that I paid too much, for already I have had more than my money's worth. During the short time we have been together, this thing has done what many elaborate entertainment syndicates have failed to do, it has raised my spirits. I am a member of the contemporary English middle classes, a family man with a precarious trade and a bourgeois conscience, and I live in a sad mist of taxes and toxins. It may be life or it may be liver (I love the sweet course), but the fact remains that my spirits frequently need raising. And again and again, already, this little piece of Japanese carving has done the trick. I was attracted to it first, when I caught sight of it on a shelf filled with such things, because the largest figure, the one on the right who is holding five others in a sort of bag, reminded me of Shakespeare. If our William, instead of dying in Stratford, had quietly sneaked off to Cathay and finally spent about fifteen years in Japan, he would have looked like this. His beard has grown; his nose has been somewhat flattened; his eyes have narrowed (though he is laughing, not foolishly, but out of the wisdom of vast experience); but otherwise it is the poet himself. He caught my eye at once, and when I had examined him and looked over the other six figures, no more than an inch high and yet crammed with character, the dealer came across to me and told me that these were the Seven Gods of Happiness. That settled it. The seven gods were mine.

I am not sure yet which is which. Is the tiny fat one, who stands underneath the five-in-the-bag, has a sack over his shoulders, and wears on his broad complacent face an expression that must have been seen at many a directors' meeting, the great Daikoku, the god of wealth? Is the one who looks like Shakespeare and stands there at the side, laughing, Fukurokuju, the god of longevity? There are two very ancient white-bearded ones in the bag, and one of them might be Fukurokuju, and the other might be Jurojin, another god of longevity. (You will notice that these people liked to live a long time, probably because they enjoyed life and laughed at all its antics.) The fierce one—his face is only a quarter of an inch square, but there is no mistaking its ferocity—is obviously Bishamon, the god of war. You will say at once, being a reader of contemporary literature, that he has no right to be there among the seven gods of happiness; but you must remember that he pre-dates the wars of barbed wire and high explosive and was probably only the god of gentlemanly warriors who enjoyed banging away at one another's armour. One of these deities is a goddess, Benten, the goddess of love, and she must be the matronly-looking little body next to Bishamon. I will confess that I am not much interested in her, for she cuts a poor figure beside Aphrodite or Venus. But now we come to two little gods whose worship should be introduced into the West—and perhaps re-introduced into the East—with all speed. These are Ebisu, the fisherman, god of disinterestedness; and Hotei, the god of magnanimity. You can see Hotei, with his sack and his fan, at the back of the bag, looking uncommonly like my friend, the London editor of our best provincial morning paper. I should like to see an image forty feet high of this god in one of our open places, and a good many people of my acquaintance compelled to do him worship. And why not? I can understand a god of magnanimity, and even if he is only an inch high, with a bald ivory head that is like a tiny bird's egg, he is more worthy of respect than some other gods, jealous gods, vindictive gods, gods with minds like mean schoolboys.

We could do with a few little gods of happiness about the place now. The universe that contemporary thought has decided to accept is far too empty for my taste, and when anything does happen in it, it seems to happen for the worst. Everything now is strangely hollow and dark. Outside us is a universe consisting of a few lonely electrons. As a spectacle it is not without a certain grandeur, but there is something very melancholy about it. When you read the fascinating works of Eddington and Jeans, you can feel this melancholy in the very rhythm of their sentences. Inside us—if I may put it that way—is the unconscious, a vast dark region above which our bits of conscious thinking are merely so many darting fire-flies.

Whether you turn to the physicist or the psychologist (and it is they who have most to say, these days), you have the same sense of a vast vague hollowness. If only a ray of sunshine would fall into it, and then light up the homely face of Ebisu the fisherman or Hotei, with his sack and his fan! The universe is old enough, in all conscience—well, then, let it take on the form and features of Fukurokuju (if that is he), and stand at the side, holding the others in a bag, laughing, and looking rather like Shakespeare. Or like Mr. Shaw, if you prefer it, though he does not deserve the honour, for he has spent too much of his time robbing us of concrete images and making the vague vaguer still, by talking about the life-force. And you can no more worship the life-force than you can worship the Gas Light and Coke Company.

Yet I will admit that it is not the deity symbolised by this ivory group that has raised my spirits so often; it is its rich humanity. There is something about these jolly, fat, grinning little gods that is irresistible. They are great accepters of life, these fellows. I know very little about old Japanese art, but I do know that I never see a good specimen of it without instantly having ordinary human life tremendously enriched for me. The zest of their little men is infectious. Everybody in their drawings and carvings is bursting with character, energy, humour, and a passion for living. There is not a single phosphorescent glimmer of that sickly death-worship which can be observed in some other kinds of art. I cannot count the number of times I have stopped a moment or two outside a shop window, stared at some Japanese print or carving, and then gone away with a richer mind and a lighter heart. I never see one of these people from the distant islands, even if they happen to be beating our local champions at lawn-tennis, without remembering with gratitude these delicious and inspiriting little works of art. (And they are art to me, even if they are commerce in Yokohama.) I am only sorry that they have Westernised themselves—as I take it, they have—for the life out of which these things bubbled into coloured ink and carved ivory must have been a very good life, richly diverse, zestful, humorous, poetic, and I cannot help but wonder darkly what it is that I and my kind have given them in exchange for their lost seven little gods of happiness.

Public Dinners

ONCE again I have sworn never never to attend another public dinner. *Decorations will be worn*—but not by me. *Ladies on the left, Gentlemen on the right* —no, I shall not be there. *Your Royal Highness, My Lords, Ladies and Gentlemen, Dinner is served*—but not to me, if I have any strength of mind left. We must all be firm about these functions. Not one of us enjoys them. We grumble to one another going in, and we growl going out. At an hour when we might be tying up a rose-bush or having a glorious whack at a tennis-ball, we find ourselves wriggling into full dress, the stiffest and starchiest objects in the whole wardrobe, tugging away at a white tie in full sunlight, and then off we go to a place where we know only too well we shall be miserable for the next two hours and a half. Why do we do it? Who sets these wheels in motion? Who has decided that we shall thus outrage our digestions and torture our eager and adventurous minds? How monstrous it is that sturgeon should be rifled, salmon plucked out of the Tay, and lambs slaughtered on the Welsh hills, for this great Bore of Babylon! What malice is this that transforms a company of pretty women and pleasant fellows into so many staring and yawning images? Who gains besides the poulterers, launderers, and purveyors of dubious vintages?

If you go to eat and drink, you are taken in. This is one of the most curious conundrums of the public dinner. Why does the food and drink never taste right? On paper, the dishes, the wines, look well, and in our days of innocence our mouths water over the menu. Even when the food appears on the table, it looks promising. But somehow it never achieves a flavour, except that of warm cardboard or damp wool. Something devilish happens between the kitchen and the table at a public dinner. There are malicious Jinns present. Go to the same hotel with a friend or two, and the identical menu will yield half a dozen delectable courses. It is the same with the wines. An old brown sherry, a Liebfraumilch, some dry champagne, port or liqueur brandy, all these will be reduced at a public dinner to one sweetish liquid of various colours. It is as if they had all come out of a conjurer's trick kettle. And I imagine that the palate promptly informs the stomach that these deceptions are being practised. Hence the resentment inside, that hot reddish feeling that all we public diners know only too well.

It would be charitable to assume that the waiters are aware of this shameful wizardry. This would explain their gloom at such functions. They are not the men we see at ordinary times. They wear a conscripted look. If their style of serving is mistaken for that of waitresses in popular tea-shops, obviously they do not care. Their tender solicitude for the belly has given place to an air of indifference that only masks a grave misgiving. "If you do not like zees stuff, sare," their abrupt gestures are proclaiming, "don't blame me. You vould come." The head waiters smile and smile, but no longer with the flawless confidence of their kind. When you see them washing their hands in invisible soap-and-water before the chairman or secretary, you may be sure the action is really symbolic. They, too, know that before the hour-hand has gone round, they will be surrounded by a hundred hot reddish feelings inside, and though a little bicarbonate would cure them of this deed, they dare not insinuate it on to the tables.

Who, I repeat, enjoys these functions? Not the diners; not the chairman, the committee, the guests of honour. The men who have to speak are miserable because now that they are actually here, they are convinced that those little humorous remarks about the Society or whatever it is will not be appreciated, and that the concluding peroration, in a nobler strain than most after-dinner speeches, will never do for this audience. "Now I mustn't talk to you too much," the ladies at their elbows are saying, "because, of course, you are thinking about your speech. I'm sure it will be awfully good." These observations, though doubtless well-meant, only deepen their misery. By the time the speakers who come first have pointed out, with what seems the very salt of malice, that everybody present has a right to expect something unusually wise and witty from the speakers who will follow, these wretched gentlemen are really suffering,

and ask themselves a hundred times why on earth
they ever consented to make a show of themselves in
front of such a stupid mob.

Those who have only to listen are in no better situation. Indeed, they are in a worse one. To make a
speech is at least to do something, to act, to undertake an adventure. For the speakers the evening has
a shape, rising to a peak, as it were, when they themselves rise to their feet. But for the listening guests
the evening goes on and on, and they have to drag
themselves across deserts of boredom. Somehow there
is no escape. You cannot dismiss the speeches altogether, and meditate upon the Brazilian forests, the
conquests of Gengis Khan, or the habits of wild-fowl.
Your mind is claimed, held, and is then beaten con-
tinuously with heavy wooden mallets. Everybody
talks too long. "I will not take your time any longer,"
says the speaker, with the simpering mock-modesty
of his tribe, and for a moment your heart leaps up,
but then, as ever, he goes on: "There is, however, one
—er—thing—that is, one point—I should like to
make. Many years ago. . . ." And for another
hundred miles of trackless waste, he rambles on.
What makes these fellows so maddening, too, is their
trick of explaining that they have been compelled by
the secretary or the chairman or some other busy-
body to speak, and that they do so against their wish.
I was at a public dinner the other week, when at least
ten speakers spent ten minutes each telling us how
they were dragooned into talking, and they all did it

with such gusto that it was impossible to believe a word they said. And the fact that I was one of the ten does not make me an apologist for the trick.

Then again, you never know when you have come to the end. There are, we will say, six speakers down on the programme. That is bad enough, but unless you are very lucky it does not stop there. The chairman suddenly goes mad and calls for new torturers. Perhaps Mr. Mumble Mumble will say a few words? We should all like to hear the views of Mr. Blather Blather. And off they go again, protesting that they had not expected to be called upon, but at the same time—with the utmost effrontery—consulting a sheet of paper black with idiotic notes they have made. The guests yawn and mutter, the waiters droop, the room grows stuffier, and cigars taste hot i' the mouth, but nevertheless Mr. Drone Drone has to reply to Messrs. Mumble Mumble and Blather Blather, and a vote of thanks must be passed, at incredible length, by old Mr. Blah Blah Blah. And outside, wide and beautiful, is the night, and slippers and books and armchairs and dressing-gowns and pipes of tobacco and whisky-and-soda that tastes like whisky-and-soda.

I have narrowed it down to one solitary person. The toast-master enjoys these dinners. He alone is happy. It is astonishing that we who suffer should pay to be there and that he, commanding, red-coated, and at his ease, should be paid for his services. "My Lords, Ladies and Gentlemen, be pleased to charge your glasses, and pray silence for your chairman."

How he rolls it out—the ass! Why should we endure such misery for him and his "Pray silence"? Let him accept an invitation from the Talkies and leave us in peace. He is an anachronism—as his speech plainly shows—and if he is to be encouraged, well, let us take some cross-bow-men into our pay, too, and invite them to use us, in full evening dress, as their targets. If there were no public dinners, there would be no toast-masters, and that, I fancy, explains why we have public dinners. These are our masters and they have us on toast. The time has come when their power must be broken. Let us all attend the last public dinner, taking to it a plan of action. When the toast-master cries "Pray silence," let us all throw pieces of bread at him and sing comic songs.

At the Tailors'

BETWEEN the chaos of Regent Street and the opulent
bustle of New Bond Street is a little region that is
curiously hushed. It is made up of short streets that
pretend to run parallel to one another, but actually
go off at all angles. At a first glance these streets
appear to be filled with the offices of very old firms
of family solicitors. Many of their windows have
severe wire screens. The establishments there have
a certain air of dignified secrecy, not unlike that of
servants of the old school, those impassive butlers
who appeared to know nothing, but really knew
everything. There is little evidence that anything is
being sold in this part of the world. The electric-
light bills must be very modest indeed, for there are
no flashing signs to assault the eye, no gaudily dressed
windows to tempt the feet to loiter. Whatever the
season, no Sales are held there. You are not invited
to stop a moment longer than you may wish to do.
Now and then you catch sight of a roll of cloth, a pair
of riding breeches, or, perhaps, a sober little drawing
of a gentleman in evening clothes, and as you pass you
can hear these things whispering: "If you are a gentleman and wish to wear the clothes that a gentleman
should wear, kindly make an appointment here and
we will see what we can do for you." Money, of
course, is not mentioned, this being impossible in all

such gentlemanly transactions. For this is the region, Savile Row, Conduit Street, Maddox Street, and the rest, of the tailors or—rather—*the* tailors. Enter it wearing a cheap ready-made suit, and immediately the poor thing begins to bag in some places and shrivel up in others. If you have the audacity (as I once had) actually to walk into one of these establishments wearing a ready-made suit, you will regret it. Nothing is said, but a glance from one of the higher officials here strips you and quietly deposits your apparel in the dust-bin.

The hush here is significant. It might be described as old-world, and for a very good reason, too. In a new world in which anything will do so long as it arrives quickly and easily, this region has fallen sadly behind the times. It is still engaged in the old quest for perfection. Behind these wire screens the search for the absolute still goes on. Tailoring here remains one of the arts. There are men in this quarter who could announce in all sincerity that trousers are beauty, beauty trousers, and that is all we know and need to know. For them the smallest seam they sew can give thoughts that do often lie too deep for tears. That they are artists and not tradesmen is proved by the fact that, unlike tradesmen, they do not labour to please their customers, but to please themselves. A tailor who is a mere shopkeeper fits you until you are satisfied. These artists go on fitting you until they are satisfied, and that means they continue long after you have lost all interest in the matter. You stand there,

a mere body or lay figure, and they still go on delicately ripping out sleeves and collars with their little
pen-knives, pinning and unpinning, and making
mysterious signs with chalk, and you have long
ceased to understand what all the bother is about.
And even then they may tell you, quietly but firmly,
that they must have another fitting. That they should
do this to me is proof positive of their disinterested
passion for the art of tailoring.

I never walk into my own tailor's without feeling
apologetic. I know I am unworthy of their efforts. It
is as if a man without an ear for music should be invited to spend an evening with the Lener Quartet. I
am the kind of man who can make any suit of clothes
look shabby and undistinguished after about a fortnight's wear. Perhaps the fact that I always carry
about with me two or three fairly large pipes, matches,
about two ounces of tobacco, a wallet, cheque-book,
diary, fountain-pen, knife, odd keys and loose change,
to say nothing of old letters, may have something to
do with it. I can never understand how a man can
contrive to look neat and spruce and do anything else.
Wearing clothes properly seems to me to be a full-
time job, and as I happen to have a great many other,
more important or more amusing things to do, I
cheerfully bag and sag and look as if I had slept in
my suits. I can say this cheerfully here, but once I
am inside my tailors' I immediately begin to feel
apologetic. They do not say anything, but there is
mournful reproach in their eyes as they turn them

upon their ruined sonnets and sonatas. One day I
shall call upon them in evening clothes because I fancy
they are not so bad as the lounge suits. But I do not
know; they may see enormities where I see nothing;
and so perhaps I had better keep the fate of their
masterpieces hidden from them. Possibly they whisper
to one another, when they see me slouching in, looking like a man who might buy his clothes through the
post: "He's one of those gentlemen who're a bit careless during the day. I shouldn't wonder," I hear them
adding wistfully, anxious to convince themselves, "if
he takes trouble at night."

They have their revenge, though, when they get me
inside one of their horrible cubicles, for a fitting. By
the time I have been inside one of those places ten
minutes I have not a shred of self-respect left. It is
worse than being at the barber's, and fully equal to
being at the dentist's. To stand like a dummy, to be
simply a shape of flesh and bone, is bad enough, but
what make it much worse are the mirrors and the
lighting. These mirrors go glimmering away into infinity. At each side is a greeny-gold tunnel. I do not
mind that, having only a slight distaste for tunnels
and hardly any at all for infinity. But I do not like
all those images of myself. Wherever I look, I see a
man whose appearance does not please me. His head
seems rather too big for his body, his body rather too
big for his legs. In that merciless bright light, his face
looks fattish and somewhat sodden. There is something vaguely dirty about him. The clothes he is

wearing, apart from the particular garment he is trying on at the moment, look baggy, wrinkled, and shabby. He does not pay enough attention to his collar, his boots. His hair wants cutting, and another and closer shave would do him good. In full face he does not inspire confidence. His profile, however, is simply ridiculous, and the back view of him is really horrible. And a woman and several children are tied to a fellow like that! Incredible that a man can take such a face and carcase about with him, and yet entertain a tolerably good opinion of himself! As I think these things, it is possible that I smile a little. That is what it feels like—smiling a little; but immediately twenty images in that cubicle break into ghostly grins, produce wrinkles from nowhere, show distorted acres of cheek and jowl. And there is no looking away.

Meanwhile, the tailors themselves, so neat, so clean, so deft, are busy with the pins and the chalk. They are at home in these little halls of mirrors, and so look well in them from every possible angle of reflection. They pretend a certain subservience, but it is the idlest of pretences. They know—and they know that I know—that I am but a shadow of myself, a puppet in their hands. Their opinions, such as they are, seem to be those of most moderate sensible men, but even if they murmured that it was high time the Spanish Inquisition was established in this island, I should have to agree with them. They are not all alike, these fitters, or cutters, or whatever they are. Thus my usual trouser man is quite different from

my usual coat man. He is smaller and livelier, more
bustling, more given to cheerful gossip. A long and
intimate acquaintance with trousers has made him far
more democratic and more of the earth earthy. There
are times when I feel I can almost hold my own with
him. On the other hand, the coat man is quietly
tremendous. He has one of those tight, healthy-look-
ing, clean-shaven faces, like a brownish apple; and
looks something between a priest, a surgeon and a
solicitor who occasionally rides to hounds. Everything about him is clear, polished and speckless. He
regards me with about the same amount of
interest that I give to another man's coat. When he
once condescended to tell me about his boy (who is at
a public school) I felt immensely flattered and rushed
to agree with everything he said. For a few minutes
I was really alive, almost sharing the honours with
my coat. But then he became serious again and took
out a pin somewhere and made another chalkmark.

I can understand the feelings of those people who
are compelled to live with great artists. I can also
understand the inner meaning of the old saying about
nine tailors making a man. They have so little
common humanity, these artists of the pins and chalk,
that it must be difficult to wring out of nine of them
folly and friendliness enough to make an ordinary
citizen. But now that the dandies are all dead and
gone, theirs must be a lonely world. Will they accept
these few words of tribute from a pocket-stuffer, a
rumpler and crumpler, a bagger?

A Musical Party

My invitation-card says ten o'clock, so I arrive at
half-past, only to find that most people—and those,
of course, the most important—have decided to make
it eleven o'clock. After putting my hat away in the
cloak-room, and standing for a moment, wiping my
damp forehead and moving my tie back into its proper
place, I ask myself gloomily why I am here. Then I
mount the fine curving staircase. My hostess is there,
waiting at the top, and gives me that special smile of
welcome which she has also given everybody else. She
has just time to slip in a phrase about one of my
books, one she has probably never read and one that
I have long ceased to admire myself. Poor woman,
she will have to make dozens of remarks of that kind
to-night, and long before midnight that special smile
will be tarnished, cracked, faded. For a second I feel
sorry for her, but the next moment that feeling instantly disappears. I have entered the large drawing-
room, and now, to my horror, I discover that this is
to be no ordinary party with a little music thrown in,
but a solemn midnight concert. There are rows and
rows of those uncomfortable gilt chairs, and on every
vacant chair is a programme. I am in for it.

I notice a good many people I know, but I do not
go and sit near them, chiefly because I am feeling
sulky and disinclined for bright talk. The programme

confirms my worst fears. There is an awful lot of it, and very little I want to hear. If somebody from the Æolian or Grotrian Hall sent me this programme and a ticket, even if I had the afternoon free, I would not go. But I have come here, at this absurd hour of night, and stiffer than starch (for you cannot call starch stiff a night like this) in full dress. And very soon, when this corner of the room fills up, there will not be a space for my legs and my little chair will proceed to torture. Moreover, I am apparently two awful hours away from tobacco, and even when I get it, it will not be in a pipe. (The real failure of Mr. Baldwin's Government was its inability to impose the pipe upon social functions.)

All the people I know seem to be in groups, cheerfully chattering away, and, overlooking the fact that I chose to sit here myself, I seem to be exiled from them, and come to the conclusion that people do not like me. I stare mournfully at the grand piano and the ridiculous palms, and turn a bilious eye upon the newcomers, who are now arriving in gangs. I do not like the look of any of them. There is a fatuous young Frenchman who kisses hands. There are one or two elderly women who seem to have been so thoroughly barbered, massaged, tinted, enamelled, powdered, that they look quite unreal, and it is quite impossible to imagine them eating. The man on my left has cultivated a Mephistophelian appearance, and I tell myself that he is an ass, but all the time I know quite well that I really think he is somebody very important, and that if he should speak to me I should give him some simpering reply.

Will they never begin the wretched concert? I see myself sitting here until the small hours. Yes, they are beginning now. I have not seen this accompanist for years. He does not look the man he was; he is having trouble with his digestive system. While he is fussing with the piano, I have time to wonder what it is like being an accompanist whose digestion is going to pieces. The singer stands before us. Before he has sung a note, I recognize that he belongs to the ultra-interpretative school, because he pulls a curious face at us. I know that he will go on pulling these faces, sometimes looking slightly mad and at other times resembling a man who has just swallowed some unpleasant liquid, because he and his singing master are under the impression that these grimaces improve Schubert, and he has been told to suggest Joy, Dismay, Wonder. I know, too, that he will not have much of a voice. And I am right in both instances, and throughout his strange facial contortions and hoarse whisperings I take a mournful pleasure in my rightness. When he has done, we applaud, and more people arrive, looking like members of the Spanish Inquisition entering a town full of notorious heretics.

The violinist is better, and indeed plays very well, so that for a few minutes I can forget my little gilt chair. But she has a friend or two, somewhere in the front row, and every now and then she opens a wickedly expressive dark eye and gleams at these friends of hers, and I know that she is mocking us all, as well she might. But we applaud her loudly, and some of us, led by the hostess, who has to keep one eye on the door and the other, rolling in ecstasy, on the performer, call out "Brava!" exactly like Italians or people in bad novels about musical life. The lady who follows her has a well-trained voice, but somehow it is not a voice capable of giving pleasure at eleven-thirty on a warm night. Moreover, her interpretative business does not suit her large and dignified features, and there are moments during her singing when she reminds me of nothing but an astonished dromedary.

By this time I am hungry, thirsty, and aching for tobacco. To my disgust, I see that I have planted myself on the wrong side of the room. From the other side you can slip away into a little ante-room, and that is precisely what several acquaintances of mine are actually doing. This is maddening. There they are, lighting cigarettes, lounging and talking, probably having a drink, while I am pinned to this chair, with apparently another hour of indifferent music in front of me. Unless I am mistaken, there are one or two men there, men I know, who have never listened to a note yet, who have been smoking and talking in that ante-room ever since they arrived. Selfish devils! What right have they to accept an invitation to a *musicale* (not to be confused—alas!—with a music 'all) and then hog it in there, as if they were in their clubs?

The male singer returns, and with him more Joy, Dismay, Wonder, but none of it reaches my heart. The lady returns, and once again transforms herself into an astonished dromedary. The three songs she has chosen, presumably on account of their brutal length, are the desert. The violinist returns, with another wicked glance at the front row, and again plays very well, but goes on far too long. The hostess is now off door-duty, but has to put in a great deal of audience work, never allowing the ecstatic look to leave her face for a moment, and having to cry "Brava!" or even "O-o-oh, brava, brava!" a second or two before anybody else does. There is so much brava towards the end that I begin to feel very uneasy indeed, for there is clearly a danger of "Just something more," even though encores are not the thing at these functions. By this time, very important people, who never stay anywhere more than an hour or so, have moved on—not to bed, of course, but to some other party that is just beginning. Night after night, while the rest of us are in bed or smoking a last pipe with our slippered feet somewhere near the mantelpiece, these important people go on and on, sacrificing themselves so that society—or that part of it which gives late parties—shall continue. Just as racing and hunting are not mere amusements because they improve the breed of horses, or at least of racers and hunters, so, too, it is necessary that some people should be sociable until nearly dawn or it would be impossible to give late parties and improve the breed of sleepy guests.

Now the music is all done, the hostess is keeping
the ecstatic expression on her face for another ten
minutes or so, and we move in a compact mass to
the supper-room. There we discover the reason for
the accompanist's indigestion. He has been engaged
at too many of these functions. Here are salmon
mayonnaise, things in aspic, strawberries and cream,
rich cakes, and iced champagne, and the hour is pre-
posterous, but we help ourselves. Happy those guests
who in the morning will not be faced with some sheets
of white paper! Unlike most men, an author cannot
pretend to work; either he is working or idling; and
a glance at his sheets of manuscript will tell you
which. I have a suspicion that all I shall see on my
white paper in the morning will be a number of little
black spots. Liver will have set them dancing there,
but they will really be the ghosts of midnight crotchets
and quavers.

A Defence of Dull Company

AT this season, the beginning of the year, we often
find ourselves in the company of people we do not see
at any other time. The festive tide floats us into the
presence of innumerable relatives and old family
friends. Our consciences recover some of their tender
bloom in the early days of January, and we hasten
to repair the neglect of the last twelve months by
issuing invitations to those persons "we really ought
to see" and by scrupulously declining to invent excuses
for not accepting their invitations. The result is, we
find ourselves in strange waters for a little while. Our
friends, our real friends retire to the background, their
places being taken by people who (if we are under
fifty) remember us when we "were only so high" and
do not scruple to make the indecent most of the
circumstance, by old school-fellows with whom we
have had nothing in common for thirty years, except
a liking for tobacco and a hatred of taxes, and by a
host of other odd solemn fish. The values of our own
little world suddenly mean nothing; we are regarded
from all manner of quaint unlikely angles; we are
treated with respect simply because our cousin is
Borough Surveyor of Little Podlington, or we are
laughed at because we made ourselves ill with pudding at the age of twelve, or we are pitied because
we have not commandeered a fortune like our wife's

sister's husband, the company promoter. We suffer a voluntary exile.

The people we meet at such a time are generally dull. This is probably the reason why our engagements with them become affairs of the newly-wakened conscience, things not to be thought of in June or September, when such persons, nothing but poor wraiths of the memory, mean less to us than the trembling shadow of a leaf. Our friends, of course, are not dull; if they were, they would not be our friends. Indeed, I flatter myself that most of my friends would not be considered dull in any company, unless it was in a company of flappers, and even then I think some of them would give a good account of themselves. One or two of them are people of such rare charm that their very appearance acts as signal to hospitality to fling its gates wide open; if they were dropped from an aeroplane into some remote and alien city, I believe they would have received half a dozen invitations to dinner before they had walked the length of the main street. Such are my friends; witty, genial, argumentative, roaring, subtle, wise and humorous souls: I rejoice in them. But, I repeat, the people I see at this time of the year, and only at this time, are not my friends, and they are dull. Everybody knows them. They are not the skeleton in everybody's cupboard, for the skeleton is usually some relative who is a cheerful wastrel and turns up at inconvenient moments to borrow five shillings; the skeleton is exciting. These people are rather the cupboard itself, the plain, deal, innocent-looking affair that conceals the skeleton. They are solidly dull folks, good rate-payers all, the backbone of the country and the suet-pudding of society.

There is much to be said in favour of their company, or at least for a measure of it once in a while. When we are with our friends, we are not in the world, that is, not in the real world, but only in a cosy little painted world of our own; we and our old friends agree to be warmed by the same sun of illusion and cooled by the same sweet rain of opinion; much talk and many experiences in common have enabled us to map out our hills and valleys, roads and rivers together, so that we always know where we are and can travel in comfort. Once out of the society of our friends and among our distant relatives and the rest, and all is changed. Our horizons are immeasurably enlarged by our Uncle George, who used to be in the coal business, who is so old and stupid, who knows nothing about our delicate fads and foibles, and cares less. When we face him, we begin to face a new world. It may be a very dull and stupid one, but contact with it will do us good. Forced to accept innumerable strange points of view, we are braced; many a drowsy spell is broken; we must willy-nilly cast into the balance much of what we have come to accept without question. We come to a short talk with our cousin the stockbroker, who thinks of literature much as we think of eau-de-Cologne, as Childe Roland came to the Dark Tower in Browning's fine poem. It is only right that such heroic encounters should be infrequent, but if we shrink from them when they do offer themselves, so much the worse for us. More than one fiery young revolutionary is ready to face the tribunals of the bloated oppressors, but is not willing to face his maiden aunt from Cheltenham.

The time we spend in this dull company is not only a period of trial, but also one of rest and refreshment. There is nothing bad in this. Even the Crusader or the Knight-errant, once he had set out, was at least free of his creditors. So while one part of us is being tried in the battle, another part is being rested and even coddled. This welcome rest in dull society will take a slightly different form with each individual, and what follows may only apply to myself. If it does, I am sorry, but it cannot be helped: in the last resort, a man can do no more than translate his own experience into words. For my own part, then, I discover a certain transient satisfaction and mental comfort in dull company because it affords me a relief from ideas. My own friends are for the most part men and women of ideas. Modern psychology has made a distinction between "stable" and "unstable" types of mind, one tending early towards settled convictions and largely working by instinct, the other being more subject to change and knowing more of reason. My friends are of the "unstable" type. In their company, I become aware of subtleties, of the more intimate relations of things; I realize that all is relative, shifting, confused, secretive, that we grope from darkness to darkness

T

and are only the more bewildered by our brief intervals of light; I am never allowed to forget that I am
a semi-crazed, two-legged thing, half ape, half god,
mumbling and staring for a little hour on a globe
that is spinning on its way through the darkness. This
is very well; I make no complaint; but one can have
too much of it. So the dull people I meet at this season
come very opportunely, for through them I can win
a little peace.

Here, in its plain lack of ideas, is the saving grace
of this dull company. On these grounds I am prepared to defend it. There is a certain air of cosiness
about it, an absence of doubt and uncertainty, that is
the very medicine I need at the New Year when I
venture into such society. The dark outer spaces are
shut out and forgotten. The abstract, so cold and
brittle, perishes, and we move among concrete things,
solid to the sight and touch. The cosmos dwindles,
becomes more warm, human and familiar, and even
begins to suggest drawn curtains and a bright fire,
tea and muffins. That perilous talk which suddenly
starts all manner of awkward self-searching questions
in the mind, is heard no more. All we hear is solid
comforting stuff! "Now getting so much a year. . . .
The eldest, Mabel, is very pretty. . . . Sold his house
for so much. . . . Managed to find an excellent
hotel. . . ." Nothing much in itself perhaps, but infinitely soothing, keeping at bay the howling wolf-
packs of ideas. And, after all, it is not so much the
talk itself as the atmosphere, the spirit, Master

Shallow, the spirit! There are no uncertainties, no changes; every one is himself or herself, the same this year as last, as splendidly dull as ever. We are free of time; we spend an evening or two in eternity, secure from trouble, in a world all fixed and constant; the very stories, heard so many times before and so very tedious, drone on for centuries, and little we care. Once again we hear how Aunt Mildred missed the 9.52; and the fire gleams upon pleasant faces, and all is snug within, while outside there is the wind and rain and death and destruction and all the ideas in the world. There we sit, cosy, untroubled, gloriously fallow, sipping our cups of lethe-water and eating our hot buttered lotus. Later, we shall awaken like children from sleep, and go out, alert, eager and re-freshed.

Sutcliffe and I

HERBERT SUTCLIFFE has had such streams of printer's ink, frequently of the vilest quality, poured over him of late that I am sure he will not be offended at the little cupful I propose to add to the torrent. I will, however, offer my apologies to this fine cricketer and fellow Yorkshireman, if only because under cover of his name, which will probably lure so many honest cricketers to this page, I am about to write a very egotistical essay. I have chosen him as my stalking-horse because he and I have many things in common. We are about the same age, come from the same part of the world (though we are not acquainted, I regret to say), and have not entirely dissimilar biographies. Thus, we both served in France, first in the ranks and afterwards as officers, and then, when the war was over, we both became professional entertainers of a rather curious kind. He earned his bread by hitting a ball hard with a shaped piece of willow. I decided to earn mine by setting down on paper various odd fancies and thoughts about men and books. Oddly enough, there are several friends of mine who tell me that they dislike his profession, that a man should not play a game for money, though they do not object to my method of earning a living. They do not seem to see that if it is ridiculous that a man should play cricket for money; it is still more ridiculous that a man

should air his feelings for money, that a professional
batsman is less absurd than a professional sonneteer.
The fact is, of course, that these friends of mine
are unjust to Sutcliffe and his fellow professionals
because they have not grasped the simple fact that
sport and art are similar activities, that none of us,
whether we are batsmen or poets, bowlers or essayists,
work away in our fields or our studies for the money
itself. We bat or write because we have a passion for
batting or writing, and only take the money so that
the butcher and baker may be paid while we are so
happily engaged. "Don't stop," the community says to
us, and hands us a cheque now and then so that we
have not to quit the cricket pitch or the writing-desk
in order to seek a livelihood. Indeed, it would not be
difficult to turn the tables on these objectors to professional sport and to prove that it is the amateur
who is in the weaker ethical position, for while he is
playing cricket from May to September it is possible
that he is neglecting the estate it is his duty to manage
or the business-house from which he draws a salary as
director.

Both of us, then, have chosen these odd but by no
means disreputable means of earning a living. On the
score of money, I do not suppose there is much difference between us. But here the likeness ends. Millions
bandy his name who have never heard of me. He himself has probably never seen my name, whereas I
know all about him and read about him every day all
through the summer. If he strains a muscle, the even-

ing papers tell me all about it in great headlines, but
if I should die, probably the tiny paragraph giving
the news would never reach the eye of this contemporary and fellow countryman of mine. Do not mis-
understand me, however; there is here no touch of
bitterness. Not only is his work harder than mine,
but he is a better performer. If I sit down, tired,
dispirited, to fill these pages, it does not very much
matter, for I can muddle through somehow. No
wickets are scattered in the middle of the second paragraph; no howl of disappointment goes from a vast
crowd, to be echoed all over England the next morning; there is, for me, no melancholy walk back to the
pavilion. If Sutcliffe were to fumble as badly at the
wicket as I have fumbled many a time down a column
of writing, his reputation would be sent flying with
the bails. I can mistime my strokes and drop catches
in page after page, but no one is any the wiser. I have
only to tell myself that I will try to do better next
time, and have not to show a shamed face to all
England and half the Antipodes. Not only must he
work under conditions far more trying to the nerves
and temper, but he is, as I have said, the better performer. Not for long years, if ever at all, shall I
achieve in this prose the grace, the lovely ease, that
shines through innings after innings of his. I may
pull off a little trick or two before I have done, but
such mastery of the medium as he shows is to me only
something gleaming on the far horizon, and long before I arrive there, before that distant gleam becomes

a full flood of light, I shall probably be a crazy dodderer or dead and forgotten.

Yet these are facts with a double edge. There may be something nerve-racking in the conditions under which he works, but there is something heartening too. If I send a sentence flying to the boundary, no shout goes up to tell me that twenty thousand of my fellow men have followed the glorious stroke. When I take up my pen, there are for me no friendly slaps on the back, no cries of "Good luck, old man." I work alone, in silence, and often when all is done I cannot say whether it has been well or badly performed. It is true that no howl greets me if I fumble, but then no cheers come my way if I am on top of the bowling; nothing but silence, broken from time to time by little whispers of stilted praise or disapproval. How curious it would be if our conditions of work were changed about! Sutcliffe would have to go on batting, week after week, without a word, let alone a cheer, reaching his ears, until at last, after he had been slogging away for about two years, a little notice would appear in some newspaper saying: "Undoubtedly Sutcliffe is proving himself to be one of the younger batsmen to be reckoned with," or "With these 2,500 runs, Sutcliffe is establishing himself as one of our younger cricketers." And these, it must be understood, would be the complimentary notices, and there would be others. Already he probably imagines that nothing could be more nonsensical than some of the criticisms passed upon him, but if this change were brought about, he would soon realize that there are no limits to solemn nonsense. Thus, I remember once bringing out a book of strictly personal essays, in which it was avowedly my intention to write about myself, yet one newspaper chided me for being egotistical and having so many I's to the page. That newspaper would complain that Sutcliffe used a bat too much during his innings: "We should like Mr. Sutcliffe better as a batsman if he did not make such unnecessary use of the bat." He would also find himself confronted by a crazy difference of opinion. One half the papers would tell him that he did not hit hard enough, the other half that he hits too hard, until at last, like the sensible fellow he is, he would decide to laugh at the whole crew of them.

Meanwhile my own position would be so much more exhilarating that it would be embarrassing. I should wake up one morning and find the country placarded with "Priestley Disappoints" or "Wonderful Essay by Priestley." Now and then the evening papers would come out with special editions: "Priestley's Essay Begun. Latest Reports. Some Good Phrases." Retired essayists, writing long reports every other day or so, would analyse every paragraph, contrast this week's essay with that of a fortnight ago, and comment at length on every change of mood and style. If anything went wrong with me, all the country would be told about it, just as it was when Sutcliffe strained a muscle a short time ago. I can see the placards and headlines: "Priestley Out of Humour. Says in No

Mood for Work. May Not Write Essay this Week,"
and there would probably follow then a long interview
with the local wine merchant, who would tell the reporters that I had just bought a bottle of Chambertin
so that there was still some chance of my writing after
all. There would be warm discussions all over the
country, in newspapers, clubs, bar-parlours, on the
subject of my possible inclusion in the England Essay
Team. Everybody would send in lists: Belloc, Lynd,
Chesterton, Beerbohm, Lucas, Tomlinson and so forth.
In the end I should probably be selected as twelfth
man, to wait in the library. Messrs. Belloc and Lynd
would probably be sent in first. But I have no intention of discussing the composition of this team: all
that I wish to point out is that it would beat Australia
in any kind of weather. This is a fact worth remembering, for after all there are other things in the world
besides games, and England is not ruined just because
sinewy brown men from a distant colony sometimes
hit a ball further and oftener than our men do. And
I am sure that Sutcliffe, to whom, after such a picture
of a life passed in the full glare of public interest, I
offer my sympathy, will agree with me, though I hope,
for his sake and mine, he will go on gracefully stealing
runs, hitting the manful boundary, with more and
more power to his elbow.

Different Inside

I HAVE been misunderstood and wrongly accused so
many times that I ought to be able now to shrug my
shoulders, not merely suffering in silence, (for I know
that protest is useless) but being indifferent, not suffering at all. Yet every other day or so something happens
and I see once more what an ill-fated fellow I am.
Only last night, for example, when we were playing
bridge at my cousin's, she accused me of being far too
pleased with myself when I contrived (not unskil-
fully, let me admit) to be four up in Spades. The fact
is, of course, that she was still rather annoyed because
she had for once been over-called, she who calls so
wildly and unscrupulously and always forgets to pay,
or at least forgets to pay me, when she loses. That is
not the point, however, and I have no intention of
discussing my cousin's fantastic ethics. The trouble
is that I know very well she had evidence enough on
which to base her accusation. No doubt my face was
one vast ill-mannered grin of triumph, a revolting
sight, and yet I was not feeling jubilant, ready to crow
at my victory, but only mildly pleased with myself. I
did not even know I was looking pleased, having forgotten for the moment the tricks my face plays on
me. I can well believe, however, that I presented to
the company a front that irritated everybody. Are
other people, I wonder, as plagued by their faces as

I am by mine, which thus monstrously exaggerates
and distorts every feeling it is called upon to express;
or do I suffer alone—a man with a calm philosophic
mind but with a face that long ago decided to go on
the stage, and the melodramatic stage at that, a man
with his heart in the right place but with his features
in Hollywood?

When I first entered adult life I imagined, like
the young idiot I then was, that I had complete control of my face. I was convinced that I could permit
myself to feel anything behind that bland disguise.
When I went out for the evening and found myself
becoming more and more bored by the company, I
was sure that nobody but myself was aware of the
fact. I set my face, as best I could from behind, to
register a polite or even eager interest; I put on a
smile and kept it there, left my eyes to sparkle away,
and so forth; and then felt, even though the smile
seemed rather stiff towards the end of the evening,
that I could relapse with safety into comfortable
boredom. As I never saw myself, it was some time
before I was disillusioned. We never lose any of our
illusions about ourselves in the company of strangers.
But I made friends, and in this, as in other matters,
they very quickly disillusioned me as they strolled,
in the usual friendly fashion, through the house of
my mind and casually opened a few windows here
and there to let in the east wind. One would say:
"Dullish at the So-and-so's the other night, I thought.
You looked dreadfully bored." A succession of such

remarks soon revealed to me the true state of things, and I realized that I had been deceiving myself. It was not for me to try to look one thing when I was thinking and feeling another. The idea of myself as one of your smooth fellows, made for diplomacy and the best society, for ever charming yet secretly tired of it all, would no longer hold, and, bearing in mind my newer and truer relations with my face, I was compelled to revise my estimate of myself.

There was, however, nothing alarming or even really disappointing in the situation. I was not sorry to be free from the strain of a diplomatic bearing, and congratulated myself on the fact that the higher types of human beings do not wear a smooth and impassive front. There is nothing better than an open, honest countenance, frankly expressing to the world its owner's feelings. I thought so then and I think so still, though now my opinion is worth more if only because it is more disinterested. I imagined then that mine was one of those open, honest faces, and was happy in this belief until the cumulative effect of a series of misunderstandings, of which that one last night is a good example, compelled me to take stock of myself once more, with the result that I was disillusioned once and for all. I found that people were always telling me not to be so angry when, in actual fact, I was only slightly annoyed, were for ever asking me why I was so jubilant when in truth I was only mildly pleased, were constantly suggesting that I should not glare furiously at strangers when I was only conscious of feeling a little curious. At last I realized the truth. My face did not even honestly reflect my mind but grossly caricatured it. I was carrying into all companies a monstrous libel of myself. It was as if I were compelled to wear a set of features that did not belong to me at all but to some other and very different kind of man. Small wonder, then, that I should be so frequently misjudged, for it is not unnatural that people should imagine that these facial antics, for which I am held responsible though they seem to be entirely beyond my control, are an indication of my state of mind. How are they to know that my face has apparently an independent existence, setting to work merely on a hint from my mind and then going on in a fashion of which I strongly disapprove.

That is the irony of the situation. My face would seem to belong to a type of man I dislike. It is a theatrical, temperamental affair, for ever rushing out to extremes, whereas I am all for moderation. I do not pretend to absolute philosophic calm and detachment, but—whatever my acquaintances, the deluded audience of this face, may say to the contrary—I am certainly not a man of strong feelings, one of those people who must be excited about something, who are not happy unless they are in the depths of misery or find all existence wretched because they do not feel ecstatic, who must be always yearning and burning, loving and hating, laughing and crying. Not only have I a contempt for such persons, but I could not imitate them if I would. Such emotions as I have are small and safe and never likely to get out of hand. Ecstasy and despair do not come my way and are never likely to be encountered in the easy rambles that my mind takes every day. My attitude towards my fellow creatures is one of timid goodwill, tempered here by tranquil affection and there by a faint hostility. Even the kind of man who ought, at this moment, to be wearing my face only arouses a dislike that stops very far short of definite hatred. When, let us say (for last night still rankles), I win a game, I am only conscious of feeling a slight pleasure, spiced by just the slightest sense of triumph; and when I lose, as I do very frequently, I am certain that I am visited by nothing stronger than a tiny feeling of disappointment, a mere mental sigh. I have been guilty, in my time, of some meannesses and may have contrived, here and there, to do a kindness, but never yet have I played either the villain or the hero. If life is a melodrama—and sometimes it has every appearance of being one—then I am certainly a very minor character. In short, I am a well-fed, comfortable, calm and not entirely unphilosophical adult male, with no desire for raging emotions and with precious few to rage.

That is what I am really like inside. Outside, apparently, everything is different, thanks to a set of features that totally misrepresent me. So far as I can gather, my face pounces on the least whisper in my mind, as it were, and transforms it into a shout.

It grins insolently and sickeningly with triumph over a mere hand at cards. It scowls ferociously at inoffensive strangers, screams "You're a bore!" at prattling callers, and twists and writhes, lights up or fades out, falls into a sodden mass of depression, glitters with mischief, gapes or grins or glares, at every fresh turn the conversation takes. It transforms every hour into a benefit performance by a bad actor of the old school, strutting and mouthing insanely in the limelight. A talking ape with a megaphone could not produce a worse caricature of its master. While the company I am in is staring at this monstrous show, I sit there innocently behind it all, an unassuming fellow with nothing but a pleasant little rise and fall of emotion, entirely forgetting that this awful travesty of my mind is taking place until some strange misunderstanding bids me remember how grotesquely and unhappily I am situated. Am I alone in my trouble or has there been a general misdeal of faces? Perhaps there are other unfortunates for whom the situation has been reversed, who find themselves possessed of the most towering emotions, yet cannot make their passion felt because their faces refuse to express anything beyond a slight feeling of annoyance or a tranquil pleasure. If there are any such persons, I should like to meet one of them for the purpose of comparing our baffled sensations and of finally forming and consolidating a friendship. We could at least enjoy one another's faces.

In Crimson Silk

You will probably declare roundly that I ought not to have bought them in the first place. But I regret nothing. I realize, even better than you do, that there was, of course, no sense in the affair. Whoever crimson silk pyjamas are intended for, they are certainly not intended for me. I am not the kind of man who robes himself sumptuously in the night watches, and for years now I have crept to my bed or down to the bathroom in the demurest shades, the most self-effacing of pale blue stripes. My friends, men of a not always happy candour, have told me more than once that I look as if I sleep in my clothes, and I have no doubt that I look even dingier at night than I do during the day. Probably if they saw me in my pyjamas they would say that I looked as if I had spent all day in them. But not only were these gorgeous red things obviously not the kind of pyjamas I usually wear, they were also quite superfluous because I had no need of another pair. An extra suit of pyjamas, of course, will always—as people say—"come in," but you could hardly imagine these opulent, regal garments merely coming in, wistfully awaiting their turn at the bottom of a drawer. Emphatically their purchase cannot be justified by common sense, but considered, as it should be considered, as a romantic gesture, a wave of defiance to

the greyness and dullness of things, it was, I think,
by no means contemptible.

It was a grey day, had been indeed a grey week;
nothing outside the day's routine had happened for
some time; and it did not look as if anything would
ever happen again. My body had gone on dressing,
and undressing itself, eating, drinking, smoking, pushing itself into buses and trains, floundering heavily
into large chairs, had gone, in short, through all its
little repertoire of tricks; but the rest of me, mind,
spirit or soul, appeared to be on the point of hiber-
nating. There I was then, going about my business
drearily this grey morning, when suddenly in passing
a shop window I caught sight of a pair of crimson
silk pyjamas, or rather of flame and treasure and
lost sunsets, the gorgeous East in fee. They were not
things meekly soliciting in a shop window, but an
event, a challenge, a blast of sartorial trumpets. The
sun and the wind, the stars in their courses, had con-
spired together to produce a world of dirty mono-
chrome, in which nothing could possibly happen, and
we had all weakly bowed to their decision with one
grand exception, the gentlemen's outfitters, who
realizing that their moment had arrived, made a
gesture of defiance and evolved these pyjamas, to
burn there, ruby-red. I knew at once that my own
moment had also arrived. There are occasions in a
man's existence when he must make something happen, must fling a splash of colour into his life, or
some part of him, perhaps the boy in him, will perish,

flying broken before the grey armies of age, timidity or boredom.

These are brave words, but candour compels me to add that if the shopman had even flicked a derisive eyelid when I inquired about those pyjamas, they would never have been mine. I am prepared to stand facing the dark tide of circumstance, making romantic gestures of defiance, but I am not prepared to stand before a counter looking a fool. However, I never saw the faintest tremor. His manner instantly set me at ease, for he produced the pyjamas with that air of grave approval, as if to say, "It is not for me to comment on your admirable taste, sir, but it is evident that you and I think alike on these matters," that air which is the secret of all old and expensive shops. He spread the crimson bravery on the counter, lovingly fingered the material, pointed out this and that, and then mentioned the price, a figure by no means unworthy of that regal magnificence, mentioned it as a mere after-thought, a curious little fact that might possibly interest me. I said I would take them along myself, and watched him fold them away into a neat paper package. For the remainder of that morning I might have been seen as a dullish solid-looking citizen clutching a small and apparently uninteresting parcel. In reality I was a kind of wild poet who had just had one adventure and would have another at the day's end, who carried with him through all the city's grey tides some night robes as vivid as a sunset, spoil of Tyre and Sidon.

My other adventure was, of course, putting them on that night. That was three days ago, but even now there is still some faint thrill in going to bed or waking in the morning, for naturally I have been enjoying my appearance in an entirely new part. Clad in crimson silk, I feel a very different person, my thoughts adapting themselves to my outward magnificence. As I survey my lustrous blood-red length at night, as I wake in the morning to see two arms that might have come from a pagoda in festival stretching before me, another personality is superimposed upon the one I know so well. I feel a wicked luxurious fellow, with Nubian slaves, a torture chamber, and a huddle of shrinking Circassian beauties, round the corner. If I had to speak, I should do it in King Cambyses's vein. I am hand in glove with the Borgias. I enjoy the thought that the poor and honest are suffering, and am all for whipping the dogs. Strong, ruthless, beautiful, I stand high above common morality and look down with a cruel smile upon the whimpering herd. Men are my counters, women my playthings, and I own no god but myself. And then, having doffed or forgotten the pyjamas, I turn back again, dwindle if you will, into the rather timid, respectable and not unkindly citizen known to my family and friends.

The least thing, it would seem, will ring up the curtain on these mental histrionics. I have only to be given one of those enormous and very expensive cigars by means of which companies are merged and

dividends declared, and immediately I find myself
turning into a different person. The mouth through
which this costly smoke slowly dribbles seems to
expand and turn grim. I feel rich, powerful, rather
cynical and sensual, one who looks with narrowed
eyes at the poor virtuous fools of this world. But
put me, in my shabby clothes, in the middle of a
richly dressed and bejewelled company, and in a
moment I am your stern moralist, your sturdy philosopher, piercing with one glance the hollow shams
of life. While they are lighting their cigars (brigands
and zanies all of them), I am smoking the honest pipe
of Thomas Carlyle and telling them under my breath
that it shall not avail them. Yet I have only to have
a Turkish cigarette and a suspicion that the lady beside me (who probably mistakes me for someone else)
thinks I am a witty dog, a clever trifler, and there
I am, airy, exquisite, now slightly wistful, now mocking, epigrammatizing the world away. But let a
genuine fellow of this breed, with a more rapid and
heartless flow of epigrams and more superbly-creased
trousers (for you must have well-creased trousers for
this part, and that is one reason why I, who bag dreadfully, can rarely play it), let one of these fellows join
us and within a minute or so I have changed again,
being now simpler, deeper, more kindly, none of your
mere witty triflers but a man with a heart and a brain
and a purpose, whose lightest word is worth more
than a bushel of epigrams and cheap wit. Thus can
cigar, pipe or cigarette play Puck with my personality,

wandering dazed in its midsummer wood. Small wonder that a suit of crimson silk should be so potent.

When I consider these and similar drolleries of the mind, for ever ransacking its wardrobes and lumber rooms and dressing up for charades, I wonder more and more at the loud intolerant persons we know so well, who have doubted nothing for years, so supremely confident of knowing all truth and virtue that they are ready, nay, eager to show their fellow creatures the rope and gallows for a word or a gesture. Are they of different stuff from me, made all of a piece? Do they never find their personalities, or at least some part of them, veering with the wind of circumstance? Does nothing ever change their point of view, at least in the secret conclaves of the mind? Have they never discovered any touch of the theatre and the masquerade in the day's grave fooling? If so —and we can never know—then there is some excuse for their amazing confidence in their infallibility, their refusal to be tolerant of any difference in minds. But is it that they are not more but less stable than most of us are, that they are not acting half-a-hundred different parts for a few odd minutes and taking pleasure in the absurd transformations, but are solemnly play-acting all the time, desperately keeping the outward appearance of one consistent character? Perhaps, unknown to us, they are wearing their crimson silk day and night.

The Berkshire Beasts

I FOUND myself walking through a large park with
an old family friend, let us call her Miss Tweedletop,
a somewhat characterless, colourless lady whom I
had not even seen for years. Such persons have a
habit of popping up in dreams years after we have
apparently ceased to give them even a passing thought.
They travel, by what devious ways we cannot imagine,
into our subconscious minds, look around them
bravely and then, shaking the mud off their shoes and
taking a deep breath, they somehow contrive to jump
up into our dreams. Miss Tweedletop and I, then,
were walking through this park, and I knew somehow
that we were really one unit of a fairly large party
of friends who had all come out for a day's pleasure
and sightseeing. How I knew this I do not know,
because the dream seemed to begin at the point when
we had either lagged behind or out-distanced the main
body, which I never saw at all. All my dreams appear
to be tiny instalments of an enormous *feuilleton:* I
never know the beginning or the end, although I am
one of the chief actors, and also, they tell me, the
dramatist, producer, and scene-shifter. But I always
know a little of what has gone before; I give myself,
as it were, a hint of the situation before I set myself
on the stage; and on this occasion I knew that we
were both members of a sightseeing party.

We were strolling down a sort of carriage drive
that swept forward, as such things usually do if there
is space for it, in a vast curve. The place was not
unlike Richmond Park but rather more trim and well-
ordered, perhaps the private park of some duke or
other. We had walked slowly forward for some time,
slowly because Miss Tweedletop is (or was) an
elderly woman; and had been idly talking of this
and that, when suddenly I saw, only a little way in
front, a most curious group, a herd of the most unlikely creatures. They were of various sizes, but the
largest would be easily twice the size of a full-grown
elephant. They were not unlike elephants in appearance, except that they tapered more noticeably from
head (their heads were enormous) to tail, and though
they had the same huge flopping ears, they had no
trunks. I am no lion tamer and I confess to being
nervous in the presence of all strange animals, but I
think that even a lion tamer or an elephant hunter
might have felt rather diffident about approaching
such creatures, who looked as if they had strayed out
of the early chapters of the *Outline of History*. Miss
Tweedletop, however, walked on even after she had
noticed the astonishing brutes we were gradually
approaching.

"Ah," she exclaimed, but rather slowly, like one
who makes small-talk, "there are the Berkshire
Beasts." She said it quite casually, just as people
say "There is the County Court" or "There is the
Albert Memorial" when they are not excited about

the matter themselves nor expect you to be excited
about it, but are simply making talk. I could see that
Miss Tweedletop thought I knew as much about
the Berkshire Beasts as she and every one else did.
By this time they were much closer, and I could see
that they were a dark green colour and rather
wrinkly and shiny, not unlike something between a
cheap kind of lady's handbag and one of those foul
and unnatural editions of the poets that are bought
only as presents; but many thousands of times bigger
than the most capacious handbag or the largest
edition of Tennyson ever known. They looked bigger
than ever. And then I noticed that every one of
them, male or female, old or young, was wearing
spectacles. Yes, spectacles, rimless spectacles of the
kind affected by very intelligent, well-informed persons. They were, of course, much larger than our
spectacles; indeed, I noticed that each lens of the
spectacles worn by the adult monsters was about the
size of an ordinary dinner plate. As the creatures
turned their heads, their glasses gleamed and flashed
in the sun. I did not see anything very droll in all
this; I remember that I thought it a little odd at the
time, but nothing more; indeed, unless I am mistaken, it appeared to me that the creatures, peering
through or over their glasses at us, looked more
sinister than ever.

All this I noticed, of course, during the brief interval
of time when Miss Tweedletop made her remark.
And then, instead of owning that I knew nothing

about the Berkshire Beasts and thus giving myself
the opportunity of learning something worth knowing
in the natural history of dreamland, like a fool, and
a cowardly fool, I allowed a bad social habit to over-
master me, and replied, equally casually, "Ah, yes.
The Berkshire Beasts." I might have been their
keeper for years; I might have spent half my lifetime
tracking them down and capturing them in their
native haunts (and what haunts they must have
had!); I might have been the crazy oculist who had
fitted them with their spectacles; so casually did I
reply. But meanwhile, I had come to the conclusion
that it was high time we turned back. One or two
of them were moving in a leisurely but awe-inspiring
fashion in our direction, and we were still walking
towards them, as if they had been mere cattle or
sheep and not monstrosities twenty feet high. True,
their spectacles suggested that they were not
ordinary monsters, that they knew something of the
decencies and courtesies of life, and even hinted, as
glasses always do, at a bookish pacifism, a ferocity
strictly confined to polemics and debate. Why we
should generally associate short sight with good
nature is rather a mystery, but we do, and there is
always something peculiarly revolting and unnatural
about a spectacled murderer, just as there would be
about a baby who was caught trying to poison its nurse.

One monster detached itself from the others, perhaps it was the leader as it was certainly one of
the largest, and moved gigantically to meet us and

then stood, with lowered head, looking at us over the top of its glasses, not ten yards away. I can see it yet with its incredible head, dark green wrinkled skin, its spectacles stretched across a broad flat nose that was at least eighteen inches from side to side. Now or never was the time to turn round and run for it, even though there was no cover, no hiding place, for quite a distance. But the protest died in my throat, for Miss Tweedletop never turned a hair but strolled on with no more concern than she would have had in passing a tobacconist's shop. She did not even seem particularly interested in the creatures; and of course if she knew them and was not afraid, there was no reason for me to fear. But I do not think it was any such piece of reasoning that led me to walk forward by her side without any protest; it was merely the fear of being laughed at by a little old maiden lady. I saw myself being squashed as a boy squashes a black beetle; in a moment or so, those astonishing spectacles would be splashed and reddened by my blood.

But nothing happened. We passed almost under the leading monster's nose and he did nothing but survey us a little sadly and sceptically. It was incredible; the rimless spectacles had won. Perhaps that is why the creatures were made to wear them; before, when they were merely ordinary monsters without glasses, they were probably the most ferocious and dangerous creatures in the world, but now, simply with the addition of these contrivances of glass and wire, they were more gentle than most of our fellow humans. Probably the females were learning to knit monstrously, and the males were cultivating philosophical interests and debated among themselves as to the Knower and the Known. But as to that, I shall never be sure. Something, however, I did learn, for Miss Tweedletop made two more remarks before she tripped back into the lumber-room of my uncared for memories. "You know," she said as casually as ever, "they're only kept now for their singing."

If she was as casual, I was as foolish as before, for instead of boldly pressing for an explanation after admitting my ignorance, I still concealed it and remarked: "Really? Only for their singing?" No doubt I thought that, later, perhaps when we had joined the others, by putting a question here and there I could learn all I wanted without confessing my ignorance. If so, I was sadly disappointed, and was rightly served for my foolishness. Miss Tweedletop seemed faintly indignant, as if the tone of my reply cast a shade of doubt upon the ability of the beasts. "Yes," she said, rather reproachfully, "but they sing so beautifully." And then not a word more, for suddenly she and the monsters and the park and the bright summer day were all huddled away into the playbox of the night and I found my nose sniffing at the cold morning, and myself further from that park than I am from Sirius. Somewhere in the limbo of dreams, there is a park in which, perhaps, the Berkshire Beasts, like the morning stars, are singing together, singing so beautifully.

Having Covered the Card Table

EVERYBODY agreed that the card table needed a new
covering. In place of that smooth green sward which
makes the tournament of hearts and spades a delight
to the eye, our card table had long been showing
us a field that looked like some dreary recreation
ground in a little industrial town, all faded, patchy,
grey, fit for nothing better than sixes of clubs. There
was talk of calling in the local carpenter, but I would
not hear of it. I told them I would do it myself.
They were surprised, humorous, indulgent, but I persisted. I had already examined the table and had
come to the conclusion that it would furnish me with
a pleasant little job, well within my very limited range
of craftsmanship. The sides, which apparently held in
position the baize or felt (actually it is felt, though
everybody thinks it is baize), were screwed on, so
that they could easily be removed, and the old cloth
torn off and the new tacked on without much difficulty. I was not to be defrauded of so much happy
screwing and tacking, so much stretching of smooth
bright green cloth, by any bored artisan. I bought
some felt and came hurrying back with it almost as
if it were some new music or a parcel of books, and
then, having surrounded myself with screwdrivers,
scissors, hammers, tacks, pipes, tobacco, and matches,
I spent a solidly happy morning.

It is very odd that I should thus find myself more and more interested in working with my hands. I would seem to have reversed the usual progress in the hobbies of men, who commonly begin with the boy's carpentering outfit (complete on card) and gradually find their way to books and ideas. When I was a boy, however, I hated handiwork, and cared for nothing but books and games. The *Boy's Own Paper* showered instructions on me in vain, and I could pass by the most glorious set of tools, rows of gleaming chisels and gouges, without a thrill. No lop-sided boat of my laborious creation ever waddled out from the shore to heel over in the middle of the park lake or village pond. I never made anything, and did not possess even a pocket-knife. Christmas and birthdays brought me books, footballs, cricket-bats, single-sticks, and the like, and the only time I ever received anything to build up (it was a gigantic loop-the-loop contrivance, made up of hundreds and hundreds of little pieces of stiff cardboard: my father finally erected it), I was disgusted. At one high school that I attended for a season there was a period set aside for what was called "manual work," when pencil-boxes and iron paper-weights came clumsily and mournfully into being, and this period was a misery to me, whose shapeless bits of wood and pieces of battered metal were for ever held up to derision. In all other matters but this of craftsmanship, I was the conventional boy, a ferocious full back, a slogging batsman, a rapturous student of pantomime, good for three helpings of suet pudding, but for the rest I preferred the inside of a book to the inside of a steam engine and never even touched a hammer if I could avoid it.

When I say that I bought my first box of tools only a few years ago, a light will be thrown on my curious history. It seems as if I am becoming more and more interested in those things that I neglected in my boyhood. Nowadays I like to know why the wheels go round. I have something of a passion, if not an openly declared one, for what my friend the etcher happily calls "gadgetry." I have not only mended a gramophone and a typewriter, but am frequently to be found boasting about it. As yet I have not achieved a workshop, but I am rapidly becoming one of those men who do the little jobs about the house. By the time I am an old man, I shall probably be completely indifferent to books, having taken to fretwork and Meccano sets. As a craftsman, I am still a blundering novice, but the enthusiasm is there and time will ripen all. My planing is still contemptible; my sawing is weak; but my screwing and nailing are now almost up to professional standard, being sure, cool, masterful. This covering of the card table was my opportunity, for there were fourteen trim screws to be taken out and put in again, and tacks innumerable to hold the smooth green felt in position. It would be hard to say which gives me the more pleasure, the tack, that little epigram of the nail-box, demanding only a tiny push with the finger and then a jolly crack with the hammer, or the screw, so subtle and so enduring, with its initial outburst of wilfulness followed by its gradual submission, until at last it seems to conquer the material almost of its own accord.

Perhaps, though, the screw gives us the finer pleasure. I enjoyed every moment with those fourteen, enjoyed their brief effort at resistance, their crescendo of easy exit, their snug re-entry. Compelled as I am to deal so largely in human stuff, is it to be wondered at that I should find such delight in screws? I spend my days poring over the records of men's thoughts and dreams, wondering at their courage and timidity and impudence and vanity, praising here and blaming there, losing myself in the shadowy Walpurgis Night that we call literature. I see my fellow creatures pretending to be better and wiser than they are or more base and foolish, counterfeiting emotions they have never really known or hiding feelings that have shaken them for years. I spend hours and hours spinning theories or absorbing some other man's ideas, only to find, on looking back, that all is moonshine. I take mind and heart to this subject and that, pour myself out and then wrestle with the stubborn sheets, yet at the end I do not know whether anything has been created, whether it is not all idle vanity. There are perhaps a few moments of intense satisfaction for me while the work is in hand; there is a brief delight in the turning of a dangerous corner; and then nothing but fret and labour that is at once hard and yet fantastic until the work is done and I am free to juggle lazily with the next dream. If I get no praise for what I have done, then I am heartsick; but if praise does come my way, then it seems to me foolish and fulsome and I am irritated or embarrassed. So it goes on. This way of life is my own choice and I would have no other, not even though I should have my "yachts and string-quartets"; but sometimes there is a joy in taking leave of it, in stretching green felt across the top of a card table, in turning home a good solid screw.

With a screw, biting its way into the woodwork and staying there if need be for half a century or, if you will, returning to your hand, the very same screw, within the next five minutes, you know where you are. It was devised for one kind of work, and that work it will do. It cheats neither itself nor you, is as definite, as rigid, as this other stuff with which I commonly deal is shifty and shadowy, maliciously protean. When you have tightened the last of your handful of screws, you can survey your work with solid contentment: something new has been created, if only the cover of a card table, and its existence cannot be argued away. My screwing and scissoring and hammering are done, and now our shining kings and queens and knaves have a new smooth lawn for their strange encounters. A man with such jobs to do daylong, measuring the work with a wise eye, now taking up his screwdriver, now his scissors, now his hammer, is in no bad case, if, that is, he has enough in his pocket at the day's end for his steak and beer and baccy and occasional visit to the play. A man so situated is a churl if he grumbles. On the other hand, if he is bundled into a roaring great factory and there has to pass the whole day holding or cutting the felt, or hammering in tacks, or putting screws in holes while another man turns the screw-driver, then we can hardly blame him if he comes to the conclusion that he is being cheated, if he turns into a man with a grievance. He thinks that he is being cheated out of money, but whether he is or not, the fact remains that he is certainly being cheated out of something even more important, namely, a decent and amusing job, that honest and engrossing work which is also great fun. There was a time when all work was of the kind that most of us at some time or other have performed purely to amuse ourselves, just as I covered the card table: we have—I speak for both sexes—dug up gardens, mown grass, picked fruit, woven and dyed cloth, sailed boats, made shelves and cupboards, knitted stockings, soled boots, cut down trees, printed books, and so forth. But I have yet to meet anybody who went to work in a factory for fun, who spent his leisure in taking part in mass production. The world will not be happy when all the economists have agreed together and have regimented us into equal hours and equal wages, but when everybody has more work, real work, to do, when we are all happily covering card tables through the long day and have just leisure enough for an odd rubber or two before we go to bed.

W

Open House

THERE was a man having dinner near me who looked like some one I used to know, and I puzzled and puzzled until suddenly I remembered. Uncle George! I knew that it could not actually be Uncle George, who must be quite old now or may, indeed, be dead; but this man looked like the Uncle George I remembered from long ago, and the sight of him started all manner of queer things from the thickets of memory. He was not my own uncle, you must understand, but the uncle of my old schoolfellow, Harold Thorlaw, and the greatest man in the Thorlaw circle. He did not live in our own little provincial town—and now I come to think of it, I never knew where he did live—but at irregular intervals he used to descend upon us, perhaps during his travels, for I remember that his business took him about a good deal. In our provincial circle he was a grand cosmopolitan figure. To his nephew and me, then in our teens, and indeed to all the Thorlaws, Uncle George was the great world. London, Paris, and New York spoke to us through him. He it was who told us about music-halls and head-waiters and card-sharpers and those lordly expresses, those ten-somethings that do it without a stop, that are the very soul of rich cosmopolitan life. You always knew when he had arrived at the Thorlaws', for you felt his presence even in the hall, and were not surprised when Harold, or his sister, or his mother, came out to you and whispered, "Uncle George's here!" There he was, oracular in the large arm-chair near the piano, perhaps having his little joke, asking the girls a riddle, suggesting a song (he liked a light cosmopolitan sort of music, and would occasionally produce a copy of something that was going well at the Gaiety), or telling us a queer thing that had happened at his London hotel, amiably keeping up a pretence of being one of us, but clearly as far removed from us—and he knew that we knew—as Haroun al Raschid himself.

It was with the Thorlaws themselves, however, rather than with Uncle George, that my memory began to play. They were the kind of people we seem to run across only in early life, perhaps because they only blossom in provincial towns and wither and change in the air of London. The shortest way of describing them is to say that they were hospitality, real warm hospitality, incarnate: they kept open house. They were worlds away from the kind of lavish entertainers you encounter in London, the lion-hunting ladies and the vulgar rich whose houses have really been turned into railway hotels. They loved nothing so much as being surrounded by relatives and friends, and the friends of their relatives, and the relatives of their friends. It was not that they had plenty of money; they were anything but rich, and Mrs. Thorlaw's worn little housekeeping purse must have been drained of its last sixpence many a time to provide such hospitality as they proffered. They never sat you down solemnly to dinner, and could not have done even if they had wanted to, for there always seemed to be three times as many people there as the tiny dining-room could possibly have held. No, their great meals were tea, in which the oddest of odd cups and saucers came floating out on a tide of hot water; and a sketchy and peripatetic kind of late supper, when there was always an enormous bustle and you were so occupied getting out of people's way and handing things round that you never noticed if you were actually having anything to eat.

Yet there shone through that house so bright a spirit of generous hospitality that it seemed to snow meat and drink there and you took part in a perpetual feast. What may have been in cold fact a cup of lukewarm tea and half a sandwich seemed a solid hour's happy guzzling. A small glass of cheap port in that house was worth whole bottles of vintage wine anywhere else. So strong was the atmosphere of festivity that material facts, actual cakes and ale, were of little or no account. You called there— "popped in" was the phrase for it—on an ordinary Saturday or Sunday evening and, if you had not known what to expect, you would have supposed that it was Christmas Eve or Old Year's Night, or that a birthday or a wedding was being celebrated. There would be two or three people in the hall, a few others having a snack in the dining-room, probably a group of ladies chattering in the best bedroom, and the drawing-room would be full. I have never known any other room like that drawing-room, for it was certainly not very large and yet there seemed to be no limit to the number of visitors it would hold. To say that it would be "full" does not mean that it would not hold any more people (it always did), but merely that it looked full—indeed, fuller than any room you had ever seen before. You would see a swarm of faces on three different levels, for some people would be standing up, others seated on chairs, and the rest would be on the floor. My friend Harold, whose idea of pleasure in music was limited to the notion of taking something very fast and loud and trying to play it faster and louder than any one else had ever played it, would be pounding away at the piano; and every one there would be very noisy, very hot and flushed, very happy.

The Thorlaws could create this atmosphere wherever they went. I remember now that they took a tiny cottage on the edge of the moors during the summer months of one year, and that I called there after a long walk on either a fine Saturday or Sunday afternoon. I could hear them shouting and laughing long before I got to the door. The tiny cottage was simply bursting with people, who were eating and drinking and passing plates and filling teapots and putting kettles on the fire and being sent for water or returning with more milk. Every one would be explaining to everyone else how it happened that he or she had "popped in," and at the sight of each newcomer a tremendous shout would go up. (I have a vague idea, though my memory may be the dupe of my innate poetical desire to have everything perfect, that Uncle George was there.) The Thorlaws, I believe, could have filled a plague-stricken hovel on a blasted heath with such a laughing crowd of visitors. It was not merely that they had a passion for gathering people round them—for many have that whose houses are visited once and then for ever shunned—but they radiated such a spirit of friendliness and good cheer that instantly they put all their visitors at their ease, made it impossible to be stiff, supercilious, or shy, and transformed every chance gathering into a kind of hilarious family reunion. With them, if you were asked to sing a song, you immediately stood up and sang it without any more ado. I myself have sung comic songs there by the hour, without shame, and may be remembered to this day by all manner of people in remote places as a budding Henry Lytton, as "Harold's friend, you know, who used to sing the comic songs." I was always being buttonholed in odd places by people who had seen me there, people whose very faces I had forgotten, let alone their names, who asked me if I had any more comic songs and were obviously prepared to roar with laughter at every remark I made.

I would give something to be able to call there again to-night, now that they have all returned so vividly to my remembrance. To see Mr. Thorlaw, a humorous and pugnacious little man with blazing blue eyes, moving round with the doubtful port, chaffing the girls and bullying their young men. To see his wife, one of those little thin, dark women who seem to be made of wire and catgut, smiling, tireless, who would go flicking in and out of the throng like a radiant shuttle; and all those flushed, noisy, and happy people I would meet there, most of whose names I never knew, whose names and faces, one and all, I have now forgotten. Foolish, funny little people, nothing like the beautiful, the clever, the distinguished persons whose acquaintance I can boast to-day, but dimly consecrated in my memory by a happiness that something seems to have withered away, shining there in a queer kind of Golden Age, strangely compounded of provincial nobodies and cheap port and chaff and comic songs. I wonder if that house, like the hospitality that gave it so much light and warmth, has gone the way of so many things and is now given over to loneliness, to darkness and dust. Here, at least, for an hour in my memory, the lights have been turned up, the fires poked into a blaze, and the doors opened wide again, the place itself a guest in the open house of remembrance.

THE END